Walks from Bristol's Severn Beach Line

Andrew Swift

AKEMAN PRESS

Published by AKEMAN PRESS
www.akemanpress.com

ISBN 978-0-9560989-5-5

Printed by Berforts Information Press, Stevenage

CONTENTS

FOREWORD

I have so enjoyed perusing Andrew Swift's brilliant book of walks, have learnt so much and look forward to discovering more by following his recommendations. Bristol surely provides greater variety than any other city in the UK, including wonderful names such as Nightingale Valley, Coalpit Heath and Paradise Bottom and of course some great historic pubs to be found on the way, such as the Seven Stars that played such an important role in the abolition of slavery. He also rightly mourns the loss of other watering holes but also triumphs the Bristol and District Footpath Preservation Society and others who have saved parks and places from rapacious developers, places and walks that we now take for granted. He weaves stories and introduces us to Bristol's characters, and points out hidden gems such as the magical lost gardens of Bishop's Knoll, the two headed goose or Nipper the dog. This is not just another book of walks but a highly knowledgable account of both the city and its railways which form such an important part of our past and must be revived for a sustainable future. *Walks from Bristol's Severn Beach Line* makes a major contribution to the city's annals and I am confident will bring huge pleasure to those of all ages.

George Ferguson, CBE
Mayor of Bristol
August 2014

INTRODUCTION

Bristol is one of the world's great cities, but it is not easy to get to know, or to love. This is not just because of its size; as Andrew Foyle explains in his guide to the city's buildings, it can sometimes be more than a little bewildering:

> The nature of Bristol's development and the traumatic after-effects of Second World War bombing have led to a mystifying disjointedness, a constant staccato in the city's rhythms often remarked upon by visitors. Bristol is quirky, revealing its charms only slowly. One plunges from sheltered medieval alleys into alienating traffic routes amidst high-rise offices and back again with alarming suddenness.[1]

The walks in this book do not try to smooth over or avoid this diversity but seek to embrace it, finding delight in disjointedness, joy in juxtaposition, inspiration in incongruity. Bristol is never going to be a showpiece city, sanitised for tourists, and, while it may revel in being Green Capital, England's first cycling city, internationally famous for street art, culture and counter-culture, with fantastic festivals, vibrant nightlife, and bars and restaurants to match any in London, it is never going to be cosy ... or dull. Bland it isn't, and, if it sometimes seems a little edgy, that is surely a price worth paying for its lack of mediocrity.

Unlike towns and cities with more obvious charms, Bristol improves with acquaintance, as it reveals – or as you uncover – the depth and richness of its history and traditions. Bristol's history is not something preserved in aspic, but part of a living, evolving continuum. Neither is it something that can be commodified into a heritage experience; it is something you need to go in search of, and much of it is to be found in places only your feet can take you.

The clue to Bristol's character lies in its role as a great port. The city docks may have closed back in 1973, with cargoes now loaded and offloaded downriver at Avonmouth and Portbury, but ports have a character all their own, and 40 years without cargo ships tying up in the city centre does not erase a spirit which took a millennium to evolve.

Ports are never going to be cosy, genteel places, but so much money was generated in Bristol's docks during their heyday that wealthy merchants could afford to move to the airy heights of Clifton, creating one of Britain's most spectacular urban landscapes, or to mansions farther out, where they lived amid parks designed by great landscape gardeners. Despite later growth and industrialisation, the eighteenth-century landscape of Clifton and of the great country estates – now open for all to enjoy – has survived remarkably well, and is explored at length in several of the walks that follow.

The Georgian period also saw Bristol transformed into one of the country's top visitor destinations. Like Bath, Bristol had a spa, with hot – or at least warm – springs, along with assembly rooms, parades and grand lodging houses. And, because Bath was only twelve miles away, many visitors who stayed there dropped into Bristol for a few days as well. One of the biggest draws was the dramatic scenery, lauded in innumerable guidebooks, of the Avon Gorge, Leigh Woods and Coombe Dingle. So celebrated did it become that, in the early nineteenth century, Bristol even had its own school of landscape artists.

The spa and the pump room where visitors once took the waters have long gone, and the Portway now runs where once they rambled in search of visions of the sublime, but much of what they came to see has survived and, where it has, these walks endeavour to take you there.

They go in search of much else as well, peeling back the layers of Bristol's history to reveal Civil War forts, prehistoric encampments, lost conduits, disused railway tunnels, ancient manor houses, medieval churches, Roman roads, abandoned mills and harbours, slipways to forgotten ferries and a pool built by medieval monks to supply them with fish.

Many of these walks are only possible because generations of Bristolians fought landowners and developers to preserve access to green spaces and keep rights of way open for the use of everyone. As a tribute to their efforts, accounts of some of their campaigns appear alongside the walks. Unfortunately, not all their efforts were crowned with success; stories of how well-loved open spaces came to lie beneath bricks and mortar serve as a reminder that the outcome of such campaigns can never be taken for granted. Nor are threats to our open spaces a thing of the past, as the stories of Royate Hill and Easter Garden (on pages 41 and 108) show.

Something else that survived against all the odds is the Severn Beach Line. Like so many branches earmarked for closure by Beeching, it could so easily have become a barely remembered thread in the city's history, its course now obliterated by redevelopment. Yet how much poorer the city would have been without it, not only as a superbly scenic and civilised way of traversing its northern suburbs, but also as a gateway to the riches explored in these walks. I hope you enjoy following them as much as I have enjoyed putting them together.

Each walk starts at a station on the Severn Beach Line and end at a station either on the Severn Beach line or with regular services to Bristol Temple Meads.

LENGTH OF WALKS:
Although I have indicated distances, I have not indicated how long each walk is likely to take. This will depend not only on how fast you walk but also on how long you take to look at things en route. Generally, though, if you walk at a reasonable pace with occasional stops you should cover around two miles an hour.

PUBS & OTHER ATTRACTIONS:
I have tried to ensure that information regarding opening times, etc is correct at time of publication. However, as this may change, you are advised to check by phone or the internet, especially if you are planning to stop for a lunch.

DOGS:
The suitability of the walks for dogs depends – unless your dog is especially fond of street-walking – on the amount of parks, fields, woods and other open spaces en route. That said, the walks only include one place, as far as I am aware, where dogs are not permitted – Royal Fort in Walk 9. Where pub listings indicate that dogs are welcome, this means that well-behaved dogs on leads are allowed in at least part of the pub. However, change of policy or management may mean that this is no longer the case, and you may wish to check beforehand.

MAPS & DIRECTIONS:
The sketch maps at the beginning of each walk indicate the route. They are not intended as navigational aids. Although I have endeavoured to make the directions in the walks as comprehensive, comprehensible and unambiguous as possible, things inevitably change, often very quickly. Landmarks disappear, pubs are renamed, footpaths are temporarily (and sometimes permanently) closed, tracks become overgrown – so you are strongly advised to arm yourself with a map in case you need to make an unscheduled diversion.

For the urban walks, the paperback-sized Geographers' A-Z Map of Bristol & Bath, with a scale of 4 inches to the mile, is recommended. This can also be used for the country sections of the walks, with the exception of Walk 16 and the first part of Walk 15. For these, Ordnance Survey (OS) Explorer Maps, at a scale of 2½ inches to a mile are recommended. OS Explorer Maps are also useful – although not essential – on the rural sections of the other walks and grid references are provided for those who want to use them.

1

BARTON HILL, ST ANNE'S VALLEY, ARNO'S VALE & WINDMILL HILL

Starts at: *Lawrence Hill station*

Ends at: *Temple Meads or Bedminster*

Distance: *8.5 miles to Temple Meads, 7 miles to Bedminster*

Terrain: *A mixture of pavements, tarmac paths and rough woodland paths*

Arno's Vale Cemetery closes at 5pm in summer and 4.30pm in winter (or dusk if earlier); dogs on leads welcome

Pubs & other amenities:

A choice of cafés in Sandy Park Road

Atrium café in Arno's Vale Cemetery (open 10am-4pm; hot food served to 3pm)

Windmill pub, 14 Windmill Hill, BS3 4LU, open all day from 12; food served all day; dogs welcome; 0117 9635440; www.thewindmillbristol. com

Map: *Geographers' A-Z*

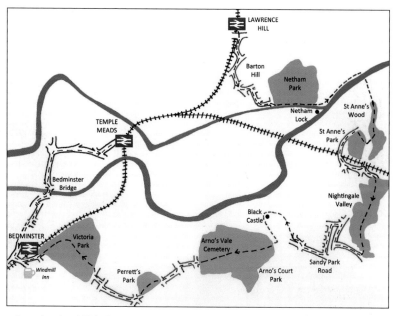

Opposite: Arno's Vale Cemetery

Starting in the old industrial heartland of Barton Hill, this walk takes in the site of one of Bristol's most noxious factories – now transformed to a green oasis – two wooded valleys, a castle built from industrial waste, the site of a long-lost tunnel built by Brunel, one of Britain's most famous cemeteries, four parks and a holy well once visited by Henry VII.

On leaving Lawrence Hill station, cross the road at the lights and turn into Morton Street, a few metres along to the left. At the end, turn left by the Russell Arms pub. After passing Cabot Green, bear right and then right again along Barton Hill Road.

Turn left along Queen Anne Road. St Luke's church, on the left, dates from 1843. Its octagonal tower originally had a stone spire on the top, which was removed in 1982.

At the mini-roundabout, cross and turn right, before turning left along Maze Street and left again along Aiken Street. The Lord Nelson pub – with its splendid bust of Nelson – is a remnant of the tight-knit community of terraced houses, mostly dating from the 1850s and 1860s, that once characterised this part of Barton Hill. In 1952, the council announced plans for a comprehensive redevelopment of the area, which were opposed by many residents. They formed the Barton Hill Planning Protection Organisation, but the council pushed the plans through anyway. Behind the Lord Nelson is Barton House, which, when officially opened on 23 June 1958, was England's tallest block of flats outside London.

Turn right by the Lord Nelson along Great Western Lane, where Bristol Creative Studio occupies part of the site of one of Bristol's largest factories, the Great Western Cotton Works, opened in 1838 and demolished in 1968.

Turn left at the end along Glendare Street and then right into Herapath Street. Follow the street round to the left past a grassy area. At the end, cross the road ahead and, a few metres along to the right, turn left into Netham Park and carry straight on along a path. The Feeder Canal, on your right, opened in 1809. It fed water from the River Avon into Bristol Harbour, which, after a lock was built at the far end, was transformed from a tidal stretch of river into a floating harbour where the water level remained constant. The river itself was diverted along a 'New Cut', which you will see later in the walk. The slope on your left marks the site of a huge waste dump for Netham Chemical Works, established in the 1840s. Among the products manufactured here were sodium carbonate (washing soda), sodium hydroxide (caustic soda), calcium oxide (quicklime) and sulphuric acid. It closed around 1950 and the site has now been landscaped to create a recreation ground. About 200m along the path is the site of a tramway terminal, where cranes transhipped goods between boats and wagons, but of the tramway, and of the transit sheds and limekilns that surrounded it, there is no trace. The chemical works stood at the other

end of the tramway, about 100m up to the left, surrounded by piles of chemical waste.

At the end of the park is Netham Lock, where the Feeder joins the river. Head straight on across two busy roads (with care because they are not pedestrian controlled) and continue alongside the river.

Netham Park, the site of Netham Chemical Works

Netham Lock and the delightfully bucolic lock-keeper's house date from 1809

As you carry on past a car park occupying a site once covered by an extension to the chemical works, look out for black blocks in the wall. These were made from slag produced during brassmaking, and you will be seeing many more of them later. As you carry on, the wall increases in height, with bricked-up arches, doors and windows recalling long-vanished workshops and warehouses. The land across the river remained undeveloped until 1912, when St Anne's Board Mill was established there. This was an offshoot of the tobacco industry and made the board for cigarette packets. It closed in 1980.

After the high wall comes to an end, look ahead to see Troopers Hill chimney, which carried noxious fumes away from copper works down by the river. When you reach a metal footbridge over the river – built in 1957 to replace a ferry in operation since medieval times – cross it. At one time this would have led you into the heart of St Anne's Board Mill, which stretched alongside the river for over 700m. Today, it leads you into a supermarket car park.

Head away from the river towards a roundabout. On the far side, look for a footpath to the right of a short row of shops and head along it. When

Three Pools, St Anne's Wood.

Pools in St Anne's Woods in the 1920s

the path forks, bear right downhill. On the other side of the fence on your right is Brislington Brook and a business park built on the site of part of the Board Mill. When the fence and business park end, you enter a broad meadow, shaded by large trees, with the brook burbling through. To your left, guarded by railings, is St Anne's Well, for centuries a site of pilgrimage.

Carry on across a footbridge and continue along the valley until you see the brook disappearing into a culvert built when Brunel brought the Great Western Railway through the valley in the 1830s. Just before the culvert, go up a flight of steps on the right. At the top follow the path as it doubles back high above the valley for 200m before climbing steps up to a road.

ST ANNE'S CHAPEL

Around 1392, a chapel was built at St Anne's well for pilgrims visiting the site. In 1480, William Worcestre described it as being 19 yards (17.4m) long, five yards (4.6m) wide, and 80 feet (24.4m) high, with two large candles – each costing five pounds – provided by the cordwainers' and weavers' guilds and renewed each year on Whit Sunday. St Anne was the patron saint of sailors, and among the offerings before the altar were, according to William Worcestre, '32 boats and little boats, and some carracks. And of the boats fashioned and made out of silver, there are five boats, the value of each boat 20 shillings'.[1] An indication of the veneration in which the well was held came six years later, when Henry VII, on a visit to the city, made a special journey to it. In 1539, however, when Henry VIII broke with Rome, the chapel was demolished and the well abandoned – at least officially. Local people continued to revere the well, and it was  eventually restored in the 1870s, with a canopy built over it in 1926. After being demolished, it was restored in 1996, only to be demolished again. Yet despite its current ignominious condition, ribbons and other tokens tied to nearby trees and railings show that the spirit that led medieval mariners to offer silver models of their boats to the well's presiding deity still survives. As for the chapel, fragmentary remains were still visible less than a century ago, but they now lie under an access road to the industrial estate.

Cross and turn left for 50m before turning right into St Anne's Park. After 50m turn right along a tarmac path and left along the road to Langton Court Hotel, an ornately-decorated jettied building dating from 1902. As you carry on, look behind it to see part

of Langton Court, dating from 1602. It was originally much larger, but most of it was demolished to build the Langton Court Hotel.

At the end, bear left along Langton Court Road. Westminster Insurance, on the corner of Maple Road, was once St Anne's Post Office. When you come to a bridge, look to the right for a spectacular view of the railway with the city beyond. When it opened in 1840, the line here ran through a tunnel, the northern portal of which was just north of the bridge. In 1889, the two tracks were increased to four, the tunnel was opened out and replaced by a cutting, the bridge you are standing on was built and a large yard, known as Bristol East Depot, was opened. Today the four tracks have reverted to two and the depot has closed, but the cutting and bridge remain.

The tunnel demolished in 1889

Bristol East Depot in the 1950s

THE FIGHT FOR ST ANNE'S WOODS

In 1883, a solicitor called James Sinnott acquired St Anne's Woods. By this time, the ferry had ceased operating on a regular basis, and in 1887, despite the paths through the woods having been rights of way since time immemorial, he closed them off, erected 'no public way' signs and padlocked the gates. After several people were prevented from walking through the woods, the Bristol & District Footpath Preservation Society organised a mass trespass on 23 June 1899, placing the following notice in local newspapers:

REOPENING OF ST ANNE'S FERRY
The ferry boat at the ancient ferry from Crew's Hole to St Anne's will be at the proper crossing place for the conveyance of passengers from two o'clock pm this day. Toll ½d each way.

Over 100 people turned up to take the ferry, walk through the woods and, according to Mr Sinnott, knock down a wall and do 'very considerable damage'. As a result, he took the organisers to court.

The case lasted 18 days, at the end of which the rights of way over Mr Sinnott's land were upheld, and he was ordered to pay the costs of the hearing. It was a landmark case, sending a clear signal to other local landowners that they interfered with ancient rights of way at their peril. And it is thanks to organisations like the Bristol & District Footpath Preservation Society that we are still able to walk through St Anne's Woods and other green spaces today.

There is another reason to be grateful to them, for the dozens of witnesses they called provide us with a record of how popular St Anne's Woods were in the nineteenth century. It is sometimes claimed that walking for pleasure was a minority pastime, confined to the leisured classes, until well into the twentieth century. The following extracts from the trial transcripts confirm that walking in St Anne's Woods was as popular then as it is today, if not more so:

Thomas Webley, an old man aged 87, stated that he first went to live at St Anne's in 1817. A good many people crossed the river in the ferry boat from both sides. On the St Anne's side there was a path five or six feet wide leading through the withy bed and the garden up to the mill, and from thence in front of the mill to Brislington. The toll was a halfpenny each way and the boat plied Sundays and weekdays.[2]

John Reach Webley, born in 1814, stated that he knew St Anne's Mill from 1818 to 1820. It was kept by his grandfather. He visited the mill several times, and he crossed the ferry and went by way of a black path through the withy bed to the mill. He saw other people crossing the ferry, and they went by the same route to St Anne's Woods. They had no business at the mill. At one time his cousin worked the ferry boat.[3]

Thomas Jones said he was born at Crew's Hole in February 1822, and he had only been away from home about 18 months all his life. He knew St Anne's Ferry at the time of the Bristol Riots. There was a landing place on the St Anne's side and a regular path to the mill and on to the wood ... It was a common road for everybody, and none of the gates was kept locked.[4]

Michael Mahony, aged 55, living at 10 Orchard Street, stated that he came to Bristol in 1851. He knew Brislington and St Anne's Woods. He first visited the place between 1880 and 1882 ... He was a Catholic. While at the well, a man whom he took to be the caretaker came to them, and he gave them a jug to drink from the well. They afterwards walked down close to the pond, passing the old ruins. He had been to the well many times since. He had an accident, and got a cataract on the left eye. He was afraid of the other becoming affected, and he visited St Anne's Well because he thought that the water from that holy well would do his sight good.[5]

William Knowlett was then called, and examined by Mr Metcalfe. The witness intimated he was rather hard of hearing.

Mr Metcalfe: Can you hear what I say?

Witness: No, sir (loud laughter). Continuing his evidence, witness stated that when he was 14 or 15 years old, he was employed by Mr Fear, a tenant of St Anne's Mill, to work the ferry boat, and he was told by his master that he was compelled to put people over any hour of the day or night, as it was a public ferry. He had taken over £1 on a Sunday, and at holiday times he had taken as much as 50/- a day. The toll was a halfpenny. There was a landing stage on the St Anne's side leading up to a path five or six feet wide, with a drain on each side, which went straight through the withy bed to the mill, and thence through a wicket gate to St Anne's Wood. There was a road to Brislington over the stone bridge and another route through Birchwood. There was a path to the old chapel. About two months after he commenced working the ferry, and six weeks after the railway work began, a notice board was placed near the ferry, stating on the side facing the river, 'Public ferry from St George to Brislington', and on the reverse side, 'Public Ferry from Brislington to St George'. The board remained five or six years, and it was then knocked down by boys and never put up again. About a year after Mr Ring took the farm, the ferry was removed about 100 yards further up the river and the withy bed on either side of the path was dug up.[6]

Joseph Hodge, 79 years of age, was born at Blacksworth Mill and lived there until 19 or 20 years old. He said he remembered a landing place there, and there was another on the St Anne's side, with a path in the wood, almost a cart road, leading by the rear of the mill house. Before 1831, the year of his marriage, he went for walks through St Anne's Wood with his sweetheart. They went the water way by the regular ferry which existed at the place, paying a halfpenny fare. At the wood, there were roads from the mill, both ways, and he had never seen the gates locked. He remembered a man named Fear keeping a public house at the mill, but he never went in there. There were regular paths in the woods and once there people could ramble about as they liked.[7]

James Hobley, engineer of the telegraph department of Bristol, stated that he was born in 1829 at Pile Marsh, St George's, where he lived for 25 years. He recollected the mill and the public house, and the common use of the ferry. People crossed the water for both business and pleasure, going to St Anne's Woods for recreation. He had seen the site of the old chapel, and his father had escorted visitors there. He revisited the place in 1888, and found the ferry changed.[8]

Carry on past the school and turn left along Salisbury Road, keeping to the right-hand side of the road. At the end, cross the main road ahead (you may find it safer to use the crossing up to the right) and turn left downhill.

Although you will be turning right down St Anne's Terrace, before you do so carry on to a bridge, built over the site of the eastern portal of the tunnel when the line was widened. Below you is the site of St Anne's station, opened in 1898 and closed in 1970, with the impressive portal of St Anne's Tunnel beyond it.

The cottage below you on the left as you turn down St Anne's Terrace was recently threatened with demolition, when a developer applied to build two blocks of flats on the site. After a concerted campaign by local residents, the application was turned down and the character of this semi-rural part of suburban Bristol was saved.

Carry straight on along a gravel track, go through a squeeze stile into Nightingale Valley and follow the path as it curves right alongside Brislington Brook. After 300m, you reach a packhorse bridge, where you have the choice of crossing and carrying on beside the brook along a broad path, or of staying on the right bank and following a rougher, muddier path. Whichever path you choose, 200m further on you will see a massive plane tree, cracked, hollow and patched with masonry, but still defiantly alive, standing beside a small waterfall and the remains of a bridge.

Just past this – on the right-hand path – the going gets tricky and somewhat sinister, as you pick your way over ground wrinkled and contorted into a sort of rubbery lava, suggesting that industry once flourished here. Old oil drums, half buried and fractured by rust, seem to tell a similar story. But industry never sullied this valley; these were the semi-ornamental

Nightingale Valley

Wick House

grounds of Wick House, which you will see shortly. The oil drums and their contents were dumped into this sylvan retreat at the end of the Second World War when a nearby American army camp was decommissioned. Given that what remains has had 60 years to be absorbed by the healing hand of nature, it is best not to dwell too deeply on the devastation wrought at the time.

Just past this – if you have been following the left bank – a metal footbridge returns you to the right bank. 150m further on, go through a gate, bear right across the grass and carry on up Hill Lawn road. After passing a scout hut, look to the right to see old walls, with an old building called Wick Cottage beyond them.

At the top turn right. At the end of the stone wall on the right is the gateway of Wick House, whose grounds once included Nightingale Valley. Built around 1790 as a scaled-down version of Arno's Court (which you will see later), it has been swamped by later extensions and is now a hostel for the homeless.

There were other grand houses nearby. If you look ahead you can see, 75m along on the right, Woodcroft House, a three-storey late Georgian building disfigured by a modern porch and now converted to sheltered housing. On the left hand side of the road, just beyond it, was the much grander Broomhill House, built in the 1760s and demolished in the 1920s.

Cross and head down Upper Sandhurst Road, take the first left along Sandringham Road, and at the end turn right down Sandy Park Road. After passing the Sandringham pub – where Sandy Park Road rises towards a bridge over the old Bristol & North Somerset Railway – head along Sand Hill, which runs parallel to it on the right. Just past a pair of large green gates, bear left along a footpath beside a green fence. At the end, bear left past concrete bollards and turn right, before crossing and heading across the car park to the right of the supermarket.

Black Castle, on the far side of the car park, is one of Bristol's most bizarre buildings. It was built in 1764 for the brassmaker William Reeve, using bricks made with slag from his brassworks. Two years later, when Horace Walpole visited Bristol (which he described as 'the dirtiest great shop I ever saw'), he wrote to a friend that,

> going into the town, I was struck with a large Gothic building, coal black and striped with white; I took it for the devil's cathedral. When I came nearer, I found it was an uniform castle, lately built, and serving for stables and offices to a smart false Gothic house on the other side of the road.[9]

Today it is a pub.

The Black Castle as it appeared around 1900

Head to the left of the Black Castle and, before reaching the road, turn left along a footpath. This would once have led through the grounds of the Black Castle to a Bath House with a colonnaded facade, which, after the building was demolished in 1957, was rescued by Clough Williams-Ellis and rebuilt at Portmeirion in North Wales.

The footpath now leads to an arch which originally stood at the southeast corner of the Black Castle before being moved to its present site in 1912. Built of Bath stone, it would originally have gleamed white against the gritty blackness of the castle. Its niches housed statues salvaged from two of Bristol's medieval gates which were demolished in 1766. The statues were, however, moved to the city's museum over a century ago; the ones you see today are replicas dating from the arch's restoration in 1995.

As you carry on past the arch, you pass, on your left, the imposing entrance to the former tram depot, built in 1901. Cross the two sets of lights at the bottom of Sandy Park Road, and turn right to cross another two sets of lights to Arno's Court, which, as you can see, was built in three distinct

The former tram depot seen through the archway

Arno's Court

stages. In the middle is the rather plain house William Reeve bought with the money he made from brassmaking; on the right is the 'smart false gothic house' he added to it; and on the left is an extension added in the mid-nineteenth century when the building became a convent.

Turn left across the entrance to the hotel and then right into Arno's Court Park. Follow the path for 50m before bearing right along an untended lane beside the wall on the right. When you reach the fence at the end, turn left uphill for 150m. When you come to a bench – ideally placed to take in the view – turn right and walk up steps to a hidden gateway leading into Arno's Vale Cemetery.

ARNO'S COURT PARK

Arno's Court is one of Bristol's newest public parks. It was originally part of the Arno's Court estate, and in the 1830s and 1840s there were moves to sell it off for development. Its future was secured in 1850 when the estate was bought by William Gillow, a Roman Catholic philanthropist, who gave it to the Order of the Good Shepherd to use as a convent. A few years later, Arno's Court was extended to house a reformatory for teenage girls. After the buildings were damaged by bombing in the Second World War, the occupants were evacuated, and the Order put the estate up for sale for £17,500. The council eventually bought it for £14,400. In 1949, after the court had been renovated, the council moved its planning and city engineer's departments in. A high wall that had surrounded the court was also demolished, so that, for the first time, it could be seen by passers-by. The court was later sold and is now a hotel, but its grounds are now one of Bristol's most popular parks, a splendid open space on the borders of Brislington and Bedminster with extensive views over the city.

Carry on up the steps and – ignoring a footpath bearing right alongside the fence – head straight on uphill until you come to a Cross of Remembrance, commemorating Second World War naval casualties.

Turn right here and carry on until you come to a wall with a steep drop on the other side.

Here you have a choice. If you already know Arno's Vale Cemetery or want to leave an exploration of it for another day, turn left alongside the wall and carry on until you come to the Top Lodge. Otherwise, turn right and, just before the wall ends, go through a gap in it and, at a T junction, turn left. A little way along, bear right along a path doubling back, and follow it down to an obelisk commemorating Thomas Doddrell. Follow the path as it swings right downhill.

ARNO'S VALE CEMETERY

Long before the Bristol General Cemetery Company acquired part of the Arno's Vale estate in the 1830s, the area was a well-known beauty spot, a natural amphitheatre with views across the city. The company laid out winding paths along the upper slopes, with formal walks and a ceremonial way on the level ground at the bottom. The Bath Road lodges and the two chapels – Anglican and Nonconformist – were designed in classical style, and trees and shrubs were planted to enhance the natural beauty of the site. By the 1980s, the trees had reached maturity and the cemetery was a superb and magical natural habitat in the heart of the city. It was also becoming increasingly dilapidated, its paths choked with brambles and its monuments crumbling. By now, the cemetery was in the hands of an individual rumoured to have plans for redeveloping it. After a lengthy campaign, with volunteers taking over responsibility for maintaining the cemetery, it was acquired by the city council and handed over to a trust, which embarked on a major restoration programme.

After descending a short flight of steps, bear right at a T junction.

At the bottom, turn right past the Church of England mortuary chapel along a broad path, where the Italianate formality of the layout is in sharp contrast to the picturesque informality of the slopes above. Follow the path as it curves past the Greek Revival lodges – the right one now housing a visitor centre – and the tomb of Raja Rammohun Ray to the Nonconformist mortuary chapel, alongside which is a cafe.

Bear right up steps to the right of the cafe, turn left at a T Junction and carry on uphill. When you come to a broad drive, turn left and climb gently uphill to Top Lodge.

Go through the gates by Top Lodge and carry straight on along Cemetery Road. Over to your right is the green copper spire of the Church of the Holy Nativity, a prominent Bristol landmark and all that survives of a Venetian-style church built in the 1880s. The rest of the church was destroyed by bombing in the Second World War and rebuilt in the 1950s. At the end of the street is Totterdown Baptist Church, built in 1880 – look out for some curious brickwork in its gable end as you approach it.

At the main road, cross a pelican crossing, turn left and then right along Crowndale Road. When you reach the crossroads with Bayham Road, go into Perrett's Park and carry on in the same direction. The park, like Arno's Vale, is a natural amphitheatre, with far-reaching views over the city. It opened in 1925, despite considerable opposition, after Councillor CR Perrett gave £500 towards the purchase of the land. In January 2013, a neighbourhood group called the Community of Perrett's Park installed a toposcope to help visitors identify landmarks visible from the park.

At the end of the park, rejoin the road and carry on in the same direction. When you come to a five-way junction, carry straight on downhill and follow Sylvia Avenue as it curves round to the right.

At the bottom, turn right, cross the zebra crossing and turn into Nottingham Street. At the end, cross over, turn right, and a little way along turn left into Victoria Park, laid out around 1890 on Windmill Hill, long a place of public resort. Follow the path straight ahead as it heads uphill. At the top, when the path bears left past the bowling and tennis club, carry straight on across the grass to the right of the tennis courts. When you come to the junction of six paths, take the second from the left, heading off at a 45-degree angle towards a lamp with a bench around it. When you reach it, carry on in roughly the same direction downhill, with the platforms of Bedminster station below you on the

The ornate drinking fountain which once stood in Victoria Park was taken away for scrap in the Second World War. As can be seen from this Edwardian postcard, children back then had not only a park keeper but also a policeman to keep them in order.

A FOUNTAIN FOR PERRETT'S PARK

On 14 April, 1930, the *Western Daily Press* reported that

the water of the handsome red granite fountain in Perrett's Park, Knowle, was turned on, on Saturday, in the course of an interesting little ceremony. The fountain is the gift of Mr CR Perrett, the donor of the park ... During the last few months the new walk on the upper part of the ground has been laid out by the district surveyor, Mr WLF Palmer, acting under the city engineer, and there are now recessed seats and a rockery planted with shrubs and plants.

The fountain was to have been started on Saturday by Sir William Howell Davies, but in his unavoidable absence the task was performed by Alderman Frank Moore. Prior to the ceremony, selections of music were provided by the Kingswood Evangel Brass Band, and there was a large gathering of residents of the district.

Mr FA Wilshire, who presided at the ceremony, pointed out that ... it was very fortunate that Bristol possessed such men as Councillor Perrett who desired to leave his city the better for his having lived in it.

Alderman Frank Moore remarked that the inhabitants of that neighbourhood would always be thankful to Mr Perrett for the thought and consideration he had given in the provision of that fountain ... Not only the present generation, but generations to come would be very grateful to Mr Perrett for his kind action. All present wished him improved health and many years in which to see the park develop and large numbers of people enjoy it. Alderman Moore concluded by declaring the fountain 'open'.

The water was then turned on, and Mr Perrett was invited to take the first drink of water. He took a cup and wished all 'good health'.

In the photograph of the ceremony below, Mr Perrett is second from the left with a white beard. The fountain disappeared from the park in the 1970s, but, after exhaustive efforts to track it down, it has recently been rediscovered in a pond at Ashton Court. A campaign is now under way to restore it to its original site.

Top: Fry's advert in Fraser Street

Above: The Apple Tree, formerly the Maltster's Arms

Below: Stillhouse Lane malthouse

right. When the path ends, look for an old Fry's cocoa advert on the wall to your right, before going through a squeeze stile and heading down Fraser Street, some of whose houses sport particularly elaborate mouldings.

At the end, you are faced with three choices – turn left up to the Windmill Inn (originally the Friendship Inn); head into Bedminster station to catch a train back to Temple Meads or Lawrence Hill; or turn right under the railway bridge to continue the walk.

If you choose the latter option, turn right when you come to the main road, cross the zebra crossing and carry on, before turning left along Clarke Street. As you carry on along a footpath, you will see, to your right, Windmill Hill City Farm, opened in 1976 by a group of local residents and the first city farm to be established outside London. At the end is the splendidly adorned Apple Tree pub, originally known as the Maltster's Arms. As you carry on past it along Stillhouse Lane, you will

see the reason for its original name – an old malthouse on the corner of Willway Street. It was built sometime after 1855 on the site of a ropewalk. As you carry on, you will see courts and alleyways, lined with old workshops, leading through to Bedminster Parade on the left.

At the far end is one of Bedminster's hidden gems – the former St Mary Redcliffe & Temple School of 1895. Turn left by the school and then right along Bedminster Parade. Carry on over the roundabout, which takes you across Bedminster Bridge, over the New Cut. Carry on up Redcliff Hill and, when you reach St Mary Redcliffe Church, turn

St Mary Redcliffe & Temple School

right along Redcliffe Way to return to Temple Meads – or alternatively, carry straight on along Redcliff Street to the city centre.

Bedminster Bridge over the New Cut in the early twentieth century

Further information online:

Arno's Park Action Group: *www.arnospark.org.uk*
Arno's Vale Cemetery Trust: *www.arnosvale.org.uk*
Friends of Nightingale Valley: *www.brislington.org/fon/fon.html*
Friends of the Avon New Cut: *www.franc.org.uk*
St Anne's Park: *www.stannespark.com*
Victoria Park Action Group: *www.vpag.org.uk;*
   see also www.treasuremind.org/sediment
Windmill Hill City Farm: *www.windmillhillcityfarm.org.uk*

2
BRISTOL'S LOST RAILWAYS

Starts at: *Lawrence Hill station*

Ends at: *Temple Meads station*

Distance: *7.5 miles*

Terrain: *Pavements and tarmac or gravel paths*

Pubs & other amenities:

M Shed Cafe, open 10-4.30 (5.30 at weekends)

Barley Mow, Barton Road, BS2 0LP, open all day from 12, food served 12-3 & 5-9; dogs welcome; 0117 9304709; www.barleymowbristol. com

Grain Barge, Mardyke Wharf, BS8 4RU, open all day from 12; food served 12-3 & 6-9 Mon-Fri; dogs welcome on top deck; 12-10 Sat; 12-4 & 6-9 Sun; 0117 9299347; www.grainbarge.co.uk

Map: *Geographers' A-Z*

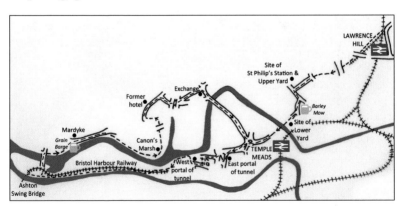

*T*his walk follows the course of two lost railway networks – the former Midland Railway lines on the east side of the city and the Bristol Harbour Railway which ran along both sides of the floating harbour. Both networks survived until the mid-1960s, but – with the exception of a preserved section of the Bristol Harbour Railway – both have now been largely obliterated. Walking the routes of these lines today is not only an exercise in nostalgia but a reminder of how much the city has changed in the last half century. You

Opposite: Bristol Harbour Railway

may also like to ponder how sections of these lines could have formed part of a metro or tramway system like those successfully adopted in other cities, had anyone had the foresight to think of it. As a diversion from railway matters, the walk also takes in an old Jewish cemetery, the site of a spa housed in a real – or royal – tennis court and the Green Men of Redcliffe.

Walk up the steps from Lawrence Hill station, turn left and then take the second left along Russell Town Avenue. By the zebra crossing at the end, carry on to the Bristol & Bath Railway Path and turn left. You are now following the course of the Bristol to Gloucestershire Railway, opened in 1835, later absorbed by the Midland Railway, and until 1969 part of the main line from Bristol to Birmingham.

As you cross a railway bridge, you have a panoramic view of Lawrence Hill station. The disused single line to the west of the running lines was a siding to a refuse transfer station on the old Midland line, which opened in 1985 but has recently closed. As you carry on, you will see the siding alongside you on the left. The width of the bridge you go under a little further along gives an idea how many tracks once ran through here. Just past the bridge was a junction, where the line to Temple Meads curved away to the left, while the original line – whose course the railway path follows – carried straight on.

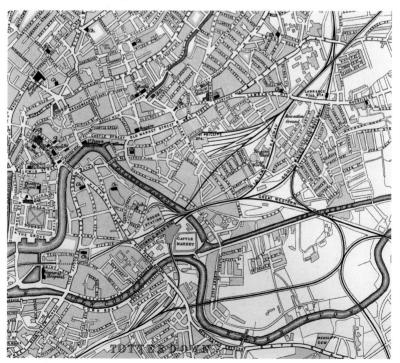

A map from around 1900 of the railway lines covered in the first part of the walk

THE BRISTOL & GLOUCESTERSHIRE RAILWAY

Bristol's first railway – the Bristol & Gloucestershire – opened on 6 August 1835. It linked collieries in the Coalpit Heath area with Bristol, where there were two depots – the Upper Yard in St Philip's, and the Lower Yard (also known as the Avonside Yard) alongside the river, where coal could be loaded into barges. Although there were plans to use locomotives on the line, most if not all of the traffic was worked by horses, except on an incline of 1 in 55 between Fishponds and Lawrence Hill, down which wagons travelled by gravity, controlled by brakesmen. Apart from the opening ceremony, when guests were conveyed in horse-drawn wagons, there seems to have been no passenger traffic.

Less than a month after the opening of the Bristol & Gloucestershire Railway, the Great Western received parliamentary approval to build a line between London and Bristol, and it was not long before there were calls for the Bristol & Gloucestershire Railway to be extended to Gloucester. A new company – the Bristol & Gloucester Railway – was formed, and Brunel was appointed chief engineer. Apart from the last two miles to Coalpit Heath, he followed the course of the Bristol & Gloucestershire Railway, which he converted from standard to broad gauge. At Bristol, a spur was opened from a junction at Lawrence Hill so that passenger trains from Gloucester could run into Temple Meads.

Although it was anticipated that the Great Western would eventually take over the line, the Great Western's offer to the Bristol & Gloucester shareholders was so niggardly that they accepted a better offer from the Midland Railway, which took over the standard-gauge Birmingham & Gloucester Railway at the same time. Although this gave them a line from Bristol to Birmingham, the change of gauge at Gloucester meant that everything – passengers and freight – had to change trains midway. This state of affairs lasted until 1854, when the line between Gloucester and Bristol was converted to standard gauge, dealing a major blow to the continued viability of Brunel's broad gauge.

In 1869, the Midland Railway opened a branch from Mangotsfield – five miles north of Bristol – to Bath, and the following year a new passenger terminus – St Philip's – opened alongside the Upper Yard. This was served by local trains between Bristol & Bath until it closed in 1953, and services were diverted to Temple Meads. The Upper Yard closed in 1967, but part of the Lower Yard remained open until the late 1980s. Passenger trains on the Midland line between Bristol and Bath were withdrawn in 1966, and in 1969 trains between Bristol and Gloucester were diverted south of Yate over former Great Western lines. The only section of the former Midland lines in Bristol still with tracks in situ is a disused siding which until recently served a refuse transfer station near Lawrence Hill, and, while much of the old system has been converted to cycle paths, St Philip's station and the Upper and Lower Yards have been comprehensively redeveloped.

Another bridge, adorned with murals, takes you under Barrow Road, after which the line divided again. One line carried straight on to the Lower Yard, while the other curved right to the Upper Yard and St Philip's station.

On your left you will see the disused refuse transfer station and the end of the siding on the course of the line to the Lower Yard. The railway path curves up to the right past industrial units built on the site of the line. When the path forks, bear left. After passing an information board and going under an arch in the form of a tree, cross and carry on along St Philip's Road, lined with large industrial units. As you near the end of the road, look to your right to see a high retaining wall. This marked the northern boundary of the Midland Railway site; St Philip's passenger station was built up against it.

St Philip's station in the 1930s

Ebenezer Chapel

Carry on to Midland Road (known as Whipping Cat Hill before the railway arrived) and cross to the site of the old Ebenezer Chapel. Dating from 1849, and latterly home to an architectural salvage company and then a cycle hire & repair business, it was demolished in July 2014 despite widespread protests and a high-profile campaign to save it.

Turn left along Midland Road. As you look ahead you can see

the road rising to a bridge which once crossed the line to the Lower Yard. Before you reach it, however, take the third right along Barton Road. This leads past the Barley Mow pub, built in 1828 as the Duke of York, and now owned by the Bristol Beer Factory, with one of the most extensive ranges of cask and craft beer in Bristol.

Just past it, behind a locked gate on the right, is a Jewish cemetery established in the mid-eighteenth century. A little further along, when you reach the point where the line to the Lower Yard crossed the road, turn right to follow its course along Chimney Steps.

Carry on across a road and along Pug's Lane, to the left of which lay the Lower Yard, while on the right – where the Ibis Hotel now stands – was the Avonside locomotive works. Carry on across another road and head towards a bridge over the river.* As you cross it, look to your left to see a recess on the left bank filled in with red brick, which was once the entrance to a railway wharf.

On the far side of the bridge carry straight on through the site of the Great Western Railway (GWR) goods yard until you reach a large roundabout. Follow the pavement as it curves left towards a pelican crossing with the disused Grosvenor Hotel, built in 1875, ahead. To the left of it, also currently empty, is the George Railway Hotel, built in 1866. A bridge carrying the Bristol Harbour Railway across Victoria Street stood next to the George. Although the bridge went decades ago, the viaduct beside the hotel was only demolished recently.

Goods wagons on the bridge linking Temple Meads goods yard with the harbour lines

---

* At the time of writing, this road was closed due to construction work. Until it reopens, you will need to divert left, turn right at the traffic lights and right alongside the floating harbour before turning left across the bridge.

THE HARBOUR LINES

The first part of the network of lines that stretched along both sides of Bristol Harbour opened in 1872. It ran from the GWR goods yard, north of Temple Meads station, crossed a bridge over Victoria Street and ran through a 267m tunnel under St Mary Redcliffe churchyard before crossing a steam-powered bascule bridge over Bathurst Basin. It ended at Princes Street Bridge, where two new wharves were built. The bridge across Victoria Street was on the site of the old Temple Gate, whose foundations were uncovered during construction.

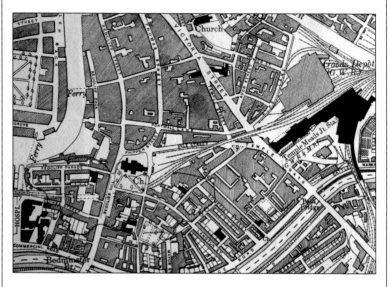

The line was extended to Wapping Wharf in 1876, and in 1906 it was extended again, along the New Cut, which it crossed on a swing bridge at Ashton, before continuing to a junction with the Portishead branch. A new line was also built north from Ashton Swing Bridge. This crossed Junction Lock on another swing bridge before heading east along the harbourside to a new goods yard at Canon's Marsh.

The line between Temple Meads and Wapping Wharf closed in 1964, and the line from Ashton Swing Bridge to Canon's Marsh closed a year later, but coal trains continued to run across Ashton Swing Bridge to Wapping Wharf until 1987. In 1978, heritage train services began operating at Wapping Wharf in connection with Bristol Industrial Museum. When coal traffic ceased, these were extended along the New Cut as far as Ashton Swing Bridge. The last train across the swing bridge, however, ran in 1996.

Although the line from Wapping Wharf to Ashton Swing Bridge still carries heritage train services, the lines from Temple Meads to Wapping Wharf and from Ashton Swing Bridge to Canon's Marsh have been largely obliterated.

Cross the road and carry on along the old street, paved with setts, beside the Grosvenor. This is a fragment of Portwall Street, which followed the line of a defensive wall built in the thirteenth century. Cross a pelican crossing ahead before turning left across Redcliffe Way and carrying on towards St Mary Redcliffe. Just before the church, turn left up Pump Lane. After passing a brick wall on the left near the top, turn left to see, on the other side of it, the bricked-up entrance to a tunnel which carried the railway under St Mary Redcliffe churchyard.

To see the other end of the tunnel, carry on to the top of Pump Lane, turn right into the churchyard and head diagonally across it. If you look to the left, you will see a fragment of tramline which was catapulted over the adjoining houses after a bomb fell on Redcliff Hill on Good Friday, 11 April 1941, and embedded itself into the ground. Go through the gate at the end, down a flight of steps and left across a pair of zebra crossings. Turn left uphill and right along Redcliffe Parade by the Colosseum pub.

The eighteenth-century terraces on Redcliffe Parade are not only among the finest in Bristol; perched on an eminence high above the harbour, they enjoy some of the best views in the city. Partway along Redcliffe Parade, turn left along Jubilee Place. Carry on along Alfred Place and at the end take a brief diversion to the left to look at Nos 10-12 Guinea Street, built around 1718 with Green Man-style keystones. Then head down to the right past the early eighteenth-century Golden Guinea pub and the former General Hospital, which closed in 2012 and is now being converted to apartments.

After turning right at the bottom, look to your right to see the western portal of the tunnel. The road here still has rails embedded in the setts. The line continued across a steam-powered bascule bridge – now replaced by a footbridge – over Bathurst Basin, beyond which its course is now covered by buildings. Cross the bridge, turn right alongside Bathhurst Basin and then left along the harbourside.

As you cross Prince's Road by the M Shed, you will see more rails embedded in the tarmac. These were sidings – to return to the course of the main harbourside line, turn left and after 20m you will see more old rails emerging from a garage on the left. Turn right to follow the line along the back of the M Shed, where bollards are now set into one of the tracks. Past the M Shed, you come to the preserved section of line along which steam-hauled services still operate. As the line continues through a locked gate to the loco shed, you need to go to the right of the building ahead and carry on along Wapping Wharf past sidings lined with old wagons. Just after passing an isolated dockside crane, turn left across the tracks along a path which then bears right to follow the line as it curves under

Wapping Wharf in 1969 ...

... and in 2014

Cumberland Road and along the New Cut.

Carry on for 900m with the line on your right, passing under Vauxhall Footbridge, until you come to a path, signposted to the Underfall Yard, crossing the line. You will be taking that path shortly, but first carry on past an old tobacco warehouse to one of the most impressive reminders of Bristol's railway heritage. Ashton Swing Bridge, which carries the path over the New Cut, opened in 1906. It originally had two decks – a road above and two railway tracks below – with a signal cabin on top. The road and signal cabin were removed in 1965, and the line, singled in 1976, was last used in 1996. There are plans to use the bridge for the Metro Bus route from Ashton Vale to Temple Meads, but a pathway at least as wide as the existing one will be retained.

Numberplate in Avon Crescent

Datestone on dock cottages

Trains crossing the bridge ran to a junction with the Portishead branch. If you look to the right, you will see the platform where steam trains from Wapping Wharf now terminate. Beyond it, another line headed north, its course now blocked by a bricked-up bridge.

To get to the other side of that bridge, you need to retrace your steps past the tobacco warehouse before crossing the line by the path you saw earlier. Carry on across two roads and turn left along Avon Crescent, built for dock workers in the 1830s and still with its original numberplates.

Just past the entrance to the Underfall Yard – originally known as the Nova Scotia Yard – look to your left to see the other side of the bricked-up bridge behind locked gates. The line continued across the road here, its course blocked once again by modern buildings.

Carry on past the Nova Scotia pub and, as you cross the bridge, look to your right to see, past a row of dock cottages, a small column marking the site of a railway bridge. Continue across a swing bridge and turn right along the dockside. Just past the Pump House – built around 1870 to provide hydraulic power for Cumberland Basin – you will see two red-brick columns, the remains of a railway swing bridge that stood here.

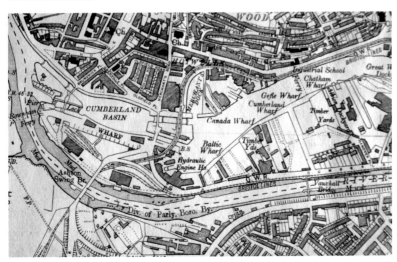

A mid twentieth-century map of Ashton Swing Bridge and the lines at the west end of the floating harbour

A 1950s view of a train heading east past Mardyke Wharf, where the Grain Barge is now moored

Looking in the other direction, a westbound train heads along Hotwells Road in 1959, with the gasworks still operational and the dock on the opposite bank still awaiting the return of the SS Great Britain.

The inlet just beyond the columns once led to a large dock, originally known as Champion's Dock but later renamed Merchant's Dock. It was built in 1765, and the railway curved round to the north of it. It has now been filled in and covered with houses. As you cross the mouth of another old dock – Poole's Wharf – look to the left to see Royal York Crescent high on the hillside above.

The railway, slowly curving back towards the harbourside, lay behind the modern buildings on your left. When you reach Mardyke Wharf (with the Mardyke pub across the road), look out for steps heading under the harbourside path to the river. This was a railway bridge and if you go down the steps you will see CMH 00 36 painted on the wall. Similar signs still appear on railway bridges to indicate their location. In this case, CMH tells us that it was on the Canon's Marsh Harbour line, while 00 36 tells us that it was 00 miles and 36 chains (724m) from the junction at Ashton Swing Bridge.

Bristol Beer Factory's Grain Barge, a little further on, is a tempting place to stop for a drink. In the eighteenth century, it was spa water that visitors came here in search of, after the short-lived Mardyke Spa opened, in a former tennis court, in June 1794:

> The medicinal qualities of the spa, originally discovered about 1786, were alleged to be superior to those of Cheltenham water, and astonishing cures were said to have been effected. Hot and cold baths were subsequently constructed [but] in July 1808, the spa, with its 'pleasant garden bordering on the river', was advertised to be let, and in January 1810, the premises were converted into 'The Mineral Spa coal wharf' by J Poole, coal wharfinger.[1]

In 1824, on the spot now occupied by the Grain Barge, the Seamen's Friend Society moored a boat called the Clifton Ark, which served as a seaman's chapel until 1833, when a church opened nearby.

From Mardyke Wharf the railway ran alongside the road, which is now lined with trees. After 250m, the road – and the line of the railway – carries on, while the harbourside path curves right along Porto Quay. You could carry on along the road and try to imagine what it must have been like when steam trains shuttled along here, but a better option is to head along Porto Quay – with views across to the SS Great Britain – past the old gasworks, established in 1823 and currently being converted to flats after years of dereliction.

The gasworks awaiting renovation in 2009

The end of the line, looking west towards the multi-coloured terraces of Clifton Wood

As you carry on along the harbourside, you eventually come to two buffers, with lines leading to them from the east. Transit sheds once stood on the left, and these sidings marked the end of the harbour railway, which, after running along Anchor Road, curved in a long loop across what is now Millennium Square and past the Lloyds building to end up facing in the opposite direction.

As you carry on, there may seem little left, apart from a few short sections of track, of the harbour railway. Carry on along the harbourside, though, and, as it curves to the north, head into Millennium Square and walk across to the At-Bristol building. This was originally part of a vast GWR goods shed, built from reinforced concrete in 1906. Head to the right of it, and ahead you will see a building dating from 1886, over 20 years before the railway arrived at Canon's Marsh. Now housing a restaurant, it was originally a leadworks.

Although that concludes our tour of Bristol's lost railways, you may be feeling short-changed by a Bristol railway walk that has managed to avoid virtually any mention of Brunel – so here, to get you back to Temple Meads, is a supplementary walk featuring two locations with links to the great man.

Head to the left of Prezzo, carry straight on over the pedestrian crossing, and, a little way along to the right, walk up the steps. Carry on along Trinity Street and turn left past the cathedral. Opposite the Central Library, turn right down College Street. The building facing you at the bottom was the Royal Western Hotel, designed by Brunel and built between 1837 and 1839. It was intended for passengers who had travelled down to Bristol on the Great Western Railway and were continuing to America in Brunel's Great Western Steamship. It seems odd that Brunel

Opposite page, from top: A map showing the lines on either side of the floating harbour in the mid-twentieth century

Canon's Marsh Goods Shed, converted to At-Bristol

A leadworks converted to a restaurant

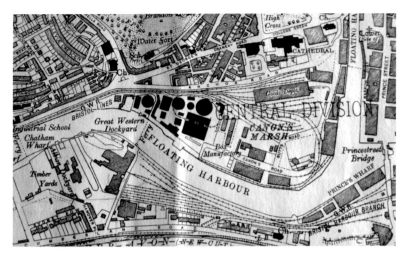

Above left: One of the grand entrances to the Royal Western Hotel, bearing more than a passing resemblance to the western portal of Brunel's Box Tunnel (above right)

decided to build it here rather than near Temple Meads or the docks, and it was never a commercial success. It closed after less than 20 years and was converted to Turkish Baths. After being rebuilt behind the façade in the 1980s it now houses council offices.

Bear right at the end of College Street along Frog Lane. There is another ocean-going connection here – the Mauretania Bar & Lounge on the left contains fittings from the RMS Mauretania, launched in 1906 and withdrawn from service in 1934.

After passing under Park Street, look up to your right to see one of Bristol's most famous – and now partially vandalised – Banksy's. Head to the right of the Hatchet Inn, dating from 1606, and turn right along Denmark Avenue. A left turn takes you into Orchard Street, and one of the finest collections of early eighteenth-century buildings in Bristol. Turn right along

Orchard Street, in the shadow of the Colston Tower

Orchard Lane, and, after passing Harvey's sherry warehouse – now converted to apartments – take the second right along Gaunt's Lane and left along Denmark Street. Turn left along St Augustine's Parade and cross at the pedestrian lights. Carry on past the Neptune statue, cross another set of lights and turn left. Cross the lights at the end of Baldwin Street and bear right along pedestrianised Clare Street. Carry on along Corn Street, and, when you come to another pedestrianised section, look up to the right to see the clock on the Exchange.

The Exchange dates from the early 1740s, and on the face of it may seem to have nothing to do with railways. Its clock, however, is a potent reminder of the impact the arrival of the Great Western had on the city. You will notice that it has two minute hands – a black one showing Greenwich Mean Time (GMT) and a red one set ten minutes earlier. When the clock was installed in 1822, it only had one minute hand, and was set to local time, ten minutes behind GMT. This was standard practice through the country, and, in an age when nothing moved faster than the fastest horse, caused few problems, as those travellers who carried watches could adjust them when they arrived at their destinations. When the Great Western Railway opened from London to Bristol in 1841, however, cutting the journey time from over twelve hours to under four, the drawbacks of this arrangement were obvious, and the GWR not unnaturally opted to use GMT at all its stations.

Bristolians, however, were having none of this and stuck resolutely to local time, with the result that a lot of people must have turned up at Temple Meads to find the train they planned to catch had already left. To try to prevent this, the clock on the Exchange, at the heart of the city's business district, was provided with an extra minute hand, set to GMT. This arrangement lasted until 1852, when GMT was officially adopted at a council meeting by a vote of 27 to 3, and the extra hand was removed, only to be restored in 1989 as a reminder of Bristol's two-timing past.

From here, carry on to the end of Corn Street, turn right, carry on across the lights and over Bristol bridge, before heading along Victoria Street to Temple Meads station.

Further information online:

Bristol Railway Archive: *www.bristol-rail.co.uk*
Bristol & Bath Railway Path: *www.bristolbathrailwaypath.org.uk*
Bristol Harbour Railway: *bristolharbourrailway.co.uk*
Friends of the Avon New Cut: *www.franc.org.uk*

3
TROOPER'S HILL, ROYATE HILL & ST GEORGE

Starts at: *Lawrence Hill station*

Ends at: *Lawrence Hill station*

Distance: *Six miles*

Terrain:

Pavements and paths, along with short sections of rough ground. The kissing gates on the approach to Troopers Hill are somewhat constricted.

Avon View cemetery is open from 9am to 4.30pm on weekdays, and from 11am to 4.30pm on weekends and Bank Holidays.

Pubs & other amenities:

Gwennie & Jack's Café kiosk, St George Park

Chelsea Inn, Chelsea Road, BS5 6AU; open daily from 1pm; dogs welcome; 0117 3291316; www.thechelseabs5.co.uk

Map: *Geographers' A-Z.*

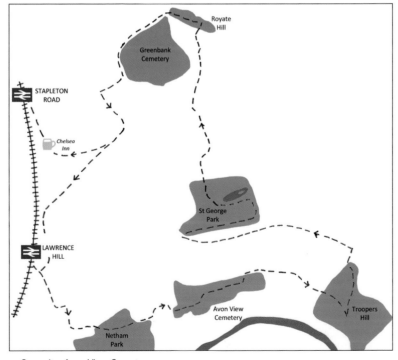

Opposite: Avon View Cemetery

*T*his walk is a green odyssey through Bristol's eastern suburbs, where old industrial sites, quarries, collieries and abandoned railways have been transformed into parks and nature reserves. Hidden corners, inspiring spaces and breathtaking views await exploration in this little-known part of the city.

Leaving Lawrence Hill station, cross the road and turn left. Take the third right along Cobden Street, carry straight on at the crossroads and bear left into Tichborne Road at the end. Turn first right along Mildred Street and left at the main road.

After 150m, cross and go up steps into Netham Park, which occupies a site once covered by Netham Chemical Works. Go to the right of the playground and follow the path straight on. After passing a netball pitch on the left, cross a drive and carry on across the grass to the right of a row of houses.

Carry straight on along a road. Turn left at the end up Netham Road, before crossing and turning right into Grindall Road. At the end, turn right along the main road for 60m, before crossing into Avon View Cemetery, opened in 1883.

At the top of the rise, bear left to a small roundabout. As you turn right again to head towards the chapel, the monuments get progressively grander. One of the grandest is an obelisk commemorating Handel Cossham, a self-made colliery owner who was also MP for Kingswood and a noted benefactor. At his funeral, on 28 April 1890, between forty and fifty thousand people gathered in and around the cemetery to pay tribute to his memory.

Turn left at the chapel, go through the gates and turn right along the road. After 150m, turn right into Strawberry Lane, and take the footpath bearing left to Troopers Hill. Carry on past allotments and up steps, bearing right when a path merges from the left. When you reach an access road, cross and carry on down between hedges, before turning left through a kissing gate (KG). Follow a path through scrubby woodland and through another KG. When you reach the open area, turn right along a path leading to Troopers Hill chimney, built around 1800 to carry poisonous fumes away from copper works at the bottom of the hill. Sitting almost on the lip of a large quarry, high above the Avon valley, it commands one of the finest views in the city.

Head back along the path, and, after passing an information board, carry on across the grass

TROOPERS HILL

Troopers Hill was once part of a royal hunting forest, but got its name because of a tradition that Parliamentary troops camped here before the second siege of Bristol in 1645. In the eighteenth and nineteenth centuries it was transformed by quarrying, mining and other industrial activities. Nevertheless, it remained one of the most popular recreational spaces in Bristol, as well as a venue for public gatherings. In 1878, when workers at the Great Western Cotton Works went on strike after their wages were cut by five per cent, they held a mass meeting here.[1] In 1889, striking quarrymen held a mass meeting here, and in 1895, several hundred boot & shoe workers marched here for a strike rally behind a brass band.[2] Religious groups also met here, sometimes facing opposition from other users of the hill. In May 1882, for example,

the Kingswood detachment of the Salvation Army, headed by a brass band and by banner-bearers, after parading the neighbourhood, made their way to the hill with the intention of holding a service there; but on arriving on the breezy plateau found that they had been preceded by a party of Bristol secularists, who were expounding their views. Some of the 'Salvationists' endeavoured to hustle the Freethinkers off the ground, and a regular melée ensued. In the course of the struggle turf and rotten eggs were thrown and sticks freely used. The disturbance lasted a considerable time, and ended in the rout of the secularists.[3]

Users of Troopers Hill were prepared to go to extraordinary lengths to preserve it as an open space. When a smallpox epidemic broke out in the city in April 1888, it was decided to build a temporary fever hospital here, with 18 beds. A mass meeting 'of the working men of Crew's Hole and neighbourhood' met on the hill to protest at the plans, and, when their wishes were ignored, someone tried to blow the half-completed hospital up with gunpowder.[4] It opened anyway, amid great acrimony, but was dismantled just over a year later.

In 1923, Troopers Hill was acquired by a Mr John Ballard, who set about trying to prevent access to it, undermining a right of way and putting up signs prohibiting trespass. Eventually, in 1928, two local residents took him to court. They won their case and access to the hill was enshrined in law.[5] There were calls for it to be turned into a public park, which came to nothing, but in 1956 the council acquired the land to preserve it as an open space, and in 1995 it was declared a Local Nature Reserve.

Old St George, clockwise from top left: the parish church; the technical school; the Don John's Cross pub; the park gates; and the public library

beside a green fence. Follow this as it swings left. At the road go through a KG and turn right. At the main road turn left.

After 350m, you come to the heart of St George. This area was largely developed in the last two decades of the nineteenth century, with some fairly grand buildings, many of which have sadly disappeared. On the corner of Cherry Orchard Lane, to your right, the Baptist church dates from 1932 but incorporates a rather fine school – later used as a drill hall – at the back. A little further along, the wall on your left – incorporating black bricks made from brass slag and a filled-in ornamental archway – is broached by a gateway leading to St George's House. This stands on the site of St George's Parish Church, a Gothic Revival building consecrated in 1880 and demolished in 1976. The Sikh Temple along to the right occupies another former school.

At the junction of Cloud's Hill Road is an ornate drinking fountain installed in 1896. Carry on across Glebe Road and Beaconsfield Road, where, according to old maps, the medieval Don John's Cross once stood. The modern library across the road stands on the site of an imposing Jacobean-style structure built in 1895. A little further on, Don John House, the modern blocks of flats by the bus shelter, stands on the site

The tree-lined avenue originally known as Church Walk

The island in the Wain Brook lake

of a pub called Don John's Cross, demolished in 2005. Just past it, the old police station on the corner of Northcote Road survives, but has been converted to flats.

Cross at the pedestrian lights a little further along. The patch of grass shaded by trees on the other side of the road is the site of the Park Picture House, demolished in 1967.

The Gurdwara Sikh Temple, 200m further on, was built in 1895 as a technical school. As you carry on round the corner to the right, you come to the main entrance to St George Park. This was laid out in the 1890s on land belonging to Fire Engine Farm. The farmhouse stood roughly where the lodge to the left of the entrance stands today, and, if you look across the road, you will see the Fire Engine Inn. The fire engine in question had nothing to do with fire-fighting. It was a steam engine – presumably impressive enough to be regarded as a local landmark – which pumped water from a coal mine whose site you will see shortly.

Head into the park and walk along the tree-lined avenue ahead. This follows the line of a thoroughfare called Church Walk, which predated the park. At the end, turn left downhill. At the bottom, go down steps

The lake in St George Park around the time of the First World War. In the background is a Co-op bakery opened in 1910

to the ornamental lake – created by damming the Wain Brook – and turn left along its southern shore. Carry on, turning right by a raised area (once topped by a bandstand) and walk up to the road. The houses over to your left, beyond the tennis courts, stand on the site of Whitehall Colliery, where the fire engine was located, which closed in 1893.

At the road, cross and head straight up Congleton Road. To your left, St Ambrose's church, known as the Cathedral of East Bristol, dates from 1913. At the main road, after crossing with care, turn right and then left into Thurston's Barton. After 40m, when the road forks, carry straight on along a footpath for 200m. When you reach a road, cross and turn left. At Gordon Road, cross and turn right. After 100m, when the road forks, bear left into a cul de sac. Carry on at the end, and, as the path swings right, turn left onto the old Midland Railway line – now a railway path – and turn right. After crossing a bridge, continue for 50m before turning left into Clay Bottom – its name recalling the brickworks that once that operated in this area, converting the clay soil into bricks. Carry on to the road, turn left and then right along Wainbrook Drive. Turn right past the backs of houses and, after 75m, cut across the grass to the entrance to

THE BATTLE OF ROYATE HILL

The five-acre nature reserve at Royate Hill may seem remarkable chiefly because part of it occupies an old railway viaduct, but the story of how local residents fought to save it against

overwhelming odds makes this one of the most inspiring open spaces in the city.

In 1990, after acquiring the land, a company called Beechgold Developments Ltd applied to demolish the viaduct and build 60 houses on the site. The application was refused and, when the company appealed, the inspector upheld the council's decision on the grounds that the site was 'an area of semi-natural vegetation, which is a scarce resource in Bristol'.

That was far from being the end of the story, however. At 6am on 23 May 1992 – the Saturday before the Spring Bank Holiday – local residents woke to find bulldozers and men with chainsaws busy clearing the site. Trying to stop the bulldozers by standing in their path was futile. Even when the police turned up and told the drivers to stop because of public safety, they were determined to carry on with the work of destruction. The only thing that could stop them was an injunction, but finding anybody to issue one on a Bank Holiday Saturday was no easy matter.

By the time an emergency injunction was eventually issued, around a third of the site had been devastated. This was at the height of the nesting season, and local residents recall birds frantically calling out to their young, now buried beneath tons of landfill. The company was unrepentant, claiming that it had merely been carrying out the council's directive to clear rubbish off the site in case it attracted vermin, and were fined a mere £400, the maximum penalty for destroying a bird's nest.

In the wake of the devastation, Avon Wildlife Trust worked with local residents to maintain a 24-hour vigil on the site, and the injunction was upheld at a public enquiry. The council tried – unsuccessfully – to negotiate with the developers to buy the land before applying for a Compulsory Purchase Order, which was granted in April 1995.

Over 20 years on from that dreadful May morning, nature, aided by a team

of volunteers, has reclaimed the site. Bully-boy tactics by big companies are nothing new, nor are they likely to diminish in the years to come, but it is heartening to know that sometimes local residents can beat them.

Above: A gravel path where trains once ran

Right: A wild rose at Royate Hill

Below: First World War headstones in Greenbank Cemetery

Royate Hill Nature Reserve, where a flight of steps leads up to the trackbed of the Clifton Extension line from Kingswood Junction to Ashley Hill Junction, along which you turn left. The section designated – after a prolonged and bitter fight – as a nature reserve includes a long and lofty viaduct. From it there are views north over the allotments in the Coombe Brook Valley and south over Greenbank Cemetery, opened in 1871. Beyond it, a narrow strip of gravel winds through a hidden world, rich in ox-eye daisies, knapweed, vetch and dog roses, and onto a grassy embankment – like a chunk of downland transplanted to suburbia – before heading down steps, past a set of mosaics, to the road.

Turn left along the pavement beside Greenbank Cemetery, where, after 350 metres, you will see a plot with 59 headstones commemorating soldiers killed in the First World War. At the junction with Robertson Road, carry straight on beside the cemetery along Thurlow Road. At the end turn right and take the second left along Kingsley Road. The extraordinary red-and-yellow-brick building on the corner was built as a Congregational church in 1902. After closing in 2008, there were plans to demolish it and build flats on the site, but it has been converted to a mosque

The railway path near Devon Road

The Chelsea

instead. As you cross Co-operation Road, look up to the left to see the Elizabeth Shaw chocolate factory, opened in 1901, closed in 2006 and still empty. At the end, turn left along Bruce Road and then right down a ramp to turn right along the railway path.

As you near the end of the walk, you have a choice of either calling into the Chelsea Inn – a lively, friendly street-corner local with an excellent range of beers and ciders – or of heading straight back to Lawrence Hill station.

To visit the Chelsea, carry on along the railway path for 200m. Just after going under Devon Road Bridge, turn right up a ramp and turn left along Colston Road. At the end, turn right along Chelsea Road for 50m and you will find the pub 30m along on the right. From here, it is quicker to return to Stapleton Road station, for which carry on along Chelsea Road, continue along Roman Road, turn left at the end along High Street and then right by St Mark's church (with the animals on the roof of the tower) to find the path up to the station.

To head back to Lawrence Hill station, carry on along the railway path for 700m, before turning left onto Russelltown Avenue. Head south to the end of the avenue, turn right along the main road and the station is 150m along on the right.

Further information online:

Friends of Troopers Hill: *www.troopers-hill.org.uk*
Friends of St George Park: *www.stgeorgenp.org.uk/friends-of-st-george-park*
Bristol & Bath Railway Path: *www.bristolbathrailwaypath.org.uk*
Royate Hill Nature Reserve: *www.avonwildlifetrust.org.uk/reserves/royate_hill.htm*
Greater Fishponds: *www.fishpondspeople.co.uk*

4
THE FROME VALLEY

Starts at: *Stapleton Road station*
Ends at: *Bristol Parkway station*
Distance: *11 miles*
Terrain: *Mostly on rough paths with some field walking*
Pubs & other amenities:
Snuff Mills Café, open 9.30-5.30 (4.30 in winter)

White Lion, Frenchay Common, BS16 1LZ; open daily from 12; food served all day; 0117 9568787; www.johnbarras.com/pub/white-lion-frenchay-bristol/m8643/

Cross Hands, Down Road, Winterbourne Down, BS36 1BZ; open daily from 12; dogs welcome; 01454 850077

Crown Inn, Bristol Road, Hambrook, BS16 1RY; open daily from 12; food served all day Mon-Sat; 12-4 Sun); 0117 9568005

Map: Geographers' A-Z & OS Explorer 155

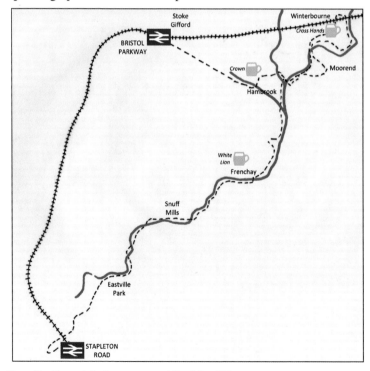

Opposite: The weir that once powered Stapleton Mill

*T*his walk follows the course of the River Frome from Stapleton Road to Winterbourne before heading west through Hambrook and Stoke Gifford to end at Parkway station. The river today is a picturesque haven for wildlife, but for centuries it was an industrial powerhouse, playing a key role in Bristol's economic growth. There were eleven mills along the Frome between Eastville and Winterbourne. Most were established by the early seventeenth century, but some were considerably older. Originally they were 'grist' mills for grinding corn, but in the eighteenth century many were converted for metalworking or snuff grinding, and several new mills were also built to serve these industries. All, though, fell into disuse in the late nineteenth or early twentieth century as they were supplanted by steam mills, and most have disappeared virtually without trace. The latter part of the walk, through the south Gloucestershire countryside, also takes in an iron age fort and an impressive railway viaduct, along with ancient manor houses, cottages, farms and inns.

On arriving at Stapleton Road station from Bristol, go down the steps at the north end of the station. On arriving at Stapleton Road from the north, cross the footbridge to the other platform and go down the steps at the north end. The battlemented turret in the wall beside the steps was a gazebo in the grounds of Stapleton Manor, which would once have looked out across the River Frome to the green fields beyond.

Turn left along Stapleton Road, where you will see early nineteenth-century houses across the road. Cross at the traffic island and bear right along Warwick Road (don't turn sharp right into Warwick Avenue). After 50m turn right along Fox Road and follow the road as it bears right to the Old Fox Inn, closed in 2004 but still with its sign bracket. Today it looks out across the M32, but originally it stood on the banks of the River Frome, and as such marks the true beginning of our walk.

Carry on past the pub and after 50m bear left into Fox Park. You are now following the old course of the river, and as you go under the stone

railway bridge, built in 1863, you can see on the right where it once flowed. The iron railway bridge a little further along was built in 1888 when the line was quadrupled. The tracks across it were taken up in 1984, but there are now plans to relay them.

Where once the river ran

The Black Swan, dating from the seventeenth century, seen here in the 1920s

Carry on along the path as it curves towards the M32, with the Purdown BT Tower ahead, and carry on beside the motorway. After 100m, turn right along a footpath between high railings and a stone wall. Turn left along Stapleton Road past the Black Swan. At the traffic lights turn left between concrete bollards. Turn right and then left under the M32. After 75m, look over the railings on the left for your first – distinctly uninspiring – glimpse of the river. Although the Frome continues to flow – albeit underground – past the Old Fox and through the centre of Bristol to the floating harbour, some of its waters are diverted, by the sluices you see here, through a three-mile tunnel which joins the Avon downstream from the Clifton Suspension Bridge. Known as the Northern Stormwater Interceptor, the tunnel was completed in the 1960s to alleviate the floods which had devastated low-lying parts of the city for centuries.

Retrace your steps, but, before you reach the M32, turn left along Napier Road, then right, before bearing left across the open space below the M32. As you carry on along Stapleton Road, beside the M32, you will see, through the railings on your left, the river running through a deep, dark, narrow gully.

Carry on along the right-hand pavement to a large roundabout. The branch of the Clifton Extension Railway from Kingswood Junction to Ashley Hill Junction crossed the valley here on a thirteen-arch viaduct, which was demolished in 1968. Carry on past the entrance to a subway and across two sets of lights before heading up a path into Eastville Park. Carry straight on along a path through an avenue of mature trees. Looking across to the right, the large expanse of parkland could almost be part of a great country estate. It was in fact farmland belonging to Greville Smyth

THE OLD FOX

Few of Bristol's lost pubs are so sadly missed as the Old Fox. Built in the early eighteenth century, it took advantage of its riverside location by providing bathing facilities. On 19 July 1755, the *Bristol Journal* advertised 'the Old Fox public house, at Broad Stoney, near Lower Easton' for sale or to let, along with 'a bathing place in the river Froom, with commodious dressing houses'.*

Matthew's *Bristol Directory* for 1793-4 listed two establishments 'for those who are fond of bathing and swimming: the spacious bath and dressing houses ... of Mr Rennison, near to Stokes-croft turnpike; and the conveniences for bathing in the River Froom, at the Fox, Baptist-mills, about half a mile from Bristol'.†

In 1857, when Henry Fletcher, the landlord of the Old Fox, was declared bankrupt, he was described as a 'licensed victualler and bathing-house proprietor', and the lease of this 'well-known house' was advertised 'with bathing houses adjoining'.[1] It was taken over by Joseph Reynolds, who two years later established a court of the Ancient Order of Foresters – known as the 'Banks of the Froom' Court – at the inn.[2] On 14 June 1860, he placed an advertisement in the *Western Daily Press*:

IMPORTANT TO BATHERS
OLD FOX INN, BAPTIST MILLS
J Reynolds begs to inform the public that the baths have been entirely cleansed and re-fitted, with every convenience for bathers, and solicits a visit.
Upper Baths (towel included), 2d; Lower Baths, 1d.
DANCING on the green every Monday and Tuesday during the summer months; should the weather prove unfavourable, the large room will be fitted up for dancing. Rifle shooting and good skittle alley on the premises.

---

* Although spelt 'Frome' today, 'Froom' was once the more usual spelling.
† The site of Rennison's Baths is visited in the fifth walk.

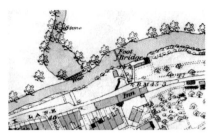

A map showing the Old Fox and its river-side pleasure grounds in the 1880s

Festivities were not confined to the summer. On 7 January the following year, the *Western Daily Press* reported that 'the low-lying meadows ... opposite the Old Fox at Baptist Mills ... were thronged with young and old of both sexes, enjoying either a slide or a skate, and fearless of a fall, knowing that the water beneath was but the shallow flood occasioned by the recent melting of the snow.' Later in the year, a 'grand fete and gala' was held in the 'pleasure ground' of the Old Fox to raise funds for the Bristol Royal Infirmary.[3] There was also a bowling green in the grounds., on which quoits matches were played.

When the Old Fox was put up for sale in 1888, it was described as

> the old-established, valuable, fully-licensed freehold premises known as the Old Fox Inn, with the skittle alley, stabling, greenhouse, well-known bathing and boating houses, extensive pleasure grounds and premises ... adjoining the River Froom ... and conveniently near the Stapleton Road station. The house contains extensive underground cellarage, bar, bar parlour, brewhouse, kitchen and offices; on first floor, large clubroom and bedroom, and four bedrooms over. The property, besides offering a good opportunity for greatly developing the present business connected with the pleasure grounds, bathing, boating and skating, possesses a valuable frontage which is very eligible for building purposes.[4]

The Old Fox's career as a bathing and boating establishment was rapidly drawing to a close, as in 1891 the council announced plans to straighten and widen the river as part of a flood prevention scheme.[5] Shortly afterwards, the pleasure grounds were sold for housing, and it was around this time that the Old Fox acquired a redbrick extension to cater for an influx of regular customers from newly-built streets nearby.

It eventually became a Courage pub, but in 1975 the brewery decided it was surplus to requirements and put it up for sale. It was snapped up by CAMRA (Real Ale) Investments Ltd, a company set up by the fledgling Campaign for Real Ale, as a flagship for real ale in the city. In 1983, CAMRA (Real Ale) Investments changed its name to Midsummer Inns, and two years later was taken over a company called Swithland Leisure, which was dissolved in 1998. The Old Fox continued in private ownership as one of the top cask-ale pubs in the city until 2004, when it was sold at auction. Unfortunately, the new owners had no intention of running it as a pub; they planned to turn it into a computer education centre. And so, on 15 May 2004, after more than 250 years, one of Bristol's most historic inns called last orders for the very last time.

Above & below: The lake in Eastville Park shortly after its construction

Left: A grey heron stands in the lake waiting for an unsuspecting fish. Kingfishers can also be seen along the River Frome, although they are somewhat harder to photograph

of Ashton Court, and there was a long campaign for a park in Eastville before the council acquired the 70-acre site in 1889.

Carry on over two crosspaths, before going down steps to a lake and walking along its left bank. The lake, constructed in 1905 by hundreds of unemployed men recruited by the council's distress relief committee, is not only surprisingly large but designed in such a way that its full extent cannot be seen from any one point.

At the end of the lake, continue on up a path, but instead of carrying on into a meadow, turn left along a footpath, where you will see the river below you on the left. After 400m, you come to an impressive weir. Stapleton Mill, also known as Lathbury Mill, stood beside it on the far bank. First recorded in 1620, it was demolished around 1880.

Carry on across a bridge built in 1937 after the footpath past the Black Rocks on the right bank was washed away. Although you need to

bear right to continue along the valley, it is worth making a short diversion left and then right up a flight of steps to see an ice house which supplied ice to nearby Stapleton House.

Continuing along the valley, you come to Wickham Bridge, built in the

The banks of the Frome around 1910

Stapleton Mill before demolition around 1880

THE PATH PAST THE BLACK ROCKS

The path between Eastville Park and Wickham Bridge has long been a tranquil retreat for Bristolians, most of whom are probably unaware of its eventful and occasionally acrimonious history. The land belonged to the Merchant Venturers, who in 1887 built a wall and employed a watchman to keep people out. After numerous complaints, the clerk of the Stapleton Local Board wrote to the Merchant Venturers 'requesting them to remove the obstruction'. They replied that the matter would 'come before the next meeting of the society', but they 'would defend their rights', adding that they 'did not object to people using the path, but they were troubled by trespassers'.[6]

At which point the National Footpath Preservation Society weighed in, asking for firm action to be taken to remove the obstruction, and explaining why the footpath was so important to local people:

The path is not only valuable as a thoroughfare, but also giving access to the only good bathing place in that part of the river. The weir which, I believe, was built for the mill which formerly stood on the site of the Colston School bath, keeps back the water, and I am informed that the public have for many years used the path in order to get to the water at this spot for bathing. The rock renders the place secluded on one side, and it is not commanded by any houses. Below the weir the water is, throughout a great part of the year, too shallow for bathing, and ... bathing under the Black Rock (before eight in the morning and after eight in the evening) has not hitherto been interfered with. I presume that the surveyor to the local board will have instructions to see that the stiles and gates at each end of the land belonging to the Merchant Venturers are put in proper order. Their present condition invites and causes the damages of which the Merchant Venturers' Society complains.[7]

The local representative of the Footpath Preservation Society later claimed that it was only the society's intervention that had 'practically prevented the Merchant Venturers from closing ... the path at Stapleton'.[8]

Even though access was now unimpeded, further problems arose due to some people bathing not wisely but too well. A correspondent in the *Bristol Mercury* summed up the problem succinctly:

Kindly allow me, through the medium of your valuable paper, to call attention to an intolerable nuisance which exists at Stapleton. Gangs of roughs are continually bathing, without any regard to decency, in the River Froom, between the Colston School baths and the Snuff Mills, and running about the fields insufficiently clothed, and hooting and using bad language. It is a public thoroughfare, and much resorted to by people of both sexes for a pleasant walk, but now it is to be avoided by all respectable people, on account of the nuisance complained of. In addition, people on their way to the parish church (particularly ladies) have to go a long distance out of their way in order to avoid the disgraceful scenes. Can nothing be done to protect the public right and abolish this great nuisance?[9]

In the early 1920s another problem arose when part of the path was washed away. In January 1926, the Bristol & District Footpaths Preservation Society was revived and the first matter to be brought before the committee was

the state of the footpath at Stapleton Glen which gives access to the beautiful walk along the Frome from the lake at Eastville Park as far as Wickham Bridge, and from there onwards to the old Snuff Mills. This path ... was one of the first rights of way to which a right was asserted by the Bristol Footpath Society ... It was then possible to walk straight along the level below the well-known Black Rock which juts out into the river immediately opposite the weir above the Colston School Baths. The Rock has been worn away precisely at the point and only a very daring and athletic person who would be prepared for a sudden immersion in case of the slightest slip would venture to go round it. In addition to this obstacle the river bank has been worn away at three or four places between the Black Rock and the entrance to Eastville Park, and the path itself has completely gone in some spots, necessitating a trespass on the adjoining land ... The Bristol Corporation ... are the

The Black Rocks around 1916

body on whom the legal duty of repair is cast, and it is thought that £50 or £60 rightly expended would be all that is required.[10]

Nothing was done, and over six years later a correspondent wrote to the *Western Daily Press* declaring it

a pity ... that the Black Rocks should be falling into a state of decay. There was at one time a footpath on which one could walk along by the side of the river, but this has now been washed away in many places ... Nothing is more delightful than in going this way to Sea Mills and Frenchay, yet one is in constant danger of personal injury through unsuitable pathways.[11]

Still nothing happened, but when, in April 1937, the chairman of the council's planning committee was asked to

consider the urgent necessity of making a path from the wicket gate at the north end of the Eastville Park lake along the side of the river to what is known as the Black Rock; also a path either around the rocks or a bridge over the river in order that pedestrians can journey along the Eastville side of the river to Snuff Mills without having to climb over the dangerous rocks,

he replied that 'plans for the bridge were in hand'. A few months later 'an artistic rural bridge' was installed, finally giving unrestricted access to the valley.[12]

early seventeenth century, which once carried the old road to Gloucester. After crossing it, turn left to follow a footpath alongside the river. As you pass allotments, look up to the right to see the gables of Wickham Court, visited in Walk 7.

When the path forks, bear right up to the road, cross and turn left along the pavement. As you cross a bridge over the river, you will see a weir on your right. A mill – variously known as Curtis Mill, Broom Mill, Wyatt's Mill and Watt's Mill – stood on the right bank. Dating from sometime before 1606, it was demolished around 1890.

On the far side of the bridge, turn right along River View. The cottage in the terrace on your left with a Gothic-style doorway and an 1886 datestone was, until 2009, a Methodist chapel. After passing the Snuff Mills Café, carry on through a car park, before gardens mark the approach to Whitwood Mill. Built sometime before 1610, this closed in the early twentieth century and, after being acquired by the council in 1926, was largely demolished. It has since been partially renovated and interpretation boards describe the work carried out. As this stretch of the river is known as 'Snuff Mills', and this is the only mill of which a fragment survives, it is commonly referred to as 'the snuff mill' – commonly but wrongly, as snuff was never ground here.

A postcard of Whitwood Mill after being acquired by the council in 1926, but before being largely demolished

Carry on along the valley and, when the path forks, bear right to stay close to the river. Just after the paths join up again before crossing

The ruins of the Lower Snuff Mill in the early twentieth century, with the footbridge in the background

a footbridge, you will see an open space on the right. This was the site of the Lower Snuff Mill, also known as Witherley's or Snuffy Jack's Mill. First recorded in 1610, it had become a snuff mill by 1790 and was acquired by HO Wills in 1805. It later became a flock

mill before closing around 1877. The buildings survived, in a ruinous state, until well into the twentieth century before being demolished.*

After crossing the river, turn left alongside it. The next weir marks the site of the Upper Snuff Mill, also known as King's Mill, which stood on the far bank. As you carry on alongside the river, the path suddenly becomes rougher and narrower. After passing a flow monitoring channel, designed to warn of impending floods, you will see an old building, much modernised, on the far bank. Frenchay Mill, which stood beside the weir to the left of it, closed in 1905 and was demolished around 1958.

Shortly after this you come to a wide flight of steps. At the top, carry on to the road and turn left across a bridge.

If you feel in need of refreshment at this stage, turn left on the other side of the bridge, follow the road uphill for 200m and turn right along Frenchay Common to the White Lion, before heading back down to the bridge to continue the walk.

To carry on, turn right on the other side of the bridge and look back to see a plaque recording the bridge's opening in 1788. Look out too for an impressive old quarry behind a cottage on the left. Frenchay Flock Mill, a little further along on the right, was built as an ironworks in 1761. It became a flock mill sometime after 1880, and was later home to a variety of light industrial units before being converted to housing in the 1990s. Just past it is Grove House, once home to the Frenchay highwayman.

A little way up the hill, turn right along Chapel Lane. Carry on through a squeeze stile and along a footpath past another former Methodist chapel converted to a house. As you approach the road, you will see Cleeve Bridge, a massive structure whose original arches, built in the eighteenth century, can be seen underneath those added in the early

* A painting of this mill from around 1822 by Francis Danby can be seen in the Museum & Art Gallery.

nineteenth century when it was raised and widened. There is another mill, still largely intact, 100m above the bridge. In the early twentieth century, there were tea gardens in its grounds, but these closed in 1956. Today it is a private house and the footpath does not run past it.

Follow the path through a squeeze stile and up to another stile. Cross the road and head uphill between high banks. After passing an old dovecote on the right – now converted to an electricity substation

A dovecote converted to an electricity substation

– turn right down Grange Park. Just past No 8, turn left down a drive and bear right through a kissing gate (KG) at the bottom. When the path forks, bear left along a muddy path to carry on along the valley. Soon you will find yourself in one of the quietest and most secluded stretches of the valley so far. Make the most of it, for, as the distant roar of traffic indicates, another close encounter with a motorway awaits.

First, though, come the twin bridges of the Avon Ring Road. Then, after crossing the Ham Brook as it flows into the Frome, comes the M4, with the raw red rocks underneath its bridges still unsoftened by vegetation.

After crossing a stile, turn right across a footbridge. If you look to the left you will see the remains of Hambrook Mill, a corn mill built sometime before 1653 and closed in the early twentieth century. Just beyond it, Bradley Brook, flowing down from Bradley Stoke, joins the River Frome. Carry on past

Moorend Mill, possibly the smallest on the River Frome

THE FRENCHAY HIGHWAYMAN

'On the 28th January 1767, a man calling himself Hickson, and living at Frenchay in the style of a country gentleman, was arrested near Lawford's Gate, on suspicion of having committed several capital offences ... He was the son of a Worcestershire farmer named Higgins, and had led, with his brothers, a vicious life from boyhood. In 1764 he was convicted of a robbery at Worcester, and, being sentenced to transportation, was shipped at Bristol for America. Within a month of his being sold there into temporary slavery, he broke into a merchant's office at Boston, and stole sufficient money to enable him to secure a berth in a ship bound for England, which he reached within three months of his departure. He then resumed his former career of crime in Worcestershire; but after one of his brothers had been hanged there in 1763, for returning from transportation, he removed into Gloucestershire, and finally took a mansion at Frenchay, set up a pack of dogs and a stable of remarkably fine hunting horses, and lived in what the Bristol Journal termed 'a splendid manner'. Suspicions having arisen that his hunters were really kept for the perpetration of highway robberies, he was carried before Sir Abraham Elton, committed for trial, and removed to Gloucester. But at the April assizes no evidence as to robberies could be obtained against him, and as the charge of returning from transportation could be tried only at Worcester, the judge liberated him upon two sureties of £60 each. Higgins then retired to Carmarthenshire, where he committed two daring burglaries before again falling into the hands of justice. In July he was conveyed in irons to Worcester, where his previous conviction was made clear; but the Crown neglected to prove his shipment at Bristol, and the judge ordered his acquittal. However, at the following assizes at Carmarthen he was sentenced to death for his latest crimes. Executions generally took place about a week after conviction; but powerful influences were exercised to rescue the 'gentleman' rogue, an 'Earl of —' being referred to in the newspapers as especially active in his behalf. The execution, repeatedly postponed, took place in November – a respite received a few days before having turned out to be a forgery. Higgins's exploits, as magnified by tradition, are recorded in Mr. Leech's Brief Romances from Bristol History; but the cleverly-told story of the highwayman's presence at a Hot Well ball, and of his subsequent robbery of a Bristol banker on the road to London, is the product of a lively imagination.'

John Latimer, *Annals of Bristol in the Eighteenth Century*, pp. 379-80

a house, part of which dates from the seventeenth century, and climb steps. Carry on along a footpath beside the motorway before turning left to head away from it. When you come to a lane, turn left along it. After passing eighteenth-century Moorend House, you come to a T junction, with the river straight ahead. Moorend Mill, which stood on the island in the middle of the stream, was built in the eighteenth century. The photograph on the left shows it in the early twentieth century, but it has since vanished virtually without trace, along with the weir that once powered it.

Turn right at the T junction and, when the lane forks, carry straight on uphill, passing an old brewhouse and maltings. A little further along is something splendid – Moorend Farm, a gabled farmhouse built in 1676 and set back behind magnificent ivy-covered gateposts. It replaced an earlier building which stood

Moorend Farm

on the other side of the road. The building across the road today is known as Old Court House and has a datestone of 1701 over the door, but looks as though it may incorporate features – such as the bull's-eye windows in the gable ends – from the earlier house.

At the crossroads, carry straight on uphill.* After 175m, follow a footpath sign through the gateway to Up Yonder on the left. 50m along the drive, turn left following a footpath waymark across a stile. Carry on through the ramparts of Bury Hill Camp, an iron age fort later used by the Romans. Like other hilltop forts, it commanded wide-ranging views, but trees have grown up, transforming it into a self-contained enclosure with no hint of what lies beyond.

Head across the camp, follow a footpath through the ramparts on the far side, and cross a stile by Camp Cottage. Carry on past it and head down a steep, narrow path, interspersed with steps, which gives an idea how well chosen the site atop the hill was for a defensive camp.

The path leads down to a lane along which you turn right (this is where you rejoin the walk if you took the easier option). Just before a bridge, turn right along a footpath by the river. Winterbourne Mill, a corn mill converted to a cider mill around

The ruins of Winterbourne Mill in the early twentieth century

* The next part of the walk is the most challenging, with tricky stiles into and out of Bury Hill Camp, and a steep and slippery downhill path. For an easier route, turn left at the crossroads just past Moorend Farm, bear right at a T junction, and after another 100m you will see the footpath heading down from the camp on your right.

1900 and closed in the 1920s, once stood on the opposite bank. It was demolished in the 1950s and the weir beside it was later swept away in floods.

Carry on alongside the river and, when you come to a footbridge, cross it. On the far side turn right, taking the muddy path alongside the river rather than the one heading uphill. Carry on past broken-down walls to the ruins of old buildings before heading up steps, going through a gap in a wall and turning right. When you come to a lane – known as the Dingle – carry on along it in the same direction. This leads to Damson's Bridge – originally Damason's Bridge – where a turnpike gate once stood.

Cross and turn right over the bridge, and on the far side turn left through a KG. Follow the path alongside the river as Huckford Viaduct comes into view ahead. This opened in 1903 as part of the GWR's route from London to South Wales. It ran from Wootton Bassett to Patchway, cost two million pounds to build, and was not only eleven miles shorter than the old route via Bristol but less steeply graded. Even without the viaduct to enliven the scene, this is one of the loveliest stretches of the River Frome.

Just before the viaduct, follow the path across a footbridge. This may be the site of Huckford Mill, which appears on a map of 1828, although no trace of it survives. Turn right uphill (although you may want to divert left into Huckford Quarry, which supplied stone for the viaduct and is now a nature reserve). The pitched stones of the path heading up under the viaduct suggest it was used by packhorses.

When the path forks, bear left uphill. At the top go through a KG and turn left – after diverting to the right for a few metres to see Harcombe Farm, another splendid mid-seventeenth-century gabled building. After crossing the railway – where there is a superb view along the line – cross the road and carry on into Winterbourne Down. At the crossroads – with the Cross Hands Inn on the right – carry straight on. At the T junction, turn right along Church Road. When you come to another junction, carry on along Church Road. After 150m, turn left down Mill Steps, once a short cut down to Winterbourne Mill.

At the bottom, cross the end of Frome Bank Gardens and bear left across the river. Carry straight on and, when the road forks, bear right alongside the river. Bear right at a T junction and, at the next junction, carry straight on and follow the lane as it bears right past Frome Cottage. After crossing the river, turn left along a footpath. At the end, go through a KG and turn right past the old Hambrook Inn. Originally a nineteenth-century beerhouse occupying the building facing the lane, it was extended in grand style after being granted a full licence. It is now the Lucky Dragon All-You-Can-Eat Chinese Restaurant & Bar.

At the main road, turn left past the eighteenth-century White Horse Inn and carry on under the M4. You will see a number of eighteenth-century buildings as you approach the T junction at the top of the hill. The two grandest, set well back from the road, are Hambrook Grove, on the left, and Hambrook Court, tucked away behind the high hedge to the left of the Crown Inn.

An animated scene outside the Crown at Hambrook around 1910

Turn left at the T junction, and after 150m you will see two large seventeenth-century buildings – the Grange and Hambrook House – on the right. Not only do they seem uncomfortably close to each other, but, although they both abut the road, their façades are at right angles to it. Just past them, cross and turn right along a lane called The Stream. The stream in question is the Ham Brook – on the right – which gave its name to the village.

After 200m, you come to a T junction with another seventeenth century building – Brook House – on the left. If you look through the gates of Baylis's Yard, to the left, you will see a barn dating from around 1800 at the far end. Hambrook's oldest building is Faber Farm, to the right of the squeeze stile straight ahead, part of which dates back to 1500.

You will be going through the squeeze stile shortly – but first, for a glimpse of Hambrook's most remarkable building, bear right along the lane for 125m

Above: The Ham Brook

Below: The former Winterbourne steeple

Bottom: The path under the M32

until you come to a gate on the right, over the top of which you should be able to glimpse a church steeple. This originally stood on the tower of Winterbourne church, but, after being struck by lightning in 1827, was found to be unsafe and dismantled. Winterbourne church got a new steeple, and the old one was re-erected here in 1853 as a garden folly atop an ice house.

Now head back to go through that stile and follow a footpath beside the brook. After 200m the path bears left between fences under the M32. Cross a stile on the far side, bear left and carry on, keeping close to the hedge – and the Ham Brook – on your left.* Carry on through a succession of KGs and over a stile. When you come to the road, cross and carry on along the road ahead. At the end, turn right at the second roundabout and right again to Parkway station.

Further information online:

Frome Valley Walkway: *www.fromewalkway.org.uk*

Snuff Mills Action Group: *snuffmills.blogspot.co.uk*

Greater Fishponds: *www.fishpondspeople.co.uk*

* A new road – the Stoke Gifford Transport Link – and housing is due to be built in this area, and, although the footpath will be retained, there will inevitably be disruptions and diversions. Work is scheduled to begin in late 2015.

5

MONTPELIER, STOKE'S CROFT, ST PAUL'S & KINGSDOWN

Starts at: *Montpelier station*

Ends at: *Montpelier station*

Distance: *4 miles*

Terrain: *Mostly on pavements or tarmaced footpaths, although with some steps*

Pubs & other amenities:

Green Man, Alfred Place, BS2 8HD; open 4-11 Mon-Fri, 2-11 Sat, 12-10.30 Sun; food served 5-11 Mon-Sat, 12-4 & 6-10.30 Sun; dogs welcome; 0117 9304824; www.dawkins-club.talktalk.net/page31.html

Hillgrove Porter Stores, Hillgrove Street North (off Dove Street), BS2 8LT; open from 4 Mon-Thu and from 2 on Sat & Sun; dogs welcome; 0117 9249818; www.dawkins-club.talktalk.net/page28.html.

Wide choice of other pubs and cafés in Picton Street, Stokes Croft, etc.

Map: Geographers' A-Z

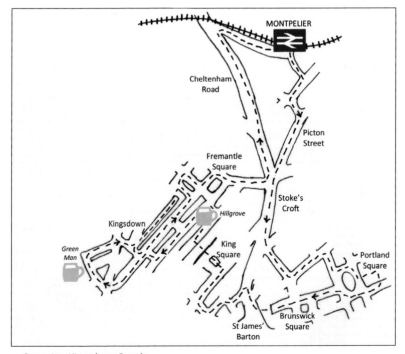

Opposite: Kingsdown Parade

*T*his predominantly urban walk visits some of Bristol's oldest and most fascinating suburbs – Montpelier, St Paul's, Stoke's Croft and Kingsdown. These are places where eclecticism, variety and vibrancy rule, where elegantly evocative Georgian terraces stand alongside some of the worst excesses of post-war brutalism, where dilapidation stands cheek by jowl with gentrification, and where the relics of the past resist, as best they can, the shock of the new. You will also see the site of a civil war fort, a celebrated well, a goose with two necks and some of the finest views in Bristol.

Montpelier was one of Bristol's earliest suburbs, although much of it remained semi-rural until the opening of Montpelier station in 1874 sparked large-scale development. Appropriately, it is at the station that our walk begins.

Turn left out of Montpelier station and walk along a footpath to St Andrew's Road, where you will see an archway leading through the building ahead. This was the Montpelier Hotel, opened at the same time as the station to cater for passengers. Its sign bracket still survives, along with some curious capitals on the pilasters, but it has long been converted to flats. To the right of it is another relic from the past – a sign for the Montpelier Toilet Saloon. A century ago, the name signified an upmarket barber's, although it is not one an aspiring hairdresser would be likely to choose today.

Turn right down St Andrew's Road past the old vicarage. The park on your right stands on the site of St Andrew's Church, consecrated in 1845 and demolished in 1969. At the T junction, look to your right to see the Old England pub, one of the oldest buildings in Montpelier. It was built in the 1760s by John Rennison, who had already established pleasure gardens and open-air baths nearby. The baths, which were later acquired by the council, closed in 1916 and a health centre now occupies the site.

Turn left along Bath Buildings and, as you carry on across a pedestrianised area, you will be welcomed to Montpelier by the splendidly decorated house ahead. Turn right along Picton Street, which follows the course of an old field track. Most of the houses along it were built

RENNISON'S BATHS

'About this time [1747] a swimming bath was opened by one Thomas Rennison, a threadmaker, at a suburban place called Territt's Mills, 'near the upper end of Stoke's Croft'. The mill was used for grinding snuff, and there was a large pond on the premises, which was probably the original bath. The public being largely

attracted to the spot, Rennison opened, in 1765, a new 'grand swimming bath, 400 feet [122m] in circumference', to which a 'ladies' swimming bath and coffee house' were added in 1767. A thread factory as well as the snuff mill still formed part of the premises. In 1774 Rennison, styling himself 'Governor of the Colony
of Newfoundland', solicited attention to his baths and coffee house, while in a somewhat later advertisement the place was called the Old England tea gardens, to which a tavern had been annexed. The spot, being quite in the country and beyond the civic jurisdiction, became a popular resort; and an annual bean feast was held, at which a mock mayor, sheriffs, and other dignitaries were elected, and various high jinks played by the not too abstemious revellers. In June 1782, evening concerts, twice a week, were announced for the summer season; admission one shilling, including tea and coffee.'

John Latimer, *The Annals of Bristol in the Eighteenth Century*, pp269-70

between 1816 and 1824, and it was named after General Picton, who was killed at Waterloo. He was held in special esteem in Bristol because of his prompt action in preventing a mutiny in the city in 1783.

Two doors along, at No 45, is a lock-up for the incarceration of miscreants, now covered in graffiti. Beside it, along Picton Mews, is the Regency elegance of Picton Lodge, in front of which Cutler's Mill Brook – now culverted – once ran. On the right-hand side of the street, No 52 has a well-preserved doorway next to an eye-catching shop window. A little further along on the left is Picton House, grander – like Picton Lodge – than the buildings around it, and set back behind railings to emphasise the point. No 21, next door, was one of the childhood homes of Archie Leach – the future Cary Grant.

Much of the character of Picton Street – especially the right-hand side – comes from the varied hues of bricks used in each building. Particularly striking is the two-tone Flemish bond of No 28, which also has a well-preserved butcher's shopfront, surrounded by tiles and with a decorative grille above the window.

Further along, No 6 – now a solicitor's – was once the General Picton pub, and the old sign still survives. Just past it, on the corner, is a Montpelier institution, the Bristolian Café, which occupies an old dairy. Unfortunately, the view ahead is dominated by the gaunt and gutted shell of Westmoreland House, one of Bristol's ugliest buildings. It is believed, however, to be subject to a compulsory purchase order, so hopefully will disappear before too long.

At the end of Picton Street, turn right for a few metres before turning left across the road to head along Stoke's Croft. The Arts House on the corner has a particularly well-preserved shopfront. Opposite, the building at the end of Cheltenham Road has a mural urging a boycott of Tesco. Further along, on the right-hand side of Stoke's Croft, is the Crofter's Rights, one of Bristol's newest craft-ale bars. Originally known as the Swan, it has been an inn since at least 1711. The ornate Victorian building next to it – now Hooper House Cafe – was originally a fishmonger's. The three-storey building next to that was another pub called the Little Swan.

On your left is the boarded-up shell of Westmoreland House, built as an extension to the splendid carriage works of 1862 beyond it, which has also been derelict for years. Further along on the right, Palmer's ironmongers, at Nos 97-99, still has its old sign but has long been boarded up. Next to it are two gabled buildings dating from the late seventeenth or early eighteenth centuries.

The former carriage works on Stoke's Croft

The changing face of Stoke's Croft: Rita's Take Away, once the North End Porter Stores

On your left, the Bank Wine Bar on the corner of Hepburn Road is housed – not surprisingly – in an old bank. Across the road, Agency 51 occupies an impressive stone building which was also a bank. Next to it is the former Blundell's department store, built in 1935.

Coming up on the left-hand side of the road is Stoke's Croft's most famous landmark, Banksy's Mild Mild West. If you look up to the right along Jamaica Street, you will see another carriage works, built between 1905 and 1909, with a groundbreaking iron-framed glass façade. Since 1993, it has been home to the Jamaica Street Artists' studio.

Many of the buildings on your right as you carry on along Stoke's Croft are Georgian, with later additions. Wolf's & Co at No 51, painted in a fetching shade of blue with horticultural embellishments, has an old sign on the wall at the side declaring it to have been established as a spirit merchant's in 1814. It was actually licensed at least as far back as 1775, and has had a variety of incarnations – Waters' Wine Lodge, the King's Arms, the Pint & Pie, and, before assuming its present name, the Junction. By contrast, the building to the right of it is less than five years old.

Carry on at the pedestrian lights and bear left along Upper York Street, past the Italianate façade of the City Road Baptist Church. On your right, on the corner of Moon Street, the vibrantly-decorated Lakota occupies a mid-nineteenth-century malthouse. The Gothic-style building behind it was built as a school in 1858, but converted to a coroner's court and mortuary in the mid-twentieth century.

Take the third left into Wilder Street and turn right along Cave Street, largely composed of Georgian buildings. Nos 2-8, towards the end on the left, still bear the name of Parsons & Co, whose boot & shoe factory was once based here. Just past it, a left turn brings you into Portland Square, laid out in 1787 but not completed until 1823, and, in contrast to the surrounding terraces, built of Bath stone. It is, despite the vicissitudes it has suffered over the years, the finest and most coherent of Bristol's squares. Provided with its own church, it was initially one of the

A charabanc outing from St Paul's in 1920

Not Pamplona but the south-east corner of Portland Square around 1910, when cattle were still driven through the streets to market

most fashionable and exclusive addresses in Bristol, but, as the nineteenth century wore on, the well-to-do deserted it for Clifton and other leafier suburbs. As property prices fell, small firms moved in, converting once grand houses to workshops and factories, and, by the end of the century, it was fashionable no longer. Today, most of the factories and workshops have gone, to be replaced by offices and newly-refurbished apartments, but the state of the Grade I listed buildings on the west side of Portland Square indicates how precipitous was its decline and how much still remains to be done.

Carry on along the north side of Portland Square and turn right along the east to St Paul's Church. Opened in 1794, and known as the 'wedding cake church' because of the way its tower is built in tiers, it closed in 1988 and lay disused until 2004, when a restoration project supported by the Churches Conservation Trust saw it converted it to the Circomedia school for contemporary circus and physical theatre. The interior, with the largest permanent flying trapeze in the country, is stunning and well worth a visit if you get a chance.

Just past the church, turn left along a footpath to the award-wining St Paul's Park, created in part of the churchyard, with play areas for children, a dedicated area for teenagers, and a space for circus and carnival performances. Turn right along a lane paved with setts to Wilson Street where a plaque marks the childhood home of Elizabeth Blackwell, the first woman to be enrolled on the British medical register. The terrace on your left, on the north side of Wilson Street – very plain, but an object lesson in how effective render scribed to look like stone, combined with stone dressings, can look – dates from around 1830. The impressive redbrick boot & shoe factory on your right was built in 1895. Turn right along Wilson Street, towards the side elevation of 13 Portland Square – built of brick rather than the more expensive Bath stone used on the façade.

Turn right and then left along the south side of Portland Square, before turning right along the west side and left along Surrey Street to Brunswick Square. This was laid out over 20 years earlier than Portland Square, in 1766. The south side and the northern part of the west side were built first, the east side followed in the mid-1780s, but houses were not built on the north side because there was a Presbyterian burial ground there. In 1835, however, a Congregational chapel was built on the north side. It was converted to offices in the 1950s. The Unitarian Meeting House beside it was originally a lodge for the burial ground.

The former lodge to the Presbyterian burial ground and, below, a range of Gibbsian surrounds in Brunswick Square

Brunswick Square's lack of coherence has not been helped by unsympathetic post-war redevelopment. It would have been far worse if the south side, long converted to industrial use and in a parlous state of repair, had been demolished as planned in the 1970s; fortunately, a sympathetic developer retained the façades and build offices behind them. The square's most memorable feature, though, is the range of Gibbsian surrounds on the doors and windows of the truncated terrace on the west side – a vibrant combination of exuberance and classical restraint.*

---

* Gibbsian surrounds were named after James Gibbs, who popularised a style of building architraves punctuated by square blocks of stone

Carry on along Cumberland Street. Built in 1770, the western end has been lost to redevelopment and what is left was largely rebuilt in 1990. Only the facades were retained, and some of those on the north side were largely reconstructed. It nevertheless remains an entrancing backwater, with an evocative shopfront, moody faces in its consoles, at No 28.

At the end, carry on along a footpath under the tower blocks, to emerge on St James's Barton Roundabout. Here you may want to divert left, to see the Spirit of Bristol statue in front of the Holiday Inn. Installed in 1971, it is reminiscent of the angular bull adopted as the logo for Birmingham's Bull Ring in the 1960s. The bull, along with the 1960s Bull Ring, has long been swept away, and, while Bristol's nod to the spirit of modernity

survives, it is screened by trees and largely forgotten. It is a monument to a different age, to an antiquated and alien vision of the future that, for the moment at least, stirs no feelings of nostalgia.

To gauge how far we have come since the early 1970s, you can look across the road to one of Bristol's newest sculptures. Ursa the Bear stands on the roof of the men's toilets in the 'Bearpit', the open space in the middle of St James's Barton Roundabout which, after years of neglect, has been reinvigorated as part of a community initiative, with market and food stalls, galleries and events, and a café housed in a vintage double-decker bus. Just as the Spirit of Bristol symbolised a shiny, thrusting, but ultimately sterile vision of the future imposed from on high, Ursa the Bear represents the spirit of regeneration driven – at least partly –from below.

Turn right under the tower blocks along North Street. The Full Moon on the right dates from around 1700 and was a major coaching

The Full Moon as drawn by Samuel Loxton in 1889; and as it appears today

Harford House before the demolition of the buildings around it; and today

inn. Despite all the changes it has seen, the affinity of this three-storey, three-gabled building to South Gloucestershire manor houses of the same period is unmistakable. If you look along Moon Street beside the inn, you will see the gloriously unrestored rubble-stone wall of the old stables at the back. The three-storey building to the left of them was built in the mid-1800s as a sawmill and has now been converted to offices.

Turn left across the dual carriageway at the pedestrian lights, and head along Cherry Lane. Modern monoliths predominate as you bear right along Barton Street and turn left into Charles Street. On the right, though, past a bit of Georgian pastiche, is a remarkable survival – a pair of mid-eighteenth-century houses, one of which was the home of the hymn writer Charles Wesley. Inside, it has been restored to look as it did when he lived there and is occasionally open to the public.

At the end of Charles Street, with the magistrates' court ahead, turn right up Montague Street, where modern buildings predominate. At the top, turn right along Dighton Street to see, above you on the left, another improbable survivor – Harford House, built of Bath stone in the mid-eighteenth century and modelled on Clifton Hill House (visited in Walks 9 and 10). Originally it stood in lordly isolation, looking out over gardens, orchards and a bowling green. Today, wedged between a multi-storey car park and an apartment block, its view is blocked by more high-rise apartments. The cross over the door at street level leading into its basement is a legacy of its conversion to a Roman Catholic convent in 1846. Further along is Llewellin's Gears – once a boot and shoe factory – with an old lane climbing up beside it.

Then comes King Square, laid out in the 1740s. Sadly, only the upper part of the south-west side – where words on the wall of No 4 recall its time as a Deaf & Dumb Institute – and the right-hand section of the north-west side are original; the rest is utilitarian or faux-Georgian infilling.

Head through the garden in the centre of the square, continue up the path between the buildings on the north-west side and climb the steps to Dove Street. You are now on the borders of Kingsdown, one of Bristol's most atmospheric corners, but one that nearly disappeared.

Around 1740, at the same time that King Square was built, streets were laid out on these slopes, following the contours of the hillside. Originally, Dove Street was called Dovecote Street, presumably because there was a

King Square

dovecote here before the houses were built.

Kingsdown was Bristol's first planned suburb. In 1794, Matthew's *Bristol Directory* reported that the slopes were 'covered with houses up to and beyond the summit. The houses are uniformly built of brick ornamented with stone; the whole area surrounded by rails and lime trees; the walks neatly gravelled.' Less grand than Clifton, but not taken over by industry like the area around Portland Square, Kingsdown survived the Blitz relatively unscathed and by the 1950s was one of Bristol's most beguiling Georgian suburbs. It was one of John Betjeman's favourite parts of the city, but, in the post-war world, untouched, unrestored and a little down at heel, it was ripe for redevelopment. In 1958, 322 houses on the lower slopes were demolished; ten years later, many more were bulldozed to build three 14-storey blocks of flats on the south-east side of Dove Street. At which

Bath-stone houses with full-height canted bays

point, local residents, backed by conservationists, decided it was time to take the planners and councillors on and fight to save what was left. The battle for Kingsdown made national headlines and ended in victory for the campaigners. In 1973 it was declared a conservation area, since when it has once again become one of Bristol's most desirable suburbs.

Modern buildings predominate as you turn right along Dove Street, but if you look up to the left you will see tall Bath-stone houses with full-height canted bays. The views across the city from here are spectacular – you can imagine how good they must be from the top floors of those houses. The Hillgrove Porter Stores,

a little way along on the left, was originally the Dublin Porter House. Today, run by Dawkin's brewery, it is one of Bristol's top cask-beer pubs. Just past it, the Hare on the Hill, a Bath Ales pub with splendid tiling, was originally the Mason's Arms.

Turn left by the Hare on the Hill up Thomas Street, looking out for an early Bansky of a flower in a rat trap – framed and glazed – on the right. Even the street art around here has gone upmarket, it seems.

At the top, as you turn left along Somerset Street, you enter what is – bar a certain amount of infilling – a Georgian enclave. Building along here started in the 1760s, but, apart from having to follow the street line, developers were free to do more or less as they liked. Not only is there an eclectic mix of building styles and materials; imposing houses for wealthy merchants rub shoulders with artisans' cottages. Bays – the ultimate way of putting your neighbours' house in the shade – come in a bewildering variety of shapes and sizes – full height, single-storey, hanging, canted and bowed. Particularly appealing is that on No 36 – a bowed first and second floor hanging bay supported somewhat improbably on two spindly iron columns. The street is still paved with setts,

Top: Afternoon sun falls on brick and Bath stone in Somerset Street

Right: The view over Bristol from Spring Hill

and, as you carry on, the gardens and imposing back elevations of the buildings on Kingsdown Parade complete the picture on the right. Somerset Street is endlessly fascinating and richly repays repeated visits. And, if you're into quirkiness, look out on the right – just after the view down Spring Hill – for Victoria Cottage, an object lesson in how to make renovation interesting – and fun. At the end, look down to your left to see, at No

23, a ponderous Greek Revival extension on the front of a mid-Georgian house, before turning right up Montague Hill.

The Bell in Alfred Place around 1950; now re-named the Green Man

At the top turn left along Kingsdown Parade. After passing the green at the end, cross the road ahead and turn right along Alfred Place, where an old grocer's shopfront has been preserved at No 15. The Green Man – originally the Bell – is another popular Dawkins' pub. Carry on past an imposing late nineteenth-century row of former shops on the right and turn right along Portland Street. On the right, after a short row of Georgian buildings, comes the Lutton Memorial Hall, built in 1883 to commemorate Anne Lutton, a famous Methodist preacher, and now converted to flats. To the left of it, modern flats stand on the site of a Methodist chapel.

At the end, cross the zebra crossing and carry on along Clevedon Terrace, built of Bath stone around 1830. Originally only the terrace on the left was known as Clevedon Terrace; that on the right was called Walton Terrace, presumably after Walton in Gordano.

After crossing St Matthew's Road – with a two-headed goose up to the right – you will see a lane on your left called 'Back of Kingsdown Parade'. This long cul-de-sac – whose name describes it admirably – is

well worth exploring. As you penetrate deeper into its untrodden recesses, past some of the few remaining gaslights in the city – it seems more and more like a lost or at least a hidden world. After No 61, the lane kinks to the left and its character changes, with many of the houses sporting hanging bays. This section, which was built later, was originally known as St James's Place and had virtually interrupted views across open country. At the end, you are only a few metres away from a street built in the mid-nineteenth century, but there seems never to have been a way through. The residents of this tranquil backwater must have been happy for it to stay just as it was, and who can blame them?

Retracing your steps, one final surprise awaits, in the shape of the Bristol Royal Infirmary chimney straight ahead, perhaps the most startling view of a structure visible from so many parts of the city.

At the end, turn left to continue along Clevedon Terrace, before turning left into Kingsdown Parade. On your left, set back behind long gardens (some now converted to car parks) are the fronts of the buildings whose backs you have just walked past. On the right, as in Somerset Street, is an eclectic mix of buildings – until you reach No 48, where vernacular disorder gives way to regularity relieved only by brick painted a variety of hues. This part of Kingsdown Parade was originally known as St James's Parade, and, if you look over to the left, you will see how it is matched by the terrace originally called St James's Place which you saw the other side of earlier.

At the end, you reach the northern limit of Georgian Kingsdown. Beyond was an open space called Nine Tree Hill, on which a fort – known as Prior's Hill Fort – was built during the Civil War. When parliamentary forces besieged the city in September 1645, Colonel Rainsborough captured the fort after two hours of bitter fighting and massacred the defenders. The taking of this strategic position was a crucial factor in the success of the parliamentary siege.

Fremantle Square

THE LEGEND AND LOSS OF MOTHER PUGSLEY'S WELL

According to John Latimer, one of the Royalist defenders killed during the siege of Prior's Hill Fort was

> *a young officer named Pugsley, who had just been married, and who, by Fairfax's orders, was buried in an adjoining field with military honours. His widow survived him for no less than 60 years. On her death, in 1705, she was, in accordance with her dying request, buried by the side of her husband in her wedding dress, without a coffin, but with girls strewing flowers and musicians playing merrily as her body was borne to the grave.[1]*

Near her grave was a well, beside which, after her husband's death, she had taken up residence, acquiring a reputation as a wise woman. It became known as Mother Pugsley's (or Dame Pugsley's) Well, and the land around it was regarded as a public park. All that changed in the early 1840s, when

> *the land known to all Bristolians as Mother Pugsley's Field, together with some adjoining plots, was disposed of in sites for building. Pedestrians had enjoyed access from time immemorial to the spring in Pugsley's Field; but ... Sir Thomas Fremantle, the owner of the land, flourished his title deeds in the face of the public, and nobody had the spirit to defend the rights of the community. A builder, named Hucker, who purchased part of the property, enclosed the spring – which had a reputation for healing virtues amongst the vulgar – for private use at his residence, Spring Villa, Nugent Hill.[2]*

The loss of this much-treasured amenity did not go entirely unchallenged, however. At a council meeting in August 1844, a Mr Herapath

> *drew attention to the present condition of the spring known as Dame Pugsley's Well ... It had been provided by a recent act of parliament that where the public had had the use of a spring of water for 20 years such use conveyed a title. Now he knew that the public had had the use of this well for 40 years. Recently, however, much building had been going on in the field in which it was situated, and the consequence had been that some person had enclosed the spring in a garden, claiming it as private property, and refusing to allow the public the use of the waters without payment ... The encroachment committee would not do its duty if it did not investigate this matter, and adopt some means for securing the public right in this spring ... Mr Visger seconded the motion, and also complained that the footpath leading to the spring had been stopped.[3]*

Five months later, the finance committee reported that they

> *had referred the subject to the law officer, who were of the opinion that no part of the borough funds could be legally expended in enforcing restoration of the use of the spring to the public; but that the remedy, if any, must be sought by the parties aggrieved by the enclosure of the well.[4]*

Despite a call for a 'public society' to be set up to challenge the enclosure, nothing was done, and one of Bristol's most cherished and time-hallowed open spaces was lost forever.

As you continue past the end of Kingsdown Parade, you come to Fremantle Square, built in the 1840s, with multi-coloured terraces on three sides, semi-detached villas on the fourth, and a shady square, curiously raised up, in the centre.

Carry on down the west side of Fremantle Square, turn right along the north side and carry on down Nine Tree Hill, with a row of wisteria-covered cottages on the left and the gaunt skeleton of Westmoreland House ahead.

At the bottom, turn left along Cheltenham Road, passing an old cinema, built in 1914, on your left. Since

The view from Nine Tree Hill

closing in 1955 it has been a church, a pub and a comedy club, and now looks set to be converted to a mosque. The row of buildings opposite, dating from around 1820, is known as Catherine Place, and shopfronts have long been built over many of the front gardens. Further along, by the traffic lights, the large, newly-renovated building whose ground floor is occupied by Boston Tea Party is one of the oldest semi-detached villas in the area. Until recently, a car showroom and garage occupied the building, which was largely hidden by a large single-storey extension that has now been swept away.

Carry on across the bottom of Arley Hill to the Arley Congregational Chapel of 1855 – now a Polish church – and continue along Cheltenham Road. On the opposite side of the road, the Dolphin School occupies a particularly elegant late Georgian villa of around 1830. A little further

One of Cheltenham Road's oldest buildings, recently transformed by the removal of a ground-floor car showroom

Arley Chapel
Cheltenham Road,
Bristol.

along, cross at the pedestrian lights. You will notice that one of the shops to your right still displays a Victorian sign for Paxman's Dye Works, despite the row now being occupied by Colston's Girls' School.[*]

Carry on along Cheltenham Road past the main school building, an eclectic, polychromatic jumble of styles from 1891. The architect was William Venn Gough, who also designed the Cabot Tower. Before the school was built there were gardens here, sloping down Cutler's Mill Brook, with paths winding through them, and a view across to Rennison's Baths and the Old England Tavern, where our walk started.

Ornamentation on Colston's
Girls' School

As you carry on towards the railway bridge – one of the visual highlights of Cheltenham Road – look out for a monolithic faux-Georgian telephone exchange across the road. A little further on, turn right up Station Road – where Montpelier Coach House, 50m along on the right, stands roughly on the site of Cutler's Mill – and carry on to the station, where the walk ends.

Further information online:

Stokes Croft: *visitstokescroft.wordpress.com*
Kingsdown Conservation Group: *kingsdownbristol.net*

---

[*] Paxman's Dye Works was one of the biggest laundry and dyeing businesses in the city, with at least seven branches. One of the firm's delivery carts has been preserved at the M Shed.

6

ST ANDREW'S, ST WERBURGH'S & MONTPELIER

Starts at: *Montpelier station*

Ends at: *Montpelier station*

Distance: *4.5 miles*

Terrain: *Pavements and tarmaced paths, along with some rough paths*

Pubs & other amenities:

St Werburgh's City Farm Café, open daily except Tuesday, 10-5 (4 in winter); 0117 9080798; www.swcityfarm.co.uk/about/cafe

The Farm pub, Hopetoun Road, BS2 9YL; open all day from 12; dogs welcome; 0117 9442384; www.eventbars.com/#/the-farm/4536642347

Miners Arms, Mina Road, BS2 9YQ; open from 4 Mon-Fri; from 2 Sat & Sun; dogs welcome; 0117 9079874; www.dawkins-club.talktalk.net/page27.html

Duke of York, Jubilee Road, BS2 9RS; open from 5 Mon-Thu; from 4 Fri; from 3 Sat & Sun; no dogs

Map: Geographers' A-Z

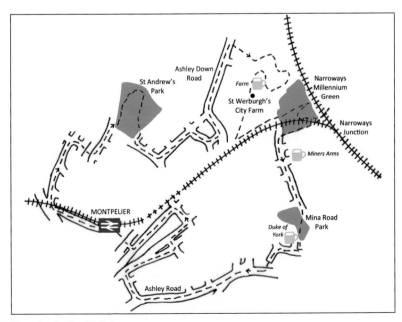

Opposite: Boiling Wells Lane

This walk is a vibrant medley of city parks, a city farm, Victorian suburbs, Georgian villas, a house from a fairy tale, a church that moved, and a secret world hemmed in by the mighty banks of an abandoned railway cutting.

Head out of Montpelier station and turn right down Station Road. At the bottom, cross the end of North Road and turn right under the stone arch of the railway bridge. After 50m, when the main road bears right, carry straight on along North Road. As you carry on past large semis, the bustle of the Cheltenham Road dies away, and you come to a row of cottages, inspired perhaps by Brunel's railway village at Swindon, but even more Gothicised and built of patterned brickwork instead of stone. Behind them, long culverted, runs Cutler's Mill Brook.

A little further along is the splendidly decorated Portico Play, showing how a building as drab as a former roofing contractors can be transformed into something uplifting and fun (as demonstrated by the elephant above). Turn right up Overton Road, where the preposterously Gothic west front of the former David Thomas Congregational Church takes full advantage of its elevated location to dominate the neighbourhood.

At the top, cross over and turn to take in the view across the valley. Head up the footpath (known as David Thomas Lane) to the right of the church – but not before taking a look at the flamboyant entrances of the houses across the road, in which Romanesque arches are combined with Gothic pillars.

As you walk along David Thomas Lane, you will see that, while the west front of the church has been retained, the rest of it has been replaced by a five-storey sheltered housing development, served by a lift in the tower.

At the end, cross and turn left along Effingham Road. A little way along on the left are a pair of half-timbered and gabled semi-detached villas from 1905. A little further along, there is an old sewer ventilation shaft at the side of the road. The terrace just beyond it has some particularly attractive terracotta mouldings.

After crossing the end of Leopold Lane, turn right into St Andrew's Park. Bear left to follow the trail – shown on the information board near the entrance – around the perimeter of the park.

St Andrew's Park dates from around the same time as the surrounding streets. Because of its elevated position, the site had long been regarded as a beauty spot, and quarrying had left it riddled with delightful dells and declivities. Many wanted it to remain as it was, an untamed wilderness amidst the regimentation of suburbia, but, when the council acquired it in 1890, they filled in the quarries with spoil from nearby building sites and laid it out as a formal park.

Two views of St Andrew's Park from around 1910

Beyond the children's play area, at the northern end of the park, is a memorial to three members of the crew of a Wellington bomber who died when it crashed here during a training exercise on 30 April 1941. As you continue along the eastern side of the park, there are good views across the valley to Redland, with its pepperpot chapel atop the hill.

Leave the park by the southernmost gateway, turn right and walk to the end of Maurice Road, before turning left along Leopold Road. At the end, turn left along Chesterfield Road. After 200m cross the zebra crossing and turn right along Somerville Road South. After passing a set of bollards, turn left to find an extraordinary survival – the gateposts of Ashley Court, an eighteenth-century mansion demolished in 1877 as its rolling acres fell victim to the onward march of suburbia. The terrace behind the gateposts, with ornate stone screens flanking the central building, gives the impression that the architect was trying to match the grandiosity of the gateposts, and has something of the look of Weston Super Mare about it. It also has superb views across to Purdown, with the BT Tower acting as a *point de vue*.

At the end, turn left up the main road, and at the mini roundabout bear right up Ashley Down Road. After 200m cross at the pedestrian lights and carry on across the top of Kathdene Gardens. A little further on is Glenfrome House, an imposing building dating from 1827, with two shallow, full-height bays flanking a gabled recess. It originally stood in splendid isolation, enjoying virtually uninterrupted views.

A little further on, turn right down a footpath signposted to St Werburgh's. After walking steeply downhill between allotments and passing a chicane, turn left along a footpath signposted to Lockleaze, UWE and Filton Abbey Wood. Take the next right along a footpath signposted to St Werburgh's and the City Centre, and, at a T junction, turn left. Mill Cottage, the early nineteenth-century building on your left, was restored in the 1980s after years of dereliction. Beside it stood Ashley Vale Mill, dating from the fourteenth century, but disused by the 1890s and later demolished.

Carry on along Boiling Wells Lane, past what must surely be many people's favourite modern building in Bristol, a woodland fairy-tale fantasy that could have been dreamt up by Friedensreich Hundertwasser but was actually designed by Graham Caine, who pioneered a technique of transforming plywood into something gloriously organic and alive.

Just before the railway bridge, turn right past a metal gate through the Ashley Vale Self-Build Co-operative site. At the end, turn left past a redbrick terrace and right along Watercress Road, whose name recalls the watercress beds that once flourished here.

Turn right along Hopetoun Road where you will find the Farm pub, originally a beerhouse called the Cress House but, when work on the Bristol & South Wales Union Railway (B&SWUR) started in 1858, renamed the South Wales Railway Tavern, a name it kept until recently. The doors to the bar also look to be by Graham Caine, and the pub itself is a quirky mixture of the traditional and the vibrantly modern, with art exhibitions and live music – a country pub in the city, but a country pub with a difference.

The Farm pub today; and as it looked when it was the South Wales Railway Tavern

BARBAROUS PLEASURES AT THE BOILING WELLS

Before St Werburgh's was developed, and the Farm pub – then known as the Cress House – stood amid open country, the fields nearby were the meeting place for some decidedly unsavoury characters, as a letter published in the *Bristol Mercury* on 21 October 1843, from James Yewen, agent to the Animals' Friend Society, reveals:

In certain fields at Baptist Mills, near the boiling well, there are, on most Sundays, dog fights and man fights; and one of the inhabitants of that neighbourhood informed me that no respectable person could pass that way at such times without being insulted by gross and blasphemous language. Last Sunday a friend accompanied me to the spot, which was indeed a scene of vice and disorder. There were present about 200 of the so-called sporting gentry. We were grieved to observe boys of eight or nine years of age, and men with grey locks, bringing dogs for the purpose of fighting. The sport, as it is called, is not confined to dog and man fights: ducks are taken thither, that they may be hunted to death with dogs ... My object in publicly stating these things is that some means may be resorted to to prevent such evils in future ... This field at Baptist Mills appeared to be a training place, where dogs are brought to try their prowess at fighting; and then follows betting upon them, to fight at public houses.

The letter roused the authorities into action. Less than two years later, on 10 May 1845, a letter from a correspondent signing himself JHR appeared in the *Bristol Mercury*. He had, he explained, visited the fields at Baptist Mills the previous Sunday and had been 'surprised to see so few men and dogs there':

On making enquiry I was told that the officers of the Society for the Prevention of Cruelty to Animals had been paying visits in that neighbourhood the last few weeks, and that the dog fighters were liable to a penalty of five pounds for fighting dogs or cocks or baiting bears or badgers. This I was very much pleased to learn, and I hope this valuable society will be well supported and that the officers will continue their services.

Happily, this was the prelude to the final eradication of such goings on. Thirty-five years later, on 20 May 1880, a leader writer in the *Bristol Mercury*, after describing how Whitsun had been celebrated in the city, recalled a time when many spent the holiday

fighting their dogs in the outskirts, and now and then, by way of change, fighting the human animal. The now brick-and-mortar covered neighbourhood of the Boiling Well was a favourite resort for those who practised the last-named sport ... In harmony with the increasing intelligence of the age ... is the more rational manner in which the people's holidays are now spent ... Instead of causing the fields to resound with the snarls and cries of contending bulldogs and the shouts and execrations of angry men, the holiday seekers nowadays use them as places of tranquil resort, feeling as they tread the turf and listen to the music of the birds, that they have left care and labour alike behind them.

If you decide to call in, leave by the top gate and turn left along the footpath. If you don't, carry on past the pub, turn left up a footpath at the end, then left along a footpath past the back of the pub. This leads to St Werburgh's City Farm Café, another Graham Caine creation, where you can eat dishes prepared with produce from the City Farm across the road.

After a visit to the City Farm, carry straight on along the footpath past the back of it and continue between allotments, passing an old cottage. At the end of the allotments, when the path bears right, go through a metal kissing gate (KG) on the left and follow a tree-lined path into Narroways Millennium Green. This path follows the trackbed of the Clifton Extension Railway branch from Ashley Hill Junction to Kingswood Junction. To your right is the Severn Beach line, while to your left are the allotments you have just walked through. After 200m you will see, through the trees on your left, Mina Road far below, with City Farm and the self-build houses in the distance.

When the path forks, take the left fork to carry straight on. Shortly after this, you emerge into a wide cutting, a self-contained haven cut off from the outside work by steep banks. In 1997, when there were plans to develop this area, over 800 people demonstrated to keep it as an open space. Enough money was raised to enable the council to buy the site from British Rail, and in 2000 it became a Millennium Green, with a 999-year lease to preserve it as a haven for wildlife.

A footpath now follows the course of the line along which, on this Edwardian postcard, a Midland Railway train from Bath to Clifton is seen approaching Ashley Hill Junction.

Carry on as far as the abutments of the bridge that carried the Clifton Extension Railway over the B&SWUR, where a fence blocks any further progress. Retrace your steps, but, just before the path re-enters the woods, turn left up wooden steps beside a fence.

When the path forks, bear right alongside the fence. After going down a short flight of steps, turn left and walk up to a bridge over the B&SWUR. This is one of the most splendid vantage points in the city, although sadly it has had to be caged in to prevent vandalism. Southwards is Narroways Junction, where Severn Beach trains branch off, while to the north are the former orphanages established by George Muller between 1849 and 1870.

Head back along the path, carry on across the Severn Beach line, and, after another 30m, go through a KG on the right and follow a well-trodden path downhill. After entering woodland, steps take you down past the entrance to St Werburgh's Community Garden to Mina Road, named after Francesco Espoz y Mina, a Spanish general who served with distinction under the Duke of Wellington. Look along to the right to see the road tunnelling under the two branches of the Clifton Extension Railway, one still open and one converted to the footpath you have just walked along.

Turn left past St Werburgh's Church, which stood in the city centre before being moved here in 1879 and giving its name to the newly-built suburb surrounding it. It closed in 1988, and has now been converted to a climbing centre. As you carry on along Mina Road, look for a flood marker from October 1882 in the wall on the left. Just past it is the Miner's Arms, another popular Dawkins' Ales pub. Carry on across the main road at the roundabout and after

St Werburgh's church on its original site in Corn Street

another 100m turn right into Mina Road Park. Opened in 1886, this originally had an ornamental lake at its centre which disappeared during the Second World War. Follow the path diagonally across the park before turning right across a bridge over Horfield Brook, where you will see the chimney of Brook's Dye Works, opened in 1870 and closed in 2007, over to the west.* Turn left alongside the brook and cross another bridge. A few metres downstream to your right, Horfield Brook is joined by the long-culverted Cutler's Mill Brook. Before turning right alongside the brook, however, look over to your left to see a green urinal, installed shortly after the park opened. St Werburgh's has two listed buildings. The church is one of them; this is the other, and, as an example of Victorian ironwork, is worth a closer inspection.[†]

* There are plans to redevelop the site and it is unclear whether the chimney will survive.
† As the urinal has been restored to working order, ladies are advised to desist from an internal inspection.

THE FLOODS OF OCTOBER 1882

'Owing to unusually heavy rains during the month of October, which attained their maximum on the 22nd and 23rd, when upwards of three inches of rainfall were measured within 48 hours, a large area of country around Bristol was deeply flooded, and much property was destroyed. The damage in the city was still more serious, thousands of houses being flooded at and near Baptist Mills, Stapleton Road, and Bedminster. On the evening of the 23rd a portion of

Stapleton Road was about four feet [1.2m] under water, and as the Froom continued to rise during the night, the district near its banks presented an extraordinary aspect on the following morning, when traffic was entirely stopped. At the Black Swan Inn, Stapleton Road, the water mounted nearly to the signboard over the door of the premises. The only means of communicating with a great number of houses in the locality was by means of rafts and boats, by which provisions and necessaries were supplied to many of the imprisoned inhabitants. In the afternoon, the accumulated waters spread in an immense lake along Newfoundland Road and Newfoundland Street to Paul Street, Portland Square. All the low-lying streets in that district were submerged several feet. When the flood receded on the following day, a deplorable sight was presented in the neighbouring dwellings, the basement floors of which were thickly covered with mud. The disaster was attended with fatal results to a young baker, named Foot, who, while delivering bread in a cart in Mina Road, was swept away by the torrent, both man and horse being drowned. A brewer's dray was carried off near the same place, but the driver escaped. Two houses in that road were undermined by the water, and fell into ruins; but the inhabitants, about twenty in number, warned by some premonitory rumblings, had escaped on rafts. The clergy and other citizens made devoted efforts on behalf of the poor who were practically ruined by the disaster, and a large fund was raised; but many of the families nevertheless suffered from sickness during the winter owing to the soaked condition of their dwellings.'

John Latimer, *Annals of Bristol in the Nineteenth Century*

Having done that, follow the brook out of the park and turn right past the splendidly decorated Duke of York pub, which, in a directory from 1828, was described as having 'Jubilee Tea Gardens' adjoining. Beside the Duke of York is Jubilee Place – named in celebration of George III's Golden Jubilee in 1809 – where there are some charming late Georgian buildings and a fine laburnum.

Carry on past the Duke of York, through a pedestrian area and past a playground overlooked by a mural of John Peel. This area was originally

The Botany Tavern

Ashley Place

known, with grim humour, as Botany Bay, after the Australian penal colony. The former pub on the corner of Jubilee Row – the Botany Tavern – is now home to the Botany Arts Studios.

Turn left along Gordon Road, and at the end carry on along a footpath to emerge on Lower Ashley Road, opposite a pair of shops with Dutch gables and Gothic-style windows. Turn right, and, after 125m, cross the end of Sussex Place. Bear left past the splendid façade of Jenner's milliners and drapers before bearing right to continue along Ashley Road, where you will see another splendid façade on the Prince of Wales pub across the road.

As you continue along Ashley Road, you pass a succession of large houses – including one dated 1825 – and grand gateways, indicating how exclusive this area once was. Bath stone is much in evidence, although many buildings are hidden behind trees, high walls and security gates.

Keeping to the right-hand side of the road, cross the end of Albert Park and bear right at the mini roundabout to continue along Ashley Road. The modern redbrick development you can see on the other side of the road stands on the site of St Barnabas's Church, consecrated in 1843, damaged by bombing in 1941 and subsequently demolished. On your right, set back and largely screened from the road, is Ashley Place, a terrace of four houses from the 1790s, unusual in that each of the three-storey houses had a single-storey annexe separating it from the adjoining house.* Infilling has unfortunately disrupted the original design.

A little further along on the right, No 77, dwarfed by the Victorian buildings on either side of it, is earlier still, having been built as a farmhouse in the mid-seventeenth century.

Turn right along Wellington Avenue, where, on the right, you will find a terrace with some elaborate ornamentation. Shaftesbury Avenue, which you cross after 100m, follows the course of Cutler's Mill Brook.

South of the brook, the land slopes gently away, but to the north it rises steeply to the breezy heights of Montpelier. These slopes are home

* A similar design was adopted at Prince's Buildings in Clifton, visited in Walk 10.

to a tightly-packed jumble of buildings, with narrow streets strung out across the hillside. The first date from around 1792, but building work continued throughout the nineteenth century, and infills are still being added today.

At the end, turn right by the Thali Cafe along York Road, past a terrace on the left built in the early 1830s. When the road forks, bear right. The last house in York Road is a delight, appearing to have only a single storey, but – by taking advantage of the sloping site – with another storey below, looking out across a large garden. The houses beyond it, in Upper Cheltenham Place, were built later, but adopted the same plan. Even more alluring are the houses up to your left, half-hidden behind luxuriant vegetation. This part of Montpelier is characterised by eclectic exuberance. Some of the buildings are grander than others, some are more striking, more charming, more evocative, or whatever, but the overall effect is one of harmonious co-existence and infinite variety.

Beyond another house from around 1830 with its upper storey level with the road, two multi-coloured terraces face each other – mid-Victorian on the left, early nineteenth century on the right.

Turn left uphill at the end and right at the top along York Road. The terrace up to your left, originally known as Waterloo Place, dates from around 1820. A little further along, a pair of late eighteenth-century semi-detached villas introduce a rare note of Bath stone into an area characterised almost exclusively by brick and render.

At the end turn left uphill, carrying straight on when the main road turns right. Before turning left along Richmond Road, look to the right to see a late Victorian terrace with Gothic-style lancets above the front doors. As you turn left, Gothicism rears its head again in the form of the brick and stone gateway of Field House on the right. A little further along, on the other side of the road, is Apsley Villa, now flanked by modern extensions. It dates from the early nineteenth century and was originally known as Montpelier Cottage.

Although there are some attractive Georgian buildings, especially on the right, as you carry on along Richmond Road, late Victoriana grows ever more prevalent, until you come to the Cadbury pub, half-timbered and with roses around the door courtesy of some nifty brushwork.

Just past the Cadbury, turn right through two archways and carry straight on to return to Montpelier station.

Further information online:

Friends of St Andrew's Park: *friendsofstandrewspark.ning.com*
Narroways Millennium Green Trust: *narroways.wordpress.com*
St Werburgh's City Farm: *www.swcityfarm.org.uk*
St Werburgh's Community Website: *www.stwerburghs.org*

7

PURDOWN, STOKE PARK, FRENCHAY, OLDBURY COURT & STAPLETON

Starts at: *Montpelier station*

Ends at: *Montpelier station*

Distance: *10 miles*

Terrain: *Mostly along rough paths through woods and fields, with some challenging stretches*

Pubs & other amenities:

White Lion, Frenchay Common, BS16 1LZ; open daily from 12; food served all day; 0117 9568787; johnbarras.com/pub/white-lion-frenchay-bristol/m8643/

Miners Arms, Mina Road, BS2 9YQ; open from 4 Mon-Fri; from 2 Sat & Sun; dogs welcome; 0117 9079874; www.dawkins-club.talktalk.net/page27.html

Map: *Geographers' A-Z & OS Explorer 155*

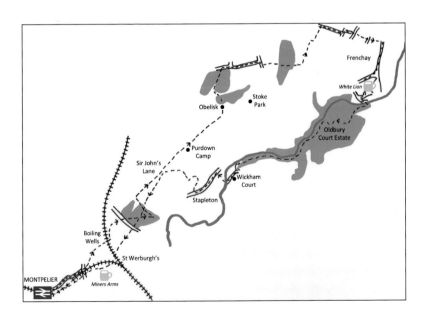

Opposite: Stoke Park from Duchess Pond

A part from short sections at the start and end, this walk is largely rural, taking in two great estates – Stoke Park and Oldbury Court – and the villages of Frenchay and Stapleton. Outward it follows the high ground on the west side of the Frome valley, returning along the high ground on the east side. Part of the return leg is fairly challenging, especially in wet weather, with stiff climbs and slippery paths. An alternative route, avoiding the most challenging section, is indicated should you wish to take it, but even so suitable footwear is essential and walking poles would be a definite advantage.

On leaving the train at Montpelier, cross the footbridge, carry on up to Cromwell Road and turn right. After 300m, you come to a crossroads. The pair of semi-detached houses on your left – Nos 128 and 130 – stand roughly on the site of Montpelier Farm, Cromwell and Fairfax's headquarters during the second siege of Bristol on 9 September 1645, but demolished in the 1890s. Carry straight on along Balmoral Road. At a T junction, turn right down Hurlingham Road and follow it as it swings round to the left. At the main road, cross and carry on down a footpath between allotments to the City Farm.

When you reach the City Farm, carry straight on to the left of the café. At a T junction, with a green fence ahead, turn right. After passing three bollards, bear left and, at a T junction, turn right following a cycle path sign to St Werburgh's and the City Centre. A few metres further on, turn left and carry straight on through the tunnel under the railway. Follow the lane as it bears left, passing the City Farm amphitheatre on your right.

Carry on as the lane turns to a rough track and, after passing a smallholding, turns sharp right uphill. At the main road, cross at the pedestrian crossing and head across the grass – bearing slightly to the right – to a gap in the hedge in the corner of the field. Go through it and bear left through another gap in the hedge. Carry straight on, following a faint track to a gap by an old stone gatepost in the hedge on the far side. Go through the gap and carry straight on, following a faint track as it curves round to the left, past a bench with a panoramic view, to follow the edge of the escarpment.

When you come to the corner of the field (with a good view of the

Sir John's Lane

Ashley Down orphanages over to your left), turn right through a gap in the hedge towards a house, before bearing left along a path beside a high wall (ST606758).

When you come to a road, turn right through a kissing gate (KG) – past a sign welcoming you to Lockleaze Open Space – into Sir John's Lane. Carry on alongside

Looking east across the Stoke Park estate to Duchess Pond

an eighteenth-century estate wall – due to be restored by Bristol City Council – and, when it ends, follow the lane to the right of Purdown BT Tower. This leads through Purdown Camp, the site of an anti-aircraft battery in the Second World War, remnants of which are still visible. After this the lane degenerates into a narrow, winding path which leads through a gateway into a large meadow. As you carry on with scrubland on your right, Stoke Park, high on a revetment above the Frome valley and painted a striking shade of ochre, comes into view ahead. Built in the mid-sixteenth century, it was substantially rebuilt in the mid-eighteenth century, when the estate was landscaped by Thomas Wright. It later became a dower house for the Dukes of Beaufort, but from 1909 to 1988 was a hospital. It was subsequently acquired, along with the estate, by a consortium of developers, and has now been converted to luxury apartments, while the area behind it, once occupied by ancillary hospital buildings, has been redeveloped. The rest of the estate was given to the council in 2012, along with an endowment to help reverse years of neglect.

The view westward from here to the far horizon, ringing by distant hills, is spectacular. In the valley below you is the spire of Stapleton Church and the grey Italianate tower of Glenside Hospital, built as a lunatic asylum in 1851, used a military hospital in the First World War and now part of the University of the West of England.

As you carry on through the next meadow, the ground starts to fall away and you can see ahead, on the far hillside, a stone monument (ST618771). Head towards it and eventually you will find yourself at the top of a slope with a lake below you. This is Duchess Pond, drained and filled in when the M32 was built in 1968 but partially reinstated by an angling club in 1993.

Head downhill and bear left up to the monument. This is all that remains of an obelisk erected in memory of Lady Elizabeth Somerset, the daughter of the Duke of Beaufort. It used to be thought that she died near this spot after falling from her horse, but it is now believed that she died from consumption. It was hit by lightning in 1940 and

A sketch of the obelisk by Samel Loxton

subsequently collapsed. What remains – including panels looking curiously like prototype QR codes – was restored in 2004. There are hopes that the obelisk, once topped by a gilded star, will one day be reinstated as well.

Just past the monument, you will see two ways into the woods, guarded by palisades. Go through the one on the left, carry straight ahead uphill for a few metres, turn left at a T junction and carry on until you come to a stile. Cross it and carry straight on, heading to the left of the spur of woodland ahead. Once past it, turn right, keeping the woods on your right before following a track into them (ST 617775). As you carry on, you will see parapets on either side of the path, with another path tunnelling beneath. There were once other ornamental garden features, such as a hermit's cell, nearby, but these have largely disappeared. A little further on, cross the ditch on your right, following a Hermitage Walk waymark. After 125m, when the path starts to swing right, bear left along a narrow path.

Go through a KG and turn right along a road past a new housing estate. At the main road, turn right for a few metres. Cross at the traffic island and cross a stile beside a gate. Cross another stile and carry straight on through a gateway. Follow the fence on your left before veering slightly to the right to follow a faint track towards a stile leading into the woods. Cross the stile and follow the path straight on.

After heading steeply downhill and narrowing between brambles, the path emerges in a meadow. Carry straight on, following a path towards the motorway. When you reach a hedge (ST630777) bear left alongside it, before carrying straight on between high hedges. Go through a metal gate and carry on along a green lane.

After 300m the lane swings sharp right and then, after going through

Bridge in Hermitage Wood

a KG, sharp left. Cross a rather difficult stile at the end and turn right along a road under the motorway. At a T junction, turn left for a few metres before crossing and turning right along Lynton Way. At the end, carry straight on along a hidden footpath on the right. After crossing a busy road, carry straight on along a footpath. After crossing a minor road – where you will see Frenchay Manor ahead – carry on along another footpath. This leads into a lane, at the end of which a left turn past Manor Cottage brings you to the classical façade of Frenchay Manor, dating from 1736. A little further on is its former stable block, now converted to housing.

From here, turn and retrace your footsteps along the road, carrying on past Manor Cottage. When the road forks, carry straight on past the Friends Meeting House of 1809 on the right and Frenchay Common on the left.* After passing a high wall and the gates of Cedar Hall, bear right again as the road forks. The west wing of Frenchay House, with a canted bay fronting the road and carved female heads in the keystones of the ground-floor windows, dates from 1772, although the rest of the building is later. Then comes Clarendon Lodge – also late eighteenth century – and Clarendon House, built around 1840.

After passing another wall, you come to the appropriately named Old House, built around 1740, and looking across to a pair of semi-detached houses dating from around 1795. Next to the Old House is something even older, a Unitarian chapel built in the late seventeenth century. The tower is thought to be a later addition, and it has been suggested that the comet weathervane indicates a date of 1758-59, when Halley's Comet appeared in the skies. Its appearance had been predicted by Edmund Halley using laws devised by Isaac Newton, and was a triumphant vindication of the validity of Newtonian physics, which many had hitherto disputed. As both Newton and Halley were Unitarians, it would have been natural for the Unitarians of Frenchay to design a weathervane to celebrate the event.

Head across the green to the right of the church – a relative newcomer, built in 1834, with a ha-ha protecting the churchyard from the livestock that once grazed the common. There is something undeniably uplifting about all this open space, and, with such august buildings looking out

---

* The Friends Meeting House has an unusual claim to fame as the place where Fred Wedlock recorded his first record in 1965.

across the greensward, this part of Frenchay Common seems, on a sunny summer's day, the very epitome of a certain type of Englishness.

Walk along the path past the churchyard gates, and at a crossroads turn right and left towards the White Lion Inn, built in 1899, and, despite many changes, still the sort of place you could imagine HG Wells's Mr Polly dropping into for a ginger beer.

Turn right by the White Lion and at the end turn left downhill past the old school house. When you come to the bridge turn right across it, then turn right into the Oldbury Court Estate, acquired by the council in 1936. Follow the path uphill, looking out for a small but impressive quarry on the left.

After levelling out, the path crosses a meadow. Carry on along the tarmaced path as it starts to head down into woodland. Just before it curves round to a small bridge, turn right along a narrow path alongside a stream

Ornamental pool on the Oldbury Court Estate

(ST636768). As you carry on down, you will see that the stream has been dammed to create two ponds. At a T junction, turn left across a footbridge, go up steps and bear right. When you come to the junction of four paths, carry straight on up steps. When you reach the top, you are at the heart of the estate – Oldbury Court stood just ahead, to the right of the sports pavilion. Dating from around 1600, it was extensively remodelled and extended in the eighteenth and nineteenth centuries, but, after falling into disrepair, was demolished in 1960.

HUMPHRY REPTON: LANDSCAPE GARDENER

Humphry Repton's name crops up several times in the course of these walks. Repton not only advised on landscaping the estates at Oldbury Court, Blaise Castle, Ashton Court, Leigh Court and Royal Fort, but had a major influence on many other projects. He was born at Bury St Edmunds in 1752 and after setting up – and failing – as a merchant, he tried a variety of other professions, before, at the age of 36, moving to the country and reinventing himself as a landscape gardener. Capability Brown had died five years earlier, and Repton had the audacity – and, more important, the ability – to set himself up as Brown's successor. He devised a novel way of presenting his ideas to his patrons, producing a series of plans and watercolour sketches which, by the ingenious use of flaps or fliers, could show what various landscape features would look like before and after his proposed improvements. These plans and sketches were presented to his clients between red binders, and Repton's 'red books' soon became famous. Unlike Capability Brown, Repton tended to work as a consultant, presenting ideas which his clients could adopt and adapt at will, rather than overseeing every aspect of creating large landscape gardens. He also wrote several books expounding his philosophy, including the influential *Sketches and Hints on Landscape Gardening* of 1794. His designs marked a transition from the picturesque naturalism of Capability Brown to the eclecticism of the nineteenth century, with flower beds and gravel walks near his patrons' houses and less formal, woodland-style landscaping beyond. In many cases, the formal, high-maintenance features of the gardens Repton was involved with have disappeared, while the woodlands – now possessed of a more thoroughgoing wildness than even he could have envisioned – have survived.

Bear right, following a signpost to Snuff Mills via Repton's Path. Bear right along a path with an old building on the left (don't go down the steps). When the path forks bear right downhill, and carry on past a fence with a sheer drop down to the river on the other side of it. The path leads under a protruding rock, maintaining a near level course along a revetment high on the precipitous slope. This superb woodland walk comes, as indicated by the signpost, courtesy of Humphry Repton, who was engaged to landscape the estate in 1800.

Oldbury Court around 1910

Eventually, the path starts to head down steps to the valley. Carry on past a steep flight of steps leading off to the right, before heading down the next flight of steps. When you reach the bottom of the valley, alongside a weir, turn left up another flight of steps and carry on, bearing left when the path forks, and continuing in roughly the same direction until the path eventually heads back down to the river.

A little way ahead you will see a bridge (ST629765). Here you have a choice. For the less challenging option, cross the bridge and carry on along the valley for 800m. When you reach the main road, turn left across the river, follow the road uphill and skip the next two paragraphs.

For the more challenging option – and a superb walk high above the valley – don't cross the bridge, but, bearing slightly to the left, head up a very steep path ahead. When you come to overhanging rocks, turn right and follow the path as it heads uphill along the side of the valley. When it levels out and meets another path, carry on in the same direction. The path continues alongside the wall of the former lunatic asylum which is now part of the University of the West of England.

When the path forks, don't branch off downhill but carry on. When the path does eventually start to head downhill, follow it down to the road, go through a gate and turn left uphill.

Cross at the traffic island and carry on uphill before turning right down Wickham Hill (ST620762). Wickham Court on the left, built around 1590 and extended in the late seventeenth century, was where Cromwell and Fairfax held a council of war before the second siege of Bristol in 1645.

After crossing Wickham Bridge, turn right along a narrow path. When it forks bear left through the remains of a KG and carry on uphill between old walls. After going through a squeeze stile – where you will see a gazebo of around 1720 on your left – carry on uphill.

At the road bear left past elegant early eighteenth-century houses – and at No 68 a cottage where the Chartist leader John Frost once lived. The Grange – on the left just before the zebra crossing – dates from the late seventeenth or early eighteenth century, while the building opposite dates from around 1730.

Cross the zebra crossing and carry on past the old Bell Inn, built in 1900, closed in 2009 and now converted to two houses. Opposite is the entrance to Colston's School, at its core an eighteenth-century house which was bought in 1840 by the Bishop of Bristol to use as a palace after the palace by the cathedral was burnt down by rioters. He liked Stapleton so much that he built the church whose spire dominates the village, but, after his death, it was decided to build a new palace at Redland and the palace in Stapleton was sold to Colston's School, which now occupies many other buildings in the village as well.

After 75m, turn right along a public footpath signposted to Purdown. After going through a tunnel, turn right up steps at a crosspath. Carry on along a path curving to the right of Beech House. Built around 1764, this was originally known as the Grove, and was the home of Raja Rammohun Roy Bahadoor between 1829 and 1833.

Turn left at a minor road, left again at a T junction, and on your right you will see Linden House, converted from a windmill in the early twentieth century.

Turn right up Heath House Lane and cross the M32. As the lane bears left, go through a KG on the right (ST611762) and follow an overgrown path diagonally uphill. When you come to a broad path at the top, turn left along it. When it forks, bear left and carry straight on through a meadow with the ruinous wall of St John's Lane on your right. The eighteenth-century building below you is Heath House, now converted to a hospital. Just before you draw parallel with it, follow a faint

An early twentieth-century view of the windmill which became Linden House

track diagonally downhill. Go through a gap in the far corner of the meadow and, after climbing down to a path, turn left along it.

When the path forks, bear right by a building and you will be confronted by a choice of paths (ST 606757). Ahead you will see a tree with a hedge to the left of it. Carry straight on following a faint track to the left of that hedge. At the end of the meadow, carry straight on along a path through woodland. After going down steps to Muller Road, cross and carry on up another flight of steps (ST604754). At the top follow the footpath as it bears left and right past Fairfield School, and when you come to a road carry straight on. At the T junction at the end, carry straight on along a footpath, crossing two railway bridges and heading downhill. When you reach Mina Road, you have a choice. A left turn will take you to the Miner's Arms, while turning right and then left along a footpath before the tunnel will take you up to Ashley Hill. When you get there, cross and carry on up another footpath. Continue along a road past the old Fairfield School on your left. Carry straight on along a footpath and ahead you will see a malthouse, built in 1876 and now converted to housing. At the end of the footpath continue along the road past the malthouse entrance. Carry on when you come to a T junction and after another 250m, when you see an archway on your left, turn right through a row of bollards to return to Montpelier station.

Further information online:
Friends of South Purdown: *friendsofsouthpurdown.weebly.com*
Stoke Park Action Group: *stokeparkactiongroup.org.uk*
Greater Fishponds: *www.fishpondspeople.co.uk*

8

REDLAND, HENLEAZE, WESTBURY & THE TRYM VALLEY

Starts at: *Redland station*

Ends at: *Sea Mills station*

Distance: *9 miles*

Terrain: *Pavements, tarmaced paths, and rough paths through woodland*

Pubs & other amenities:

Cambridge Arms, Coldharbour Road, Redland BS6 7JS; open daily from 12; food served 12-3 & 6-9 Mon-Fri, all day from 12 Sat & Sun; dogs welcome; 0117 9739786; www.cambridgearms.co.uk

Port of Call, York Street, Clifton BS8 2YE; open daily from 12; dogs welcome; 0117 9733600

Victoria, Chock Lane, Westbury on Trym BS9 3EX; open 12-2.30 & 6-11 Mon-Sat, 12-3 & 7-10.30 Sun; food served 12-2 daily, 6-9 Mon-Sat; 0117 9500441; www.thevictoriapub.co.uk

Map: *Geographers' A-Z & OS Explorer 155*

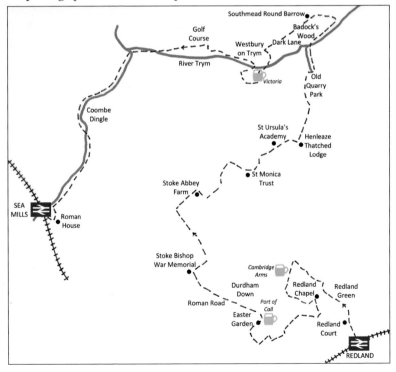

Opposite: Hollybush Lane

After exploring Redland, this walk skirts the north end of Clifton before crossing Durdham Down to Henleaze and the upper reaches of the River Trym. A walk round historic Westbury on Trym – older than Bristol itself – is followed by a walk down the valley of the Trym to its junction with the Avon at Sea Mills. As well as glimpses of Bristol's somewhat scant Roman heritage, the walk takes in a couple of extraordinary quarries, a 3,000-year-old round barrow and other hidden treasures.

Head out of Redland station, turn left and, just before the main road, turn right along Lovers' Walk. This tree-lined avenue leads to Redland Court, built for John Cossins in 1735, and since 1885 home to Redland High School for Girls. It replaced an earlier Redland Court, which may have started life as a monastic guest house for the college at Westbury on Trym (which you will be visiting later). The avenue, which probably dated from the time of Cossins' rebuilding, is a remarkable survival. As late as 1855, it still stood in open country, but, less than 20 years later, the railway had cut through it and streets had sprung up around. Fortunately, the developers regarded it as an asset rather than an obstacle to be swept away and its upper and lower sections, linked by a railway bridge, survive today as one of Redland's most endearing features.

At the end, cross the zebra crossing to the court – with gateposts carved to resemble icicles – and head to the right of it up Redland Court Road. If you keep to the right-hand pavement, you will have a better view of Redland Court as you climb the hill. After 400m, when the road forks, you will see two gateposts ahead, with a fence and hedge between them. Behind them stood the palace of the Bishop of Bristol, built in 1898 but destroyed by bombing in 1940. In 1968, a college hostel was built on the site, but this has now been replaced by apartment blocks.

Bear to the left of the gateposts and a few metres further on bear right along a footpath. Carry on past a playground before bearing right at a crosspath to Redland Green Farm, one of the oldest buildings in the area. For centuries Redland Green was common land, but in 1902 seven and a half acres of it was given to the council, who bought out the remaining commoners' rights and created a park.

Retrace your steps, and at the crosspath turn right downhill. As the path starts to rise again, you will see a fragment of an old boundary wall ahead. Bear to the left of it, across the grass, heading for the houses at the far end of the Green. Just before you reach a tarmac path, look to the left to see a large stone – of unknown origin and significance – lying in the grass.

Turn left up the path and right along a road at the top. At the T junction, turn left along Coldharbour Road. The Cambridge Arms on your left, with its superb plasterwork, was built in 1900 when a nearby beerhouse was demolished to widen the road. Just past it are some cottages dating from the early eighteenth century. Turn left at the end along Redland Road. If you look up to the right at the mini-roundabout, you will see a tall house with canted bays. This is Ashley Hill House, built in 1761, and now the Bristol Steiner School. It was originally a pair of semi-detached houses, but the matching wing with canted bays at the far end was demolished in 1933.

Bear left at the mini roundabout to continue along Redland Road. No 157 on the left – now the Redland Office Centre – was built in the 1740s as a vicarage and stood in extensive grounds, with views across open country.

On the corner of Redland Green Road – where there is a particularly well-designed drinking fountain – cross and turn left along a tree-shaded path towards Redland Chapel, built as a private chapel for John Cossins in the 1740s and now the parish church. As you bear right alongside the wall, you will see Cabot Tower straight ahead. On the grass at the end you will see another large stone, its origin unknown, although numerous legends surround it. In the late nineteenth century, it was removed by the vicar 'because children played on it and were a nuisance'. Following 'agitation ... in the local press for the restoration of the stone to its original site' it was reinstated in 1913.[1]

Turn right along the road and, as you turn left down Redland Road, look to your left to see an enigmatic milestone. The first part – '1 mile from Stoke's Croft' – is straightforward; it is the

'XI' that follows it that is puzzling. Fortunately, an Ordnance Survey map from the 1880s solves the mystery, revealing that the milestone was one mile from Stoke's Croft and eleven miles from Aust. Aust was the embarkation point for the Old Passage Ferry across the Severn, and Redland Road was part of the road linking it with Bristol. The relevant lettering on the milestone has presumably been covered up by the pavement.

If you walk downhill for 150m, you will come across a reminder of an even older – and more enigmatic – road. If you look across to the convenience store on the corner of Lower Redland Road, you will see 'Via Julia 1901' above its first-floor windows. 'Via Julia' was the name given to the Roman road from Aquae Sulis (Bath) to Portus Abonae (Sea Mills), which was believed to pass through here.* So comprehensively was this area developed in the late nineteenth and early twentieth centuries, however, that any evidence for this is unlikely to survive. You will, however, be coming across a slightly more tangible reminder of this long-lost road later.

Cross to the Via Julia building and head to the left of it up Lower Redland Road. The Shakespeare pub, on the left, was built in 1903 to replace an earlier inn, dating, like Woolcott Street alongside it, from around 1860. A little further along Lower Redland Road are Woolcott Cottages, a particularly attractive example of early nineteenth-century picturesque style.

A little further along, look up Luccombe Hill to see one of Bristol's most extraordinary buildings, half-timbered, battlemented, and flying the Jolly Roger. Built as a barn around 1675, it fell into disrepair in the early twentieth century before being converted to a dwelling by the Rev Robert Springett-Nicholson. He incorporated into it a variety of salvaged material, including some from bombed churches, and in 1974, to mark Bristol's absorption into the county of Avon, hoisted a black flag over it. The cottage above it, with a semi-circular headed door, is also believed to date from the seventeenth century, but was refronted – somewhat more conventionally – in the nineteenth.

Carry on along Lower Redland Road past imposing nineteenth-century houses. The ironwork on the balcony of Cromarty House (No 75) on the right is particularly striking. At a T junction bear left to continue along Lower Redland Road, passing the old Redland Police

---

* This was not the name given to it by the Romans, who numbered rather than named their roads, much as we do today. This road was Highway 14. Via Julia was a name coined by an eighteenth-century forger called Charles Julius Bertram, who claimed to have discovered an ancient manuscript giving details of the Roman roads of Britain.

Station, now converted to a school. Turn left along Exeter Buildings and right into Burlington Road, with one of Clifton's grander terraces, dating from around 1845, on the right.

Cross Whiteladies Road at the pedestrian lights to St John's Church. Consecrated in 1841, this closed in 1984 and became an auction house, but is now home to a range of businesses. Turn right across the end of Apsley Road, continue up Whiteladies Road and take the next left along Wellington Park. A little way along, turn right along Mornington Road and follow it round to the left, past the back of nineteenth-century villas. This little-known byway, still paved with grass-grown setts, has a charming row of four mid-nineteenth-century cottages at the end. Turn right along Anglesea Place, a colourful terrace built around 1847. A plaque on No 29 marks the birthplace of Randolph Sutton, a famous music-hall artist. Opposite are the blocked-up windows of a school that now occupies modern buildings further back.

At the top – with some delightful early nineteenth-century cottages ahead on Caroline Row – cross and head down Sutherland Place. As you turn right into Quarry Steps, you can see the aforementioned steps at the end of the street. Instead of continuing towards them, however, turn left into Quarry Road for one of Bristol's most dramatic visual surprises. This area,

as its name indicates, was once a quarry, and the revetment ahead marks the limit of its encroachment into the hillside. The scene is somehow very un-English; it could almost have been transplanted from southern Europe. And there is a striking discontinuity of scale; with high houses all around – especially atop the cliff – the cottages on the right in Richmond Dale seem almost perversely diminutive.

If you carry on to the end of Quarry Road, you will see where houses were once built right up against the face of the revetment, with traces of old walls and plaster, and, in the corner, a door leading into a dark vault. From here, head back a little way and turn left up Richmond Dale, past the superbly polychromatic brickwork of the old mission house and reading room.

At the top, a right turn leads to one of Clifton's most delightful hidden corners. Easter Garden occupies a site on which ruinous cottages – demolished in the 1950s – once stood. Although permission was granted to redevelop the site in 1994, ownership of it was in dispute and over the Easter weekend in 1997 local residents laid out a garden here. Today it is a wonderful natural space – like an open-air living room – amid streets of densely-packed houses, yet battles between residents, who have worked to make it a focal point for the community, and a succession of developers eager to shoehorn tenements onto the site, have rumbled on. In 2010 they erupted in a confrontation when the landowner attempted to close off the site and subsequently submitted a planning application. Although this was refused in January 2011, efforts to safeguard Easter Gardens received a setback early in 2013 when a government inspector refused to designate it a town green. Bristol City Council responded by ordering an inquiry into the dispute. For the sake of the residents – and the city – we can only hope that this precious amenity is preserved for future generations.

Walk up through the garden, and at the top turn right and then left down York Street past the Port of Call, originally a beerhouse called the Down Porter House. At the bottom, turn left up Whiteladies Road. A little further on, look across to see a drinking fountain erected in 1904 and housed in an octagonal structure like a market cross. Just past it is a former school, dating from 1850. As the pavement curves, cross ahead at the lights over Upper Belgrave Road. Carry on across two more sets of lights and continue along the west side of Stoke Road.

As you carry on, you will see a water tower and reservoir to your right, along with a drinking fountain adorned with terracotta heads of farm

Above: Drinking fountain on Stoke Road

Left: Easter Garden

animals. It was erected in 1877 by the Bath & West Agricultural Society for the Royal Agricultural Show held on the Downs the following year.

After crossing the end of Ladies Mile, diverge onto the grass on your left, and look to the left of the trees ahead, where you will see some buildings. Head directly for the one on the far right. You are now walking along the course of the Roman road from Aquae Sulis to Portus Abonae, from where soldiers embarked for the legionary fortress at Caerleon.

Although the course of the road was still clearly visible until the mid-nineteenth century, it has now all but disappeared, and, as you set out across the grass, there is nothing to indicate its route. Carry on,

---

THE DEATH OF A ROMAN ROAD

On 13 October 1855, a correspondent in the *Bristol Mercury* drew attention to the

> *old Roman road [leading] from the top of the hill at Redland, just above the Black Boy Tavern, across Durdham Down ... The line of the road can be distinctly traced across the down, and at one place it is the only safe passage by which a pedestrian can cross it at night, intercepted as it is by a vast number of small pits, many of them filled with brushwood, and having a very large open quarry contiguous to the beaten track. At night the white paving stones which crop up through the turf are the only guide by which the traveller can tread his way across the down, when going in the direction of the Sea Mills.*

His aim was not to celebrate the road's survival, however, but to warn of its imminent destruction:

> *To my immense surprise and astonishment this day, when passing over the down to the post office at Redland, I found the old road, at the very critical point I have mentioned, cut in two by a dyke of the most formidable proportions, so as to render it impossible for any vehicle of any description to get across the down in this direction, and to make it dangerous in the extreme for any pedestrian to attempt it after dark. Now this is so direct an attack upon what I have always been led to consider as the right and privilege of the citizens of Bristol, that I appeal to the authorities at once to take the matter in hand. It does not concern any one individual in particular, but is of vital moment to the whole mass of the inhabitants. Is their right to cross the down for purposes of health and recreation fanciful and imaginary? Do they walk, and ride, and drive on it by sufferance only? If so the Merchant Venturers and lords of the manor of Henbury, who claim to be proprietors of the soil, may not only dig trenches, but build houses, and enclose it in every way they may deem fit. But if, as appears to be the better opinion, the use of the down appertains to the inhabitants of Bristol, every moment during which they neglect to vindicate their right, appears to me to denote an extent of apathy of which, until I came among them, I could have formed no conception.*

Although the downs were eventually saved, the destruction of the Roman road continued apace, so that, one and half centuries later, the distinct track, marked with white paving stones, has virtually disappeared into the ground through which it ran.

though, and about halfway across you should gradually become aware of walking along a broad ridge – almost indiscernible, and almost certainly not something you would notice unless you were looking for it. As you approach the buildings it disappears again. And, if you look back, you probably will not be able to make it out. It is only when you are walking along it that you become aware of it, and even then it would probably be futile to try to take a photograph as a record. It is said, however, that a visit at sunrise when the ridge casts a shadow across the grass yields somewhat better results.

Carry on across the road to the building known as the Old Halt. Although much altered, this dates from the eighteenth century, when, known as Durdham Lodge, it was one of the very few buildings in this remote and inhospitable spot. Carry on along the grass beside the road to Stoke Bishop war memorial. Cross to the right to a lodge with a slag-topped wall and a Gothic arch braced with iron. Walk along the grass beside the private road to the right of it for 200m, and, when you come to Hollybush Lane, turn left.

Carry on along Hollybush Lane for 650m, when, after heading steeply downhill and levelling out, it meets a crosspath, where there is also access to a road. Turn right along the crosspath for 250m, to emerge by a large disused yard on the right. The gabled building beyond the yard is Stoke Abbey Farm, dating from 1670. For a better view of it, and of the charming gazebo beside it, turn right along the road.

Carry on across the end of Shaplands, cross at the traffic island, and, a little further along, turn left along Elmlea Avenue. After 175m, turn right up a footpath signposted 'To the Downs' (the signpost is on the left-hand side of the road). After 125m, when you come to a fork, bear left. After another 125m, the path bears right up steps before bearing left alongside a wall. At the end of the footpath, cross a slab stile and bear right up Cote Lane, past some large wooden buildings. On your right are the buildings of the St Monica Trust, originally St Monica's Home of Rest, founded in the 1920s by HH Wills as a retirement home for Anglican women.

At the end, turn left past the entrance to Badminton School, cross the zebra crossing and carry on along Westbury Road. After 150m, turn

The Convent, Henleaze.

right along Brecon Road, where there are some impressive vernacular-style buildings, reminiscent of the Arts and Crafts movement. St Ursula's Academy, on the left, has grown up around Westmead House, built sometime before 1823 for a merchant called John Irving.[4] In 1831 it was acquired by a community of nuns, and a major expansion, including an Italianate tower, was completed in 1862. It became a school in 1897.

At the end of Brecon Road, cross and carry on along Antrim Road. The thatched cottage orné at the end of the road – with a roof reminiscent

of Darth Vader's helmet but clearly inspired by John Nash's cottages at Blaise Hamlet – was a lodge for Henleaze Park, an eighteenth-century mansion which, after becoming a school, was demolished in the 1960s.

Turn left along Henleaze Road, passing the Eastfield Inn, built in the mid-1930s on the site of a Victorian beerhouse which had been granted a full licence in 1932. Limestone quarrying was the main source of employment in this area in the nineteenth century, and 100m past the inn you will see some old quarrymen's cottages on the left. Eastfield Terrace, which you cross a little further along, was also built around 1860 for quarrymen and their families.

Just after this, turn left through a gate into Old Quarry Park. Although one of the city's smallest and newest parks, it has a surprising history. The quarry here was abandoned in 1916 because of coal shortages. Coal was needed to power the machines which pumped water out of the quarry, which in places was up to 30m deep. Once they stopped working, it rapidly filled with water, making its reopening impossible. The lake thus formed was by all accounts remarkably picturesque, but in 1930 the corporation acquired it as a rubbish dump. Tipping continued for over 20 years, and, in the aftermath of the Blitz, large quantities of rubble from the city centre were disposed of here. By the 1970s, tipping had long ceased, and, with nature having reclaimed much of the site, the council agreed

Old Quarry Park

to turn it into a park. Since then, with the active involvement of the Henleaze Society, Old Quarry Park has become a much-loved amenity.

Follow the path through the park and climb the steps at the end. Turn right, then left at the main road.

Left: Badock's Wood

Below: Southmead Round Barrow

Cross at the pedestrian crossing and head back along the road before turning left along Clover Ground. After 150m, turn right down Vintery Leys. At the bottom turn left along Lakewood Road, and after 50m go through a kissing gate (KG) into Badock's Wood. This is named after Sir Stanley Badock, a businessman and philanthropist, who in 1937, when Southmead was being developed, gave part of his Holmwood Estate to the council to be preserved as a public open space in perpetuity.

Follow a path alongside a tributary stream for 250m. When it forks, bear left alongside the stream and turn left across a bridge just before it joins the River Trym. Follow the Trym downstream for 100m, and, when the way ahead is blocked by a fence, cross a bridge and head upstream for 500m until your way is once again blocked by a fence. Turn left and follow the tarmaced path as it curves uphill, ending at a crosspath, with a mosaic over to the right. Carry straight on and follow the path ahead as it curves through the trees. In the aftermath of the Second World War, 81 prefabs were built in the field to your left. Named Bowness Gardens, and with a network of roads running through it, the site was cleared between 1979 and 1982. So successfully has it been landscaped and replanted that little now remains to indicate its brief career as a housing estate. A little further on you come to the Southmead Round Barrow. At around two metres high, it may not be that impressive, but, at around 3,000 years old, it is a remarkable survival.

Head past it and carry on through a playing field with a high hedge on your right. At the end go through a KG and carry straight on along a path known as Dark Lane. At the end turn left up Channell's Hill and carry on down between stone walls to the village of Westbury on Trym.

The cottages at the bottom of the hill include Dial House, a former turnpike house with a clock painted on its wall. The story goes that a young lady who lived here, after being jilted by her lover, had it painted showing the time he jilted her as a reminder – to him and the village – of his breach of promise. Just past it, cross a small bridge over the Trym on your left, follow the path through a garden onto Chock Lane, cross over and head

Dial House & Old Bridge, Westbury-on-Trym.

up a footpath by old cottages to the church – although, if you have timed it right, you may elect to divert up to the left to call into the Victoria Inn.

The entrance to the church is at the west end, under the tower, and if it is open is worth a visit. Like St David's Cathedral in Wales – another ancient place of worship – it slopes uphill, although here steps have been installed to make the floor level. Successive rebuildings and refurbishments

– most notably in the fifteenth century, when it was briefly raised to the status of a cathedral – have created a building of great interest and variety, and the walls are lined with some fascinating memorials, including the reclining effigy of Sir Richard Hill of Redland Court who died in 1627.

Carry on past the church and, after going through the gates at the far end, you will see the House of Prayer, built as a church house in the fifteenth century. Go up steps (signposted to the Garden of Remembrance) beside it. Carry on along the footpath and, at the end of the churchyard, carry on for a few metres before turning left along a path winding through a grassy area. At the end, go through a gate and turn right. At the road, with the Mouse pub – originally the Royal Oak – on your right, and the imposing village hall of 1869 on your left, cross with care, and carry straight on along Eastfield Road. On the right, at No 12, is the late eighteenth-century vicarage. The house at the end of the road on the left, with a Gothic window, is the early nineteenth-century lodge for Burfield House, now part of the Red Maids' School. Cross the main road at the traffic island and turn right downhill. The Post Office Tavern of 1889 still proudly proclaims itself a George's house, although the brewery was absorbed by Courage's over 50 years ago.

As you carry on downhill, look across to see the door of the old lock-up in the wall. Here rowdy drunks were incarcerated overnight to let them cool off – hence its local nickname of 'the

THE VILLAGE ON THE TRYM

Westbury on Trym has only been part of Bristol since 1904, yet is not only the city's oldest suburb, but predates Bristol itself. A monastery founded here in the eighth century had a somewhat erratic history before being re-established as a college of secular priests in the late twelfth century. The collegiate church built at this time survives as the parish church. In the mid-fifteenth century, the college was rebuilt in fortress-like style, with a high wall, turrets and fortified gatehouse. After the Reformation, the college became a private house but was largely destroyed by Royalist forces in 1645 to prevent it being occupied by advancing Parliamentary troops. It was rebuilt as a private house, but, after falling into disrepair, was bought by public subscription and given to the National Trust in 1907. Other ancient buildings, including a fifteenth-century church house, coaching inns, a turnpike house and several cottages, also survive, so that, although Westbury has long been absorbed by the expanding city, it still retains the atmosphere of a village with a distinguished past.

cooler'. A little further down on the left is No 37, a particularly attractive early nineteenth-century house. The old Foresters Arms at the bottom of the hill is now a Tesco Express.

At the war memorial, cross and bear right along the High Street. The White Horse Inn on the corner of Church Road is – with the exception of the King's Head on Victoria Street – probably the least altered pub in the city. With its warren of wood-panelled rooms, furnished haphazardly with grandfather clocks, chaises-longues and settles, and beer served through hatches from barrels lined up in a vaulted cellar, it really is an untouched, unrestored blast from the past.

Turn right along Church Road and at the end, after admiring the floral display outside the Villager restaurant, turn left along College Road to find the remains of the fifteenth-century college. Facing you at the end of the road is Whitney House, a splendid piece of Georgian asymmetry.

Turn right along the High Street and first left into Westfield Road. Take the footpath on the right alongside the river. When the way ahead is blocked, turn left, then right, and when the road ends continue along a footpath.

At the main road, turn left past some of the city's surviving prefabs, cross at the lights, turn right across

One of the towers of Westbury College with the church tower in the distance

In the valley of the Trym

the end of Canford Road, carry on for 60m and turn left along a footpath to continue down the valley of the Trym.

After 200m, turn right at a T junction for 40m before going through a KG on the left into a golf course. Carry straight on, heading to the left of a large bank of trees and undergrowth, with the river on your left.

After passing an artificial pond, you come to the end of the golf course. Cross a stile, carry on through a meadow and go over a metal bridge with no handrail (ST562776). Cross the lane and continue along the footpath on the other side. Care is needed on this section, as the path is on a ledge high above the river.

After passing a metal gate, the path forks. Take the lower path, leading down to the river. Go through two KGs and cross a metal bridge. Carry on alongside the river before crossing another bridge on the left (ST558776). Carry on to the left alongside the river. The path leads into a meadow and then a car park, at the end of which you cross the road before carrying straight on along a footpath into the woods. This section of the valley can flood, but the path is raised on a causeway.

After 200m the path goes under a bridge. Carry on along the valley and when you come to a tarmac path, turn left along it. Cross a bridge and when the path forks bear right. At the next fork, turn left through a squeeze stile. At the main road, cross at the zebra crossing up to the left, head back along the road and turn left along Sea Mills Lane.

After 800m, there is a final diversion to see the most tangible legacy of the Roman settlement of Portus Abonae. Just before the Portway crosses Sea Mills Lane, turn left following a footpath sign up a side road. Carry on along the footpath and at the end turn right along a road. After 100m you will see the foundations of a Roman house on the left.

Cross the Portway at the lights, turn right down the road beyond it and turn left at the bottom for the station.

Further information online:

Redland & Cotham Amenities Society: *www.rcas.org.uk*
Easter Garden: *www.eastergarden.moonfruit.com*
Friends of Badock's Wood: *www.fobw.org.uk*
Westbury on Trym Society: *www.westburyontrymsociety.org.uk*

THE SAVING OF CLIFTON & DURDHAM DOWNS

Clifton and Durdham Downs are among Bristol's most treasured assets, yet in the mid-nineteenth century there was a real danger that they might be lost forever to developers. John Latimer describes how much common land in the surrounding parishes was lost in this way:

> Large tracts of commonable land in the parishes of Henbury and Westbury were inclosed [in 1811] under the provisions of an Act promoted by Mr E Sampson, solicitor, of Henbury, on behalf of himself and other landowners, who appropriated nearly the whole extent, with the utmost indifference to the claims of the resident labourers and of the public at large. Similar inclosures – for the most part unauthorized by Parliament – had been made in other suburban parishes, those in Clifton being especially obnoxious to Bristolians; but except a few timid grumbles in the newspapers, nothing was said or done in defence of public rights. In 1813 another Act swept into the hands of landed gentry a large extent of commonable land in the parishes of Long Ashton, Wraxall, Nailsea, and Bourton, and further extensive inclosures were made at Portishead, Dundry, and Almondsbury by subsequent statutes. Even before those 'conveyances' were effected, a writer in the Bristol Gazette of 13 August 1812 says: 'They who remember Ashton, Leigh, Westbury, Kingsweston, Clifton, and Stapleton 20 years ago, will need no description to recall to their minds the delightful and healthy walks now untrodden by vulgar feet – then open to the public for exercise or pleasure. [2]

When it came to the Downs, however, the council was not prepared to stand by and do nothing:

> At a meeting of the council on 12 February 1850, a discussion took place upon the extensive encroachments which had been recently made upon the valuable common land in the neighbourhood of Clifton. Mr Visger observed that measures were in progress which would eventually terminate in the inclosure of Clifton Down. A considerable portion, indeed, had been already built upon. 'These encroachments,' he said, 'had all been gradual. When he was a boy a great part of Clifton was open, and consisted chiefly of sheep walks. A few rails were put up, ostensibly to prevent the sheep from wandering. These soon gave way to iron stanchions; by-and-by a wall was built, and then houses were erected. Opposite these houses small shrubs were planted, and under pretence of protecting them, posts were put up. Within a few years the posts were pulled down and regular plantations formed. He well remembered having ridden up and down places that were now inclosed.' Mr Visger's remarks called forth no contradiction; but when Alderman Pinney advised the purchase of the downs, Mr Powell protested against the council interfering with the property of others. If the Merchants' Society, he said, chose to build upon Clifton Down, they would be dealing with their own property, and the council had no more right to intervene than to pull down Badminton House. It was resolved to represent to the Board of Health inspector, then holding his inquiry in the city, the great

value of these open spaces, and the danger to which they were exposed from systematic encroachments. In the following August, the lords of the manor of Henbury, 'doing what they liked with their own', disposed of a portion of Durdham Down to the authorities of St John's district church for the purpose of building a schoolhouse. Other encroachments were made from time to time, and in 1856 some enterprising individual, as an experiment, built a cottage in one of the five quarries which were then being worked in various parts of the downs. This step excited so much indignation, however, that the building was forthwith removed. In the course of the following year, the corporation succeeded in purchasing, for £450, a small property at Westbury, to which commonable rights on Durdham Down were attached, whereby it was hoped a title had been obtained to resist further encroachments in that direction. Soon afterwards Mr Baker, as owner of the Sneyd Park estate, claimed, and apparently made good his claim to, a strip of ground at Sea Walls, which had hitherto been a favourite promenade for pedestrians. In 1859 the public were startled by another unexpected proceeding – the inclosure by a Mr Samuel Worrall, descendant of a former clerk of the Merchants' Society, of two large pieces of common land which had been popularly considered to form part of Clifton Down. His action was the subject of indignant reprobation in the council; but according to legal authorities the inclosures could not be prevented,

and the utmost the public could claim was a footpath over the plots. Further encroachments being reported as imminent, a committee was appointed to negotiate with the Merchants' Society and the lords of Henbury Manor. In the result, the Society, while refusing to sell their rights over either the turf or the minerals of Clifton Down, expressed willingness to see the public assured of the free enjoyment of the open space, whilst the lords consented to sell in fee simple their estate in Durdham Down, including the quarries, for £15,000. A resolution empowering the committee to arrange with the parties on those terms was passed by the council on 24 May 1860; and an Act of Parliament legalising the settlement received the royal assent a year later. The lordship of the manor of Henbury was divided between two persons: Sir J Greville Smyth, who held three-fourths, and who therefore received £11,250; and the trustees of Mrs Colston, of Roundway, Wilts, who obtained £3,750 in right of the remaining quarter. The expense of obtaining the statute raised the total cost of the transaction to £16,296. The area over which the public acquired a right of perpetual enjoyment was 442 acres – 230 acres of which belong to Clifton Down, and 212 to that of Durdham.[3]

9

COTHAM, CLIFTON WOOD, HOTWELLS & CLIFTON

Starts at: *Redland station*

Ends at: *Clifton Down station*

Distance: *6 miles*

Terrain: *Mostly on pavements or tarmaced paths, although with some steps*

Access Restrictions: *Dogs are not permitted in the grounds of Royal Fort*

Pubs & other amenities:

Highbury Vaults, St Michael's Hill, BS2 8DE; open from 12; food served 12-2.30 Sat; 12-3 Sun; dogs welcome in front bar; 01179 733203; www.youngs.co.uk/pubs/highbury-vaults

Beerd, St Michael's Hill, BS2 8DB; open from 11.30; food served all day from 12; 0117 9743567; www.beerdbristol.com

Adam & Eve, Hope Chapel Hill, BS8 4ND; open from 5.30 Tue-Fri, from 12 Sat & Sun, closed Mon; dog friendly; 0117 3292025

Hophouse, King's Road, BS8 4AB; open from 5 Mon; from 12 Tue-Sun; dogs welcome; 0117 9237390

Map: *Geographers' A-Z*

A defiantly urban walk that includes more than its fair share of hidden corners. Along the way you will see: a civil war fort, landscaped and graced with magnificent buildings – and a maze of mirrors; the spot at the city's northern edge where criminals hanged in chains and Protestant martyrs burned at the stake; the place where the warm waters of Hotwell Spa sprang forth; lodging houses built to entice the gentry away from the hot springs at Bath; a cathedral that never was; grand houses built by wealthy merchants eager to escape the smoke and squalor of the city below; a cliff railway that ran through a tunnel; and much more.

Walk out of Redland station, turn left up the road and left across a footbridge over the railway. Carry on along Lovers' Walk, with Cotham Gardens on your left. This park was given to the city by the Fry family in 1879. It opened two years later, and some of the original plantings survive at the southern end.

At the top, cross (you may find it easier to use the zebra crossing ahead and walk back) and turn right along Cotham Park North. At the top, cross and carry on along Cotham Park, where the succession of grand villas built in the 1860s and 1870s continues. Follow Cotham Park as it

Opposite: Birdcage Walk, St Andrew's Churchyard, Clifton

119

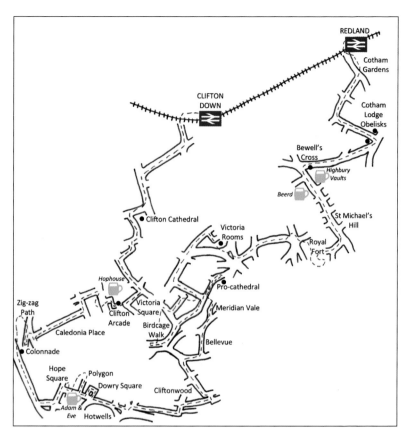

swings to the left and carry straight on. On the left, at No 16, is Ashley Down House, built around 1850. This stands on the site of an eighteenth-century mansion, surrounded by parkland, which was demolished in 1846 when Cotham started to be developed. If you carry on to the end of the road, you will see the obelisks that flanked the entrance to the estate.

Across the road is one of Cotham's oldest buildings, an extraordinary Jacobean-style row of three houses with exaggerated Dutch gables. Turn right by the obelisks and bear right up Cotham Road, passing an imposing row of semi-detached villas, reminiscent of Cheltenham, on the right.

The school buildings on the right as you pass the bottom of Hartfield Avenue stand on the site of several older buildings, including a seventeenth-century windmill converted to an observatory by the owner of Cotham Lodge. It was demolished in 1953, despite protests from the Civic Society.

Cotham Parish Church, at the end of the road, was built as a Congregational chapel in 1842 and taken over by the Church of England in the 1970s. A memorial on the wall of the church commemorates five

One of Cotham's obelisks; and Western College as it appeared when new

Protestant martyrs burnt at the stake here during the reign of Queen Mary. Just past the second gateway, a plaque indicates the remains of Bewell's Cross, erected to mark the boundary when the county of Bristol was created in 1373. Nearby was a gallows where public executions were carried out, with all the implications for public order that entailed. In 1749, the *Bristol Intelligencer* reported that

> *crowds of dissolute and disorderly persons have been entertained at about seven or eight unruly public houses near the gallows on St Michael's Hill and many insults and robberies committed on the market people and others travelling thereabout, but the gentlemen of that parish having bravely prosecuted and caused several penalties to be levied on the keepers of the houses, they are all routed away.[1]*

Unfortunately, public executions were great crowd pullers, and troublemakers just kept coming back. In 1773, local residents were so fed up with the damage to their property every time there was a hanging that they sent a petition to the council asking them to move the gallows to Brandon Hill. The request fell on deaf ears and the executions continued until they were finally stopped in 1820.

The half-timbered Arts and Crafts building facing the church was the house of the principal of Western Congregational College, opened in 1906, which you can see if you walk along to the corner. It now houses

a doctor's surgery. Hampton House Health Centre, on the other side of the road, was originally a homeopathic hospital. The future Edward VIII laid its foundation stone in June 1921.

Turn left down St Michael's Hill, where, at the end of an early nineteenth-century terrace, you will find the Highbury Vaults, worth a visit not only for its selection of cask ales but also to see the tiny snug that survives at the front of the building. A little further along on the right is the popular craft-beer and pizza bar,

Beerd. Further along again is the White Bear, an old coaching inn with the life-size figure of a polar bear holding a pint above the entrance.* Paul Street, opposite the White Bear, has an especially attractive row of early nineteenth-century buildings.

The terrace beyond the White Bear also dates from the early nineteenth century, although the gabled building at the end is much older. It dates from around 1670; the doorway with its Gibbsian surround was added a century or so later. Beyond it, the 1970s university library on the south side of St Michael's Park looks across to an elegant late eighteenth-century house on the corner of Myrtle Road.

After continuing down St Michael's Hill past the new university life science building on the right and more Georgian buildings on the left, you come to two hospitals – the Tudor-style Hospital for Sick Children, built around 1880, on the right and the non-Tudor-style St Michael's on the left.

Celestial adornments on the Wills Physics Laboratory

Royal Fort House reflected in the mirror maze

Take the next turning right into Royal Fort Road and at the top bear right through a gatehouse to enter the grounds of the Royal Fort. Apart from a short section of perimeter wall, the gatehouse is all that remains of a fort built by Royalist troops around 1644 to defend the city, but demolished after the triumph of the Parliamentary cause. Several grand villas were later built in the grounds, but most of the site remained undeveloped, apart from some sporadic quarrying, until it was landscaped, with the help of Humphry Repton, in 1804. In

* Needless to say, none of these hostelries suffer from the problems associated with their eighteenth-century predecessors.

1917, the estate was purchased and bequeathed to the university by HH Wills.

As you go through the gate, the Wills Physics Laboratory, built in the 1920s but harking back to the sixteenth century, towers above you on the right. Stuart House, on the left, is eighteenth century, but is thought to incorporate an earlier building. Beyond it is Royal Fort House, built around 1760, and one of the finest Georgian buildings in Bristol. Unusually, it has three façades, in different styles, on its north, west and south sides. After walking along the north side, turn left along the west and continue along the south, before following the path as it curves along the line of the fort's perimeter walls. After circling round below the house, past a disorienting mirror maze, carry on to the drive, turn left along it and go through the gates at the end.

Cross Tyndall Avenue and turn left across the zebra crossing, before bearing left and rounding the corner into Elton Road. At the end of Elton Road, carry straight on down Queen's Avenue. Turn right at the end and cross two zebra crossings to the memorial fountains in front of the Victoria Rooms.

As you look back, you can see three very different mid-nineteenth century buildings. On the left is the Victoria Methodist Church, built in the French Gothic style in 1863, to the right of it is the Renaissance-style Royal West of England Academy of 1857, while on the corner of Queen's Road is the former Queen's Hotel, opened in 1854, and until recently a branch of Habitat. The Victoria Rooms – 'the noblest classical erection in the city' according to John Latimer – predated them all, opening on 24 May 1842 to provide 'the inhabitants with spacious and convenient apartments

The Queen's Hotel during the First World War, when it was the headquarters of the 3rd Officer Cadet Battalion

for public entertainments'.[2] The statue of Edward VII and the fountains were added in 1913.

Walk past the fountains, turn right through a gateway and walk along the west side of the Victoria Rooms. The single-storey lodge ahead was built in the 1870s, possibly in connection with tennis courts at the back of the rooms which have now been built over.

Carry on through an archway and along Sunderland Place, turning left at the end along St Paul's Road. When you reach the mini-roundabout

Richmond Lane

at the end, bear round to the left, cross the zebra crossing and bear right. Cross the end of Richmond Hill and carry on along Queen's Road, where the monolithic student's union building of 1965 looks across to the elegance of Buckingham Place, built around 1845, with several houses at either end recessed behind stone colonnades. Beyond it is the French Renaissance-inspired extravagance of Buckingham Baptist Chapel, opened in 1847.

Before reaching the chapel, however, turn left along Gordon Road past the Richmond pub. There has been a pub on this site at least since the 1850s, but the present building – or at least its façade – dates from around 1910. Next to it is a terrace of around 1820 with a pediment in the centre and a bay at one end. Beyond it – and across the road – are some neoclassical-style semi-detacheds of around the same date. Further along is a somewhat later mini-terrace (Nos 5-9) of three buildings in Greek Revival-style. Just beyond it, turn right along a footpath called Hanover Lane and follow it around the back of the terrace. When you emerge on Richmond Lane, bear left alongside the raised pavement of Richmond Terrace. On your left, what was once a garden for the residents of Richmond Terrace has largely been taken over by the electricity board, with modern flats built at the far end.

AVENUE CLIFTON PARISH CHURCH

When you come to the steps, walk up to the raised pavement and carry on along it. Work started on Richmond Terrace in 1790, but, because of the financial crash of 1793, it took some time to complete. It is unusual in that it continues around three sides of a rectangle – like a square turned inside out. At the end, turn right along its west side – past some superb doorways and fanlights – before heading down the second flight of steps by No 16.

Cross a narrow strip of road, carry on past a dry drinking fountain and bear left along Birdcage Walk, a tunnel of lime trees running through St Andrew's churchyard. At the far end, a few stones on the left mark the site of St Andrew's church, damaged in the Blitz and demolished in 1954. It dated from around 1820, but stood on the site of a much older church, around which wealthy merchants built grand houses in the early eighteenth century. One of the earliest, known as Bishop's House and dating from 1711, can be seen beyond the site of the church. As you go through the gateway at the end, the grandest of them, Goldney House, built in the 1720s, can be seen ahead, on the other side of the green. Unfortunately, what you are looking at is its uninspiring rear extension, which was added over a century later.*

If you turn right, past a pair of houses built in 1765, you will come to Clifton Court, built around 1743 and recently refurbished as the Chesterfield Hospital. Turn and head back past the entrance to the churchyard and carry on to the T junction at the end. Richmond House, which you can see ahead (with the sign for Clifton Road on its wall), was built around 1703 and is probably the earliest of these grand houses. Beyond it, bearing the date of 1747, is Clifton Hill House.

Turn left along Clifton Road, following it round to the right past the Mew House of 1995 with its delightful cupola, before turning right along York Place, built around 1790. York Place leads into Tottenham Place, built around 50 years later, with steps up to the pavement. Across the road is Dover Place, built around 1863 with a style of window rarely seen in residential buildings.† After crossing the end of Gordon Road, carry on along Meridian Place. The grand terrace on your left, set back behind gardens, dates from around 1827. Further along on the right, the row of six buildings with three-storey, Greek temple-style porches was built around

1835. The buildings either side of it were added later.

Carry on past Frederick Place, on the left, and follow the road round to the right past a barber's shop to find the cathedral that never was. The Roman Catholic cathedral on

* Since 1956, the building has been owned by the university, but the gardens, which contain a fabulous grotto, a bastion leading to a Gothic summerhouse, an embattled water tower, a canal and much more, are generally open to the public once a year and a visit is highly recommended.

† Similar windows can, however, be found in churches (like Arley Chapel) and other public buildings, such as schools and hospitals, from around this time.

which work started in 1834 was to have towered over Bristol as the Basilica of Sacré Coeur towers over Paris. Sadly, the money ran out and, when it was eventually finished 14 years later, the plans had been so modified and the resulting building was so modest that it was decided not to accord it the status of cathedral. It was designated a pro-cathedral instead – a stand-in until a proper cathedral could be built, which it eventually was, in 1973. The pro-cathedral then closed and, after lying empty for many years, has now been converted to student accommodation.

On the other side of the road – as a contrast to all the grand buildings – are a rubble-stone cottage with a Gothic-style doorway and the Quinton House pub, still bearing the name of George's Brewery.

Now retrace your steps as far as the end of Meridian Place, before turning left down steep and uneven steps to Meridian Vale, built in an old quarry in the 1830s. At the end, turn right uphill and left along Bellevue – started around 1792 and finished around 1815. At the end, turn right up Constitution Hill.

Meridian Vale

Bellevue

An intriguing group of buildings at the top of Constitution Hill includes Fairfold House, dated 1726. Turn left along Clifton Wood Road, and, after passing an eclectic row of buildings on the left, look back to see a lodge of around 1800 with Gothic windows and a Dutch-style gable. Across the road is the stable block for Clifton Wood House, which can be seen just beyond it. Both date from the 1720s.

Carry on down past early twentieth-century buildings to an imposing Bath-stone house with two full-height canted bays, built in the late eighteenth century as a single villa, but converted into two by the insertion of an extra door. The house next to it, covered in Virginia creeper, dates from the 1730s but was refronted in the nineteenth century.

Follow the road round to the left and turn right along Southernhay Crescent. Turn left down Church Lane and, when you reach the steps, with a superb view of the harbour, turn right along Clifton Wood Terrace. After passing some modern buildings, you come to a row of six buildings with one of the finest views in the city. Most of them are early nineteenth century, but the two at the end are early eighteenth.

Carry on along Rosemont Terrace, past the back of the former Spring Gardens pub, dating – as its twin gables indicate – from the late seventeenth century, and carry on along Crosby Row. At the end, cross the road ahead, turn left down to Hotwell Road and turn right.

Although this is one of the busiest roads in Bristol, there is plenty to see. Holy Trinity Church on the right, with its spectacular classical façade, dates from 1830. As you carry on, you will see some very old buildings on

Holy Trinity, Hotwells

Dowry Square

the left. The Bear Inn, with the archway that once ran through to its coachyard still intact, dates from around 1730, as does the rest of the row. Further along on the right, the former pub on the corner of Dowry Square was the York Hotel, which opened some time before 1816.

Dowry Square itself was laid out in 1721, with buildings on three sides and a delightful lack of regularity. It was built to provide fashionable lodgings for visitors to the spa – whose site you will see shortly – and assembly rooms and pleasure gardens (both long gone) were established nearby. Dowry Square's chief claim to fame, however, is as the place where, in 1799, Humphry Davy conducted his groundbreaking experiments into the use of nitrous oxide – laughing gas – at Thomas Beddoes' Pneumatic Institute. As you take a leisurely walk round the square, look out for the plaque recording his achievements on No 6, as well as the old surgeon's plate on No 2. Dowry Square ends at the bottom of Hope Chapel Hill, although the three houses beyond, on what was known as Chapel Row, were built at the same time. The long terrace on the other side of Hotwell Road, however, known as Dowry Parade, was built in the 1760s to provide more lodgings for wealthy visitors.

Turn right up Hope Chapel Hill – originally known as Power Street

Dowry Parade

– and right again by the Adam & Eve pub along North Green Street. At the end, look up to see the Polygon – a crescent built in the 1820s – curving high above you. Carry on up the footpath and turn left along the Polygon. With its gardens rising above you on the right, this is surely one of Bristol's most idyllic backwaters.

Walk up the steps at the end and carry on past Hope Chapel to return to Hope Chapel Hill. Ahead is Albemarle Row, built in the 1760s. Turn right uphill past Hope Square, of which all that survives are seven houses on the north side and one on the west.

At the top of Hope Chapel Hill is Rutland House, built around 1760, with canted bays and wonderful carving around a door that is a door

The Polygon

Freeland Place

no longer. Take a look up Granby Hill to see a streetscape that could have been transplanted from Brighton – and which, like Hope Square, was only saved from demolition by a concerted campaign – before turning left downhill. After 100m, turn right down Freeland Place. Multi-coloured terraces are common enough in Bristol, as are decorative balconies, but rarely do either achieve such harmonious effect as they do here, with the houses flowing gracefully downhill. The first ten buildings were built by 1825, the ones below followed shortly afterwards.

At the bottom turn right along the Portway. Hard though it is to imagine, when Freeland Place was new this was a quiet riverside promenade known as Ashton Place, along which visitors strolled to take the waters at Hotwell Spa. They would not have seen the suspension bridge ahead of them, work on which only started in 1831, but high above they would have seen the most improbable bit of civil engineering in Bristol. Visually at least, Windsor Terrace was the most audacious project of Bristol's late eighteenth-century building boom; it was also, when boom turned to

THE SORRY SAGA OF HOPE SQUARE

Hope Square was named after nearby Hope Chapel, one of whose founders was Lady Hope. The chapel opened in 1788, and work started on Hope Square around the same time. The builder was William Bleuden, a journeyman carpenter from Taunton who arrived in Bristol in 1782 and, despite being illiterate, began leasing plots of land, building houses and selling them at a handsome profit. At first it was single houses, but by the late 1780s, as Bristol's biggest building boom got under way, he had moved on to terraces and squares. Hope Square – on which he planned to build 20 houses – was only one of those he was working on when boom turned to bust in 1792 and, like many others, he was bankrupted. Even had it been completed, Hope Square would have been a square in little more than name. Well proportioned though the individual buildings were, there was no attempt to mitigate or capitalise on the difficulties of the site: the two sides of the square that were completed stepped steeply and gracelessly uphill to meet – or nearly meet – in a V-shape at the top. But, as the plaque on No 11 records, it was fashionable enough to attract the likes of Thomas Beddoes, who lived here before moving to Dowry Square.

In the decades that followed, the area gradually became less fashionable, and by 1948 the condition of the properties was such that the council served a compulsory purchase order on them, to redevelop the site. The block on the east was demolished – all except for the last house – to make way for modern flats, but a campaign managed to persuade the council to spare the seven houses on the north side, which were eventually restored in 1972.

bust, one of the biggest casualties, and was never completed to anything like the original specifications.*

After passing below Windsor Terrace, you come to the Georgian elegance of St Vincent's Parade, started in 1789 as a row of lodging houses in one of the most desirable locations, and with one of the finest views, in Bristol. Across the road is another reminder of faded glories – a row of derelict, disintegrating landing stages, where daytrippers once caught paddle steamers to Clevedon, Weston, Minehead, Ilfracombe, Porthcawl, Tenby and other Bristol Channel resorts.

After passing a nineteenth-century terrace you come to Rock House, built around 1740. Beyond it, steps lead down to the Colonnade, a two-

---

* There is an opportunity for a closer look at Windsor Terrace in the next walk.

HOTWELL SPA

The spring which supplied warm water to the pump room at Hotwells could hardly have been in a worse situation. It lay at the foot of precipitous cliffs and at high tide was covered by the river. Some travellers who visited it in 1634 described picking their way down 'near 200 slippery steps' to reach it, but were amazed to find that 'when the tide is gone [there] never wants good store of company to wash in this well, and to drink of that warm and medicinable water'.[3] Its fame slowly grew and the seal was set on its success when Catherine of Braganza, the wife of Charles II, visited in 1677. In 1695, the Merchant Venturers, who owned the spring, leased it to a consortium who built 'a convenient pump room and lodging house' and 'walks to shelter and entertain visitors'.

During the eighteenth century, the spa at Hotwells came to rival that at Bath. Among its visitors were the Duke of York, who came in 1767, and the novelist Tobias Smollett, who featured Hotwells in *The Adventures of Humphrey Clinker* in 1771. Matthew Bramble, one of the characters in the novel, was less than impressed, declaring that 'the man deserves to be fitted with a cap and bells, who for such a paltry advantage as this spring affords, sacrifices his precious time, which might be employed in taking more effectual remedies, and exposes himself to the dirt, the stench, the chilling blasts, and perpetual rains, that render this place to me intolerable.'

By contrast, JC Ibbetson, who visited around 20 years later, was favourably impressed, leaving an enticing description of social life at the spa:

The Parade, leading to the Hot-well house, is sheltered on each side by trees ... The Well-house is situated at the foot of the romantic rocks of St Vincent, and under the steep crags of Clifton ... The crescent that extends towards what is called the Rock-house ... is backed by abrupt rocks, well covered with verdure ... Passing under the piazza ...the view is grand, even to a degree of awfulness. Those who resort hither for health, drink the water early in the morning, and about five in the evening, using gentle exercise after it ... The wells have the necessary attendant of such a place, gaiety. The resort to them is great, and during the summer months a band of music attends every morning. Here is a master of ceremonies, who conducts the public balls and breakfasts, which are given twice a week.[4]

Despite its popularity, it was clear that the spa needed upgrading if it was to survive. The work proved so expensive, however, that charges had to be hiked up to recoup the cost, precipitating a devastating loss of business. By 1816, Dr Andrew Carrick, a local physician, was complaining that it had 'the silence of the grave, to which it seems the inlet'.[5] In an attempt to revive its fortunes, the old pump room was demolished in 1822 and replaced by a larger one set further back from the river. Although this was moderately successful, it lasted only until 1867, when it was demolished to widen the river.

storey crescent built in 1786 as a row of upmarket shops for visitors to the spa. The pump room, where visitors took the waters, stood just north of the Colonnade, where now the Portway runs. The first pump room, built in the 1690s, was replaced by a grander edifice in 1822, but this only lasted until 1867, when it too was demolished.

Carry on past the entrance to the Clifton Rocks Railway. This cliff railway, which opened in 1893 and closed in 1934, climbed through a tunnel to emerge at the top of the gorge. It was built by the same company that built the cliff railway between Lynton and Lynmouth.

Just beyond it, head up a zig-zag path. At the top, turn right down

Princes Lane to look at the caryatids on the Clifton Spa Pump Room, built in 1894 in a last attempt to revive the spa's fortunes. It closed in 1922 and was used as a cinema

Above: The original buildings at Hotwell Spa

Right: A caryatid on the Clifton Spa Pump Room

Below: A photograph of the second pump room, with Clifton station in the distance, taken sometime between 1865, when the railway opened, and 1867, when the pump room was demolished

before becoming a ballroom until the 1960s, since when it has been boarded up. The decorations are said to be as elaborate inside as they are out, but after 50 years neglect they are probably in need of urgent attention.

Head back up Princes Lane and turn right past the top station of the cliff railway, which, thanks to the efforts of the group of volunteers who are trying to reopen it, looks in remarkably good shape. Cross and turn left along Caledonia Place, with whimsically elegant arrow struts in its balconies. This end of the terrace dates from the 1830s, and is an extension to a terrace built around 1790, which begins at No 32. At the end, turn left along the Mall, past the Clifton Club – opened as assembly rooms and a hotel in 1811 – and turn right along Portland Street. At

Caledonia Place

Clifton Arcade

the end of Portland Street, turn right between gateposts along Rodney Place, built in the 1780s, where you will see another plaque recording the residence of the peripatetic Thomas Beddoes and Humphry Davy.

At the end of Rodney Place, cross the main road (you may want to carry on to use the zebra crossing by Caffè Nero) and head along King's Road. On your left is Mortimer House, almost certainly modelled on Clifton Hill House, which you saw earlier, and recently converted from a hospital to flats. Turn right by the Hophouse, and at the end turn left along Boyce's Avenue, then left again into Clifton Arcade. This architectural extravaganza opened as the Royal Bazaar & Winter Gardens on 12 April 1879, but within weeks the proprietor had gone bankrupt, and in early July the entire contents were auctioned off and the building became a furniture warehouse. For over a century, it lay forgotten, few people even suspecting what dusty delights lay behind its padlocked doors. It could so easily have been lost, but fortunately was acquired by sympathetic developers who, after carrying out a thorough refurbishment, reopened it as a shopping arcade in 1992.

After exploring the arcade, head back out onto Boyce's Avenue and turn left. After going through an archway, look left to see the unadorned exterior wall of the arcade, looking rather like a railway goods shed.

Continue along the north side of Victoria Square, built around 1850, and turn left at the end along Lansdown Road, where late nineteenth-century buildings predominate. After 150m, look out on the right for the Bristol School of Dancing, a forward-looking building dating from 1893, which, as you can see from the inscription, was originally a Swedish Gymnasium. This was set up by Theodora Johnson, who campaigned to improve the standard of physical education in schools, using methods pioneered in Sweden. She not only wrote books, but gave lectures throughout the British Empire and had an important influence on educational policy. This was the nerve centre of her operations.

Just beyond it, turn right past the imposing façade of Vyvyan Terrace, started in 1833 and finished around 15 years later. At the end, cross and head north along Clifton Park. The Roman Catholic cathedral, which you pass on the right, opened in 1973, replacing the pro-cathedral you saw earlier. As you pass

The Roman Catholic cathedral

Edward's Van Garage

it, look to the left along Worcester Terrace, built around 1850.

At the end of Clifton Park, cross and turn right along Worcester Road. Turn left at the end along Pembroke Road, crossing at the traffic island and carrying on to the corner of Alma Vale Road. All Saints Church, on the opposite corner, was built in 1863, bombed in 1940 and rebuilt in the 1960s incorporating several parts of the old building, most notably the tower.

Turn right along Alma Vale Road, past Edward's Van Garage, built in 1899 and displaying all the exuberance and confidence of its age. It bears more than a passing resemblance to the stations built for the Great Central Railway – Britain's last main line – at around the same time.

Carry on past the Alma Tavern and turn left along St John's Road. After crossing the railway bridge, turn right to Clifton Down station and the end of the walk.

Further information online:
Redland & Cotham Amenities Society: *www.rcas.org.uk*
Clifton Rocks Railway: *www.cliftonrocksrailway.org.uk*

10

CLIFTON, BRANDON HILL, CHRISTMAS STEPS & THE WALLED CITY

Starts at: *Clifton Down*

Ends at: *Temple Meads station*

Distance: *5 miles*

Terrain: *Mostly on pavements or tarmaced paths, although with some steps*

Pubs & other amenities:

Vittoria, Whiteladies Road, BS8 2LY; open from 4 Mon-Fri; from 1 Sat; from 12 Sun; dogs welcome; 0117 9732319

Victoria, Southleigh Road, BS8 2BH; open from 4 Mon-Fri, from 12 Sat & Sun; dogs welcome; 0117 9745675; www.dawkins-club.talktalk.net/page29.html

Portcullis, Wellington Terrace, BS8 4LE; open from 4.30 Mon-Fri; from 12 Sat & Sun; tapas menu; dogs welcome; 0117 9085536; www.dawkins-club.talktalk.net/page30.html

Hope & Anchor, Jacob's Well Road; open all day from 12; food served all day; dogs welcome; 0117 9292987; www.hopeandanchor.net

Gryphon, Colston Street, BS1 5AP; open from 12 Mon-Sat; from 4 Sun; food served 5-9 Tue-Sat; dogs welcome; 0117 9830843; www.gryphonbristol.co.uk

Map: Geographers' A-Z

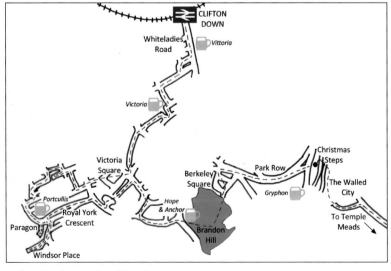

Opposite: Steps to Royal York Crescent

An urban walk featuring parts of Clifton not covered in the last walk, including the city's most vertiginous building, a lost arcade and tenements that could be have been transplanted from a Northern mill town, before heading down the old road to Bristol, past a replica – hidden in a forgotten corner – of its medieval cross, and from there down Christmas Steps and around the city walls to journey's end.

Head out of Clifton Down station onto Whiteladies Road and turn right. The shopping mall on your right stands on the site of a large coal yard served by the railway. The building across the road, curving round the corner into Cotham Hill, is known as Whiteladies Gate. Its name recalls the turnpike gate that once stood here, while the little statues of medieval kings above the shopfronts indicate the building's origins as part of the Royal Arcade. This opened in 1873 and ran through what is now the Penny Beer House – so, if you have ever wondered why the pub was set back at a curious angle, now you know. It was built by Joseph King, who, six years later, opened the arcade on Boyce's Avenue (visited in the last walk), and shortly afterwards went bankrupt. The Royal Arcade later became a linen drapers and then a bank before opening as a pub.

As you carry on along Whiteladies Road, you come to the former Whiteladies Picture House on the corner of Melrose Place. Dating from 1921, its tower is one of Bristol's finest examples of Art Deco architecture. After it closed in 2001, it was sold to a property developer, but various plans for conversion have failed to materialise, and a campaign group is now fighting to reopen it as a cinema and centre for the performing arts. The high-windowed houses on the south side of Melrose Place date from the 1850s.

Among the statues of medieval kings on the former Royal Arcade is one of Queen Isabella

Further along, on the other side of the road, the Sasparilla Bar at No 65 was built in the early twentieth century as a car showroom. All the way along Whiteladies Road you can see early nineteenth-century houses converted to shops by having single-storey extensions built over their front gardens, but the row beyond No 65 is especially

The former White-ladies Picture House

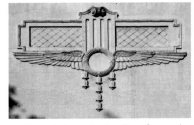

intriguing. Adjoining No 65 is a pair of semi-detached villas from the 1830s. Next to it is an elaborately carved building with a belvedere. The two buildings beyond that, including the Vittoria pub, are all that survive

of Vittoria Place, originally a terrace of five buildings built shortly after the British victory at Vittoria in 1813. Until about 1890, not only did all these buildings still have their front gardens, but the site of the building with a belvedere was a garden as well. The building to the left of it was owned by a well-known artist and photographer called James Fisher, who commissioned the extension with the belvedere around 1890. When Mr Fisher died in 1896, the Alexandra Drapery Company, which already occupied the three buildings to the right of the Vittoria pub, acquired those to the left of it as well and built shopfronts over the gardens. The date of 1911 on the Vittoria pub, incidentally, is misleading – it records not the date it was built nor the date it became a pub, but the date the bay window was added.

Just past the zebra crossing, turn right past the elegant façade of South Parade, built in the 1840s. At the end, look across to Brighton Park – originally known as Brighton Place – a curious development of imposing semi-detached villas in various styles strung together as a terrace. Carry on past Oakfield Unitarian Church, built of bright banded stone in 1864 and now converted to offices. Cross and carry on past two water-board buildings, behind which lies the Victoria Reservoir, opened in the mid-nineteenth century.

Turn left into Southleigh Road, built around 1850 – light, multi-hued, mini-balconied, and stepping gently down to the Clifton Lido at the far end. Opened in 1850 as the Clifton Victoria Baths, with Egyptian-style architraves around the entrances, it was taken over by the council in 1897, closed around 1990 and sold to a developer. Permission for demolition was granted, and it looked as though it would follow Rennison's Baths at Montpelier into oblivion. In 1998, however, local residents persuaded

English Heritage to award it Grade II* listing, forcing the developer to apply for further consent to demolish, which was refused. In 2005, it was acquired by new owners and, after refurbishment, it reopened in 2008 with a restaurant and poolside bar. The Victoria pub next door, built as part of the complex, has long been independently owned. It is now a Dawkins' Ales pub and not only has a fine range of cask ales but also one of the most comprehensive selections of Belgian beers in the city.

Turn right by the Victoria along Oakfield Place and left at the end. At St Paul's Road turn right and right again beside St Paul's Church into Arlington Villas. The church opened in 1853, and this sequestered development followed soon afterwards. First comes a charming villa tucked behind the church, then three blocks of three houses – two of them now linked by a modern extension – and finally a series of semi-detacheds with some jaw-droppingly brutalist additions.

At the end, cross a zebra crossing and look up to the right to take in Channings Hotel – originally Pembroke Hall – built around 1880 on a prime but problematic site, prompting the architect to design not one but two façades, which jostle against each other with turrets reminiscent of semi-deflated bouncy castles.

Turn into Richmond Park Road, where there are more grand buildings – prominent among them Albion Villa, high on the corner of Pembroke Grove, a superb example of picturesque asymmetry from around 1840.

On the left is the back of Buckingham Chapel, while on the right is Carlton Place, dating from the early 1840s. When part of it was converted to flats around 1900 and graced with a stair block, 'Carlton Mansions'

A Victorian view of Richmond Terrace

was chiselled portentously over the door. At the end, you have a good view across to Richmond Terrace high above the road, its vaults housing, among other things, a night club, bar and shop.

Turn right and follow the pavement as it swings round to the right into the grandeur of Lansdown Place, built around 1835. Cross the end of Lansdown Place and, a little further on, turn right between iron bollards to cross the garden, screened by trees and somewhat untended, in the centre of Victoria Square. The curious piece of sculpture you pass on the right is part of a Victorian bird bath. From here you can see a badly-weathered lion and unicorn on the north side, which was built around 1850 in an opulent, forward-looking Italianate style.

On the far side of the square, carry on past a house once occupied by WG Grace and go through an archway. The origins of the Albion pub, on the left, are somewhat obscure. It has been a pub since at least 1851, but was probably built around 1770 as a coach house for Boyce's Buildings (which you will see shortly). Despite its recent gentrification it is still possible to imagine the open space in front of it as a busy stable yard. Carry on past the entrance to Clifton Arcade (visited in the last walk) and, at the end of Boyce's Avenue, cross the zebra crossing and turn left and then right into Princess Victoria Street. The Quadrant bar on the corner was a wine merchant's for over a century, and was probably built as such, while the fish bar next to it – previously a butcher's – has a particularly fine shopfront.

If you turn round and look back, you will see, behind the row of shops on the other side of the road, the oldest development in this part of

A Victorian view of Lansdown Place

Clifton. Despite all the vicissitudes it has endured, and the company it is now forced to keep, Boyce's Buildings still manages to look magnificent. Built by a wigmaker called Thomas Boyce, who went bankrupt shortly after it was completed in 1772, it originally consisted of three lodging houses, standing in lordly isolation, for wealthy visitors to the spa. Gradually, other buildings sprang up around, and by the 1870s the gardens at the front had been built over to create shops. Then the left-hand house was split into two, the right-hand one was demolished, and until recently one of Clifton's most important buildings looked more than a little down at heel. Now, though, the right-hand house has been rebuilt – a particularly convincing piece of architectural recreation – and the whole has been refurbished and painted to look like one building, as it would have done originally.

Boyce's Buildings

Christ Church Schools, on the left as you carry on along Princess Victoria Street, was built in 1852 and now houses a library. Turn right along Waterloo Street, a quirky but busy back street whose name indicates it was built shortly after 1815. The shop on the left-hand corner at the end of the street was once the Commercial Inn and still has a classic Victorian pub façade. Turn left here, cross the Mall and continue along Portland Street. The range of tenements on the right, arranged around three courts, dates from around 1793, and is typical of high-density working-class housing built around the same time in the industrial cities of the Midlands and the North. The clue as to why these tenements were built here lies in their name – Carter's Buildings. John Carter owned the Royal York Brewery, which stood just south of Boyce's Buildings, and it seems that he built Carter's Buildings partly as a speculative development and partly as somewhere to house his workforce. In 1858, the brewery was acquired by the Merchant Venturers, who pulled it down to build Merchant's Road.

Around the same time, Carter's Buildings was redeveloped, with part demolished to build the large warehouse at No 38, now Christchurch Studios. The rest, though, survives as a little-known window onto a world that seems to have more in common with the novels of Dickens than the genteel bustle of Clifton.

At the end of the street is the Coronation Tap, whose half-hipped roof suggests that it dates from the early eighteenth century. It may, however, be much older. Unlike Carter's Buildings, it is not listed, presumably because it has changed so much over the years, but its owners claim that it was originally known as Clifton Farm, and was surrounded by fields, orchards and grazing land. By 1806, however, it had become 'a beerhouse and premises with a cottage adjoining', and it remains one of Bristol's most atmospheric cider houses today.

Head back along Portland Street, turning first left along the Mall and left again into Gloucester Street. The rather forbidding building ahead was the Clifton Down Hotel, opened in 1865 and built on the site of the doubtless far more elegant and neighbourly Bath Hotel. Requisitioned by the military for offices in the Second World War, it is now apartments.

Carry on past it and turn left by one of Bristol's most recently lost pubs, the Grapes, originally the Clifton Down Hotel Tap. Carry on past the front entrance to the Coronation Tap and bear right along Westfield Place, a small-scale crescent built in the 1830s. Turn left at the end past the mews buildings of Sion Hill to emerge on West Mall. The first 14 houses on West Mall – at the far end – were built around 1790; the banking crash of 1793 brought work to a stop, and the rest of the terrace was not completed until the 1830s.

Carry on, turn right along Caledonia Place and then left along Sion Hill to find one of Clifton's most whimsical buildings. St Vincent's

Priory, with two weather-beaten sphinxes over the entrance, dates from the 1830s. The contorted figures on the building are said to be copies of carvings in St Mary Redcliffe, yet the designation of it as a priory is as fanciful as its design. Its first recorded owner, in 1838, was a judge called Samuel Milford, who went on to achieve great things in Australia, and its name reflects its proximity to St Vincent's Rocks in the gorge below.

Cross the end of Princess Victoria Street and continue along the raised pavement. Opposite you will see Prince's Buildings, built around 1790, and described on a map of 1803 as Prince of Wales Crescent – as indeed it is, although of a rather singular kind. It was essentially a row of a semi-detacheds linked by single-storey wings, which have since been extended

Right: St George slays the dragon on Prince's Buildings

Below: The Paragon

Below right: The house wedged between Prince's Buildings and the Paragon

Bottom: The Paragon from below

upwards in heterogeneous ways. Only at the far end can any semblance of the original layout be discerned. Curious too is the pediment, which is not in the middle, but over Nos 7 & 8 in a block of ten, and features St George – looking alarmingly like a soft toy – slaying the dragon.

The terrace on the left-hand side of the road came later. Its name – Wellington Terrace – suggests it was built shortly after the Battle of Waterloo. After passing the Portcullis pub – another part of the Dawkins' empire, with an entrance below – go down a flight of steps, cross the road and head along the Paragon.

Built between 1809 and 1814, it was named after the Paragon in Bath, built over 30 years earlier. Like that Paragon, it is a crescent, but a crescent of a very distinctive kind, with the views at the back. As you walk along, it feels like a hidden backwater. You cannot even walk all the way to the end because the gates of a private garden stand in the way, and, apart from fugitive glimpses through ground-floor windows, it is difficult to get any real sense of what lies on the other side.

As you retrace your steps, you will notice a rather curious house on the left with two full-height bays and the end of Prince's Buildings towering above it. It predates the Paragon, almost certainly predates Prince's Buildings, and, when built, would have had unparalleled views in almost every direction.

You will shortly be heading back across the road to continue along the raised pavement, but first a brief detour to see the other side of the Paragon – and Bristol's most vertiginous building. For this, turn right and follow the pavement as it curves downhill. As you carry on past a private road, the views up to the Paragon become ever more spectacular. Its name may have been borrowed from the Paragon in Bath, but that Paragon – dramatic though it is – cannot compare to this. Nothing like it had been built in Britain since the middle ages, when fortresses were built on inhospitable crags to keep their occupants safe from attack. Towns and monasteries in southern Europe and Asia were built on similar sites for the same reasons – or, in the case of monasteries, to underline their retreat from the temptations and vanities of the world. This terrace in the clouds, by contrast, grew out of a sense of swagger – to impress those who saw it from below and to provide its residents with the best views in Bristol – and is as awe-inspiring today as it was two centuries ago.

Carry on downhill, bearing right along Windsor Place, carry on along Windsor Terrace, and, at the end, look not up, but down, over the railings, at a sheer drop of 21 metres. Windsor Terrace was the brainchild of a plumber called William Watts, who had come up with a revolutionary way of making lead shot by dribbling molten lead into cold water from a great height. He built a tower in Redcliff to manufacture it, grew very rich and planned to become even richer by investing in property.* Inspired

* The shot tower in Redcliff was demolished in 1968 for road widening.

WATT'S FOLLY

In 1819, shortly after Windsor Terrace had been completed, the indefatigable traveller Pierce Egan left a description of this 'fine handsome range of buildings' which offers another possible explanation of how it came to be built. He described it as 'Watt's Folly', explaining that it was 'built upon a rock of immense height':

The ruggedness of the rock has been cleaned off so smoothly, that it has now the appearance of elegant brickwork. The 'Folly', as it is termed, was originally commenced by the proprietor of the Patent Shot Manufactory; but it completely ruined him before it was half built, and remained in an unfinished state for some years. A story is very prevalent at Clifton respecting this Folly; indeed, it is vouched for as fact, that Mr Watts was induced to undertake these buildings in consequence of a dream that had some allusion to the process of making shot; which, it appears, must fall from an immense height before it can acquire a finish. The story goes on to say, that out of one of these fallen shot, which rebounded from the ground, an immense range of high houses instantly appeared, which promised an accession of fortune. Mr Watts being at Clifton at the time, and this rock appearing to accord with his dream, the erections were instantly set about: unfortunately for himself and his family, this favourable interpretation was never realised; but, on the contrary, destruction and misery.[1]

perhaps by his tower-building enterprise in Redcliff – perhaps even with thoughts of incorporating another shot tower into the development – he opted to build on one of the most dramatic and difficult sites in Bristol. Construction of the revetment on which Windsor Terrace stands began in 1790, but was such a major undertaking that it swallowed all of Watt's capital, and in October 1792 the unfinished terrace was advertised for sale. Soon afterwards came the financial crash precipitated by war with France, and in 1794 Watts was declared bankrupt. Windsor Terrace was eventually completed some 15 years later, but, for all the monumentality of its conception, it has the unmistakable air of having been finished on the cheap. The revetment slopes – or rather sags – downward, and, while the central houses – finished before work was abandoned in 1792 – are impressive enough, the remainder do not match up. If there is one feature that encapsulates the gulf between Watts' vision and what eventually materialised, it is the way the capitals of the pilasters on all but the central houses stop some way short of the cornice. That said, Windsor Terrace remains one of the most spectacular and memorable buildings in Bristol, while its picturesque disarray is certainly more endearing than symmetry and perfection would have been.

Now it is time to head back up to the steps by the Portcullis. On the way, look over to your right at Cornwallis Crescent, started in 1791, abandoned because of the financial crisis of 1793 and not completed until many years later.

Climb the steps at the west end of Royal York Crescent and head east along it. Work on this, the longest crescent in Europe, started in 1791, and, although its site was nowhere near as problematic as the one chosen by William Watts, the lie of the land and the length of the crescent meant that, although it was raised up less than three metres at the east end, at the

Windsor Terrace
Royal York Crescent

west it was much higher. When the developer was forced into bankruptcy in 1793, only ten houses had been built, with 15 more in various stages of completion. In 1801, the government acquired the unfinished portion of the crescent – around four-fifths of it – to erect an army barracks, but representations from local residents led to the abandonment of the scheme. In 1809 the government put the site up for auction and the crescent was eventually completed around ten years later.

Some architectural critics have been less than enthusiastic about Royal York Crescent. Individually, the houses may be unremarkable, and it lacks a central feature, but to criticise it for these defects is to miss the point. It is the long, sweeping and unhindered curve of Royal York Crescent that elevates it to the level of great architecture, combined with its lightness, its line of balconies, and that characteristic Bristol feature, stucco in motley pastel shades, which here reaches its highest expression. There is nothing like it anywhere else, not in Bristol, not in Bath, not in Brighton, and certainly not in Cheltenham. Walking along this pavement, wide as a road, high above the surrounding terrain, looking south-east to Kelston Round Hill and south-west to Dundry tower, is one of Bristol's greatest visual and aesthetic experiences.

At the end, turn right along Regent Street, and cross at the zebra crossing before turning left into Saville Place. Bear left and follow the road round to emerge in front of a terrace built in two distinct styles. The eastern part was started in 1790, abandoned in 1793, and eventually completed to the original design in 1838. The western part was also built in 1838, but to a new design. It is instructive to see, side by side like this,

buildings reflecting the changes in architectural style over almost half a century. On No 2, a plaque records the residency of EH Young, a best-selling writer who set her novels in a thinly-disguised version of Clifton called Upper Radstowe.

At the end of Saville Place turn left along a footpath past Millar House, a modern block of flats on the site of the mid-Victorian church of St James. Carry on along the Fosseway – a somewhat puzzling appellation as the Roman road of that name runs nowhere near it. On your left are the backs of the villas on the south side of Victoria Square, while on your right, towards the end, is St Andrew's churchyard.

Saville Place

A nineteenth-century view down Constitution Hill, with the path winding up Brandon Hill in the distance

At the end, turn right along Clifton Road, and carry on as it curves right past the Lansdown pub. After it swings to the left, head down a path past a dumbbell-shaped bollard on the left, cross the road to Clifton Hill House (with its 1747 datestone) and turn right. At the T junction, bear left down Constitution Hill. At the bottom, where two lions guard the entrance to No 2, is the site of Jacob's Well, for centuries one of Bristol's best-known natural springs. An archaeological investigation here in 1987 discovered what appears to be a ritual bath used by the Jewish community in Bristol before their expulsion from England by Edward I in 1290.

Cross Jacob's Well Road to the Hope & Anchor pub (which has a popular terraced beer garden at the back). A few metres down from the pub, turn left up a flight of steps. Just past the Avon Wildlife Trust HQ – housed in an old police station – the path forks. Take the right-hand fork along a broad path which follows the course of the old road from Clifton to Bristol across Brandon Hill. Just after passing a reed-choked pond on your left, bear left up a couple of steps and follow a path uphill along the line of a civil war fortification, with a trench on your left, and Cabot Tower ahead. At a crosspath, carry straight on. Continue along the path and, when you come to the end of the park, carry on alongside on a wall on your right. Carry on past steps down into Charlotte Street, before turning right, 50 metres further on, into Berkeley Square.

Berkeley Square was laid out 1786, but took a while to complete; half-built houses were still being advertised in 1799. Originally, it only had buildings on three sides; the faux-Georgian block on the right is quite

THE TRIBULATIONS OF BRISTOL'S HIGH CROSS

The High Cross originally stood at the crossroads where Corn Street, Broad Street, Wine Street and High Street met. It was built in the late fourteenth or early fifteenth century, restored in 1525, enlarged in 1663 and taken down – as 'a ruinous and superstitious relic' – in 1733. Although some were glad to see it go, many were unhappy and in 1736 a subscription was raised to re-erect it on College Green. In 1757, however, only 21 years after it had been unveiled on its new site, the cathedral authorities announced plans for improvements to College Green, and it was dismantled in 1762. Two years later, the dean, anxious to pre-empt calls for it to be re-erected once the improvements had been completed, offered it to Henry Hoare, a collector of antiquities, who re-erected it on his estate at Stourhead.

Top: The original High Cross at Stourhead

Above: The replica cross in its original position on College Green

Below: After it was moved to the centre of College Green to make way for the statue of Queen Victoria

If the cathedral authorities thought they had seen the last of the cross they were wrong, for in the mid-nineteenth century a campaign was launched to build a replica of it on College Green. The foundation stone was laid on 8 August 1850, but the fundraising appeal raised rather less than expected. Not only did the promoters have to make do with Nailsworth stone, whose 'vaunted durability ... was not verified by experience', but they could not afford statues to fill the eight niches. Eventually, one statue – of Edward II – was added in 1855, but it was not until 1888, when the cross was moved to the centre of College Green to make way for a statue of Queen Victoria, that the other seven were added.

There it stayed until 1950, when, once again, improvements to College Green meant that the cross – along with the statue of Queen Victoria – were taken down. The statue of the queen was eventually returned, but the stones of the cross languished in a council yard, where they were damaged by vandals. In 1956, the Civic Society salvaged what they could and re-erected the top of the cross in Berkeley Square.

Left: Queen Elizabeth on the replica of the High Cross

Below: The Coliseum, built as a roller-skating rink but converted to an aircraft factory in the First World War

Below left: Nipper, the HMV dog

recent. That is not the only reason Berkeley Square does not feel like a coherent whole, however. None of its sides are equal or parallel, it has a pronounced slope, and, even before the need for post-war reconstruction, it was a mishmash of styles. Bear left and then right into the garden in the centre of the square and head downhill to the remains of the replica of the old High Cross.

Turn left along the north side of the garden, go through a gate, head to the corner of the square and walk down past Berkeley Crescent – a brick-built gem of around 1800, now half-hidden by shops – to Queen's Road. Cross the two pedestrian crossings straight ahead to Browns – built as a museum and library in 1872 – and turn right.

After passing the Museum & Art Gallery and the Wills' Memorial Building, you come to a less celebrated building. Originally known as the Coliseum, it had a variety of roles – roller-skating rink, cinema and aircraft factory – before being bombed in 1940. The façade survived and has now been incorporated into a building called University Gate East. Nipper, the HMV dog, whose statue occupies pride of place on the corner, belonged to a scenery designer at the Prince's Theatre opposite. The theatre was bombed in 1940 and a petrol station now occupies the site.

Carry on along Park Row, past some well-designed – and now closed – public toilets opened in 1904. Across the road are some delightfully whimsical shops built shortly after 1900 – the date of 1864 on one of them is a red herring. Above you on the left, the home of the university drama department was until 1964 the Van Dyck Printing Works.

Just past it, cross at the lights and carry on to the Red Lodge, built around 1580 as a garden lodge to a mansion demolished to make way for Colston Hall. Now owned by the council, it houses a fascinating museum, and admission is free. Opposite is a synagogue, built in 1871.

After passing the top of Lodge Street, bear right down Lower Park Row. At one time, it was only the houses at the top, dating from around 1790, that constituted Lower Park Row. The rest of the street was called Griffin Lane after an inn called the Griffin which stood near the bottom on the left. It disappeared when the road was widened in the 1870s.

Just beyond the Ship Inn – open by 1775 – is a building dating from around 1600. In the eighteenth century, however, it was refronted to make it look newly built. So successful was the makeover that nobody suspected it was anything other than what it appeared until 1978, when its secret was discovered. The Georgian façade has now been removed and one of Bristol's oldest buildings, forgotten for over two centuries, stands revealed in all its rubble-stone glory.

The Zero Degrees brewpub, at the bottom, opened in an old horse-tram depot in 2004. The shops opposite were built at various dates from the early eighteenth century onwards. Foster's Almshouses, to the right of Christmas Steps, were founded in 1483 but rebuilt in the nineteenth century. If you look down to the right, you will see a pub called the Gryphon on the corner of Trenchard Street. Originally known as the Griffin, it opened to replace the Griffin that stood where Zero Degrees stands today, and is one of the city's top cask-ale pubs.*

Cross the road and head down Christmas Steps, whose buildings date from the seventeenth to the nineteenth centuries. Partway down, look out on the right for two figures from the Merchant Venturer's Hall, which was destroyed in the Blitz. The Christmas Steps pub at the bottom – known until recently as the Three Sugar Loaves, but now splendidly refurbished – was built as a bakery in 1748. The fish & chip shop on the opposite corner is seventeenth century but is believed to have been built around a fifteenth-century building, traces of which survive. It has been a fish and chip shop for well over a century.

As you turn left along what remains of Christmas Street, you pass the entrance to St Bartholomew's Hospital, built in the thirteenth century. The Madonna and Child you can see through the arch, with their heads allegedly hacked off by Cromwell's soldiers, once stood outside the arch, where passers-by rubbed the Madonna's left foot for luck – hence its worn appearance.

Christmas Street once curved right to a bridge across the River Frome, which was guarded by the Frome Gate, once the principal entrance to the city from the north. To get to the other side of the long-culverted river, carry on through a covered walkway to a 1984 statue of a cloaked horseman. Cross the dual carriageway at the lights, turn right for a few metres and then left along the other remaining section of

---

* It is also home to Brew Bristol, a newly-opened beer and home-brew shop (www.brewbristol.com).

Christmas Street. The gate which led into the city – still with its slot for
lowering the portcullis – runs through the fourteenth-century church of
St John on the Wall.

Once through the gate, turn right to follow the course of the medieval
Bell Lane along the line of the city walls. When you reach Small Street,
head through the small archway opposite, beneath ancient beams. This

HOW CHRISTMAS STEPS GOT THEIR NAME

Christmas Steps is one of Bristol's most celebrated byways, its charm only heightened by the suspicion that it owes its name to some delightful Yuletide legend. Sadly, the truth is more prosaic. Christmas Street, which led from St John's Gate to the bottom of the steps, was originally known as Knifesmith Street, because of the cutlers and armourers who had their workshops along it. Its name had already been

Christmas Steps, Bristol.

corrupted to the more familiar Christmas Street by 1480, when William Worcestre wrote of 'Christmastret called Knyfsmythstret'. It was not until 1669, however, that Christmas Steps as we know them today took shape, as John Latimer explains:

> *Down to this date the thoroughfare now known as Christmas Steps was merely a breakneck footpath, very perilous to passengers in winter weather and dark nights. The improvement of the track had been undertaken early in the year by the directions and at the expense of Jonathan Blackwell, a wealthy vintner, who ... had removed to the city of London, of which he was now an alderman. A calendar in the Council House describes the alterations made by his orders: 'Going up, there is steps, on the last of which there is a turned style, or whirligig, over which there is a lantern; then about 100 feet [30m] pitched; and then steps, with a court with six seats on each side; and then steps and a turnstyle like the former.' [In September 1669] the new thoroughfare was opened by the mayor and the members of the corporation, who went in solemn procession for the purpose.[2]*

leads into St Leonard's Lane, which continues along the line of the walls. After going under a corrugated-iron walkway, and passing a flight of steps down to St Stephen's Street, look up to see stones marking the boundary between St Stephen's and St Lawrence's parishes.

The lane emerges in Corn Street next to Stanford's map and travel store. Here another church – St Leonard's – straddled the street with an archway running through it. Carry straight on along St Nicholas Street, which once again follows the line of the walls, and is one of the most fascinating streets in the old city. The Old India restaurant on the left was built as a stock exchange in 1903. Further along on the right, Revolution was originally a fish market, opened in 1873. Look

over to the left to see some fine carvings: the elephant on the pub and the veiled woman on the shop next door date from the 1860s. If you look down the steps to the right, you will see two fish over the side entrance to the fish market. Further along on the left, look for Queen Victoria gracing a drinking fountain of 1859 by the entrance to St Nicholas Market. At the end is St Nicholas church, built on the crypt of a medieval

church in the 1760s. After being badly damaged by bombing, it was restored as a museum but now houses offices.

At the end, if you look up to the left you will see the spire of Christ Church, in front of which stood the original High Cross. A right turn, on the other hand, will take you across the traffic lights, over Bristol Bridge and into Victoria Street, at the end of which is Temple Meads.

Further information online:
Clifton & Hotwells Improvement Society: *www.cliftonhotwells.org.uk*

11

LEIGH WOODS, ABBOT'S POOL & ASHTON COURT

Starts at: *Clifton Down station*

Ends at: *Clifton Down station*

Distance: *13 miles*

Terrain: *Rough country paths, with pavements at the start and end*

Pubs & other amenities:

George Inn, Abbot's Leigh, BS8 3RP; open from 12; food served 12-3 & 6-9.30 Mon-Fri; 12-9.30 Sat; 12-4 Sun; dogs welcome in the bar area; 01275 376985; www.thegeorgeinnbristol.co.uk

Victoria, Southleigh Road, Clifton, BS8 2BH; open from 4 Mon-Fri, from 12 Sat & Sun; dogs welcome; 0117 9745675; www.dawkins-club.talktalk.net/page29.html

Ashton Court, courtyard café, open 9-5 daily April-October; 10-3 (Mon-Fri) & 9-4 (Sat & Sun), November-March

Map: *Geographers' A-Z & OS Explorer 155*

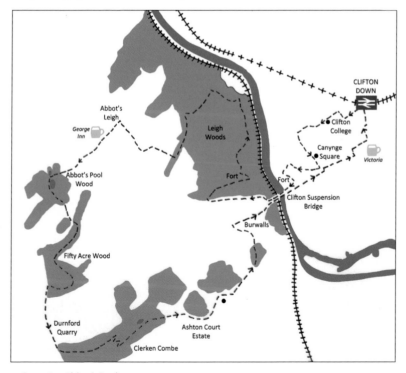

Opposite: Abbot's Pool

Although it starts and ends in the streets of Clifton, after crossing the suspension bridge this turns into a proper country walk, largely through woods and parkland. Along the way you will visit a hidden pool created by medieval monks, the faded glories of the Ashton Court estate – its deer parks still stocked with deer – and tracts of woodland whose preservation is largely due to members of the Wills tobacco dynasty. There is also a country inn ideally placed for a lunchtime break, while the café at Ashton Court is handy for a stop later in the afternoon.

Arriving at Clifton Down station from Bristol, cross the footbridge and turn left through the car park. Arriving from the Avonmouth direction, go through the gate at the west end of the platform and walk up through the car park.

At the road, turn left across the railway bridge and then right along All Saints Road. At the end – with the copper-clad lantern of Clifton College Chapel ahead – turn right along Pembroke Road. After 200m, cross at a traffic island and turn left into Guthrie Road. Emmanuel Church, built in 1869, once stood on the left. Most of it was demolished in 1976, but the tower was incorporated into a sheltered housing development.

Further along on the left is Clifton College, founded in 1860, while on the right is the high wall surrounding Clifton Zoo.

At the end turn right along College Road and first left along Cecil Road. Some of Clifton's grandest mid-nineteenth-century houses can be found in this area. At the end of Cecil Road, turn left along Canynge Road. Opposite is the Mansion House, official residence of the Lord Mayor. Behind the blocked-up archway in the wall on your left was a building – possibly a farmhouse – which predated all the others in the area. It was demolished in the late nineteenth century when Clifton College established playing fields here. After carrying straight on across Percival Road, late nineteenth-century houses give way to early nineteenth century buildings. Those on the left face into Canynge Square, whose entrance is a little further along. Despite its name, Canynge Square is triangular. With only one way in and out, it is also a delightfully secluded hidden corner, and still lit by gaslight.

Towards the end of Canynge Road, there is a particularly attractive early nineteenth-century terrace on the left with semi-circular-headed windows. Just beyond it, on the corner, is Harley Lodge, built around 1740.

Canynge Square

Turn right along Harley Place, a grand terrace started – like so many – around 1788, but abandoned due to the financial crisis of 1793 and not completed until around 30 years later. As you cross the top of Camp Road, look down it to see a modernist house built in the 1970s, before carrying on past a succession of sumptuous villas.

The architect responsible for the first of them – Charles Dyer – was so proud of his handiwork that he engraved his name on the Doric portico. The semi-detached pair beyond it – which may also be by Dyer – are distinguished by superb ironwork. Perhaps the most remarkable of this collection of grand villas is Dorset House, a few doors along, with its first two floors recessed behind giant order Doric columns.

Just past the Engineer's House, which also bears Charles Dyer's name and a date of 1831, bear left across the road, climb a couple of steps and turn left along a broad path. Carry on past the first path branching off to the right, but, 125m further on, turn right along the second. This takes you along the ditch within the outer rampart of Clifton Down Camp. At a T junction turn left uphill and follow the path as it winds round to the right. When the path forks, bear right to see the panoramic view down the gorge, hidden until now by vegetation, suddenly open up. Follow the path as it curves round the edge of the escarpment to take in the view across to Leigh Woods and the deep cleft of Nightingale Valley, followed by a view over the Suspension Bridge. The viewing platform, protected by railings, you can see in the cliff below is at the mouth of the Giant's Cave, and can be reached via the observatory above it.

As you carry on along the path, there is a real sense of the site having been an iron age fort, protected by ramparts on three sides, with a sheer drop on the fourth. Continue along the edge of the escarpment, past rocks worn smooth by generations of boys sliding down them. As the path starts heading downhill, bear right, head down to the road and turn right across the bridge.

CLIFTON OBSERVATORY

In 1819, Pierce Egan visited Clifton, where he saw 'the remains of an old tower, a circular building containing some windows, but without any roof; the interior of which has only to boast of a brick floor and a fire-place'. It had, he added, 'three open spaces, which were formerly doors', and 'from the centre of this building are three most delightful views through the above openings.'[1]

Nine years later, in April 1828,

the Society of Merchants granted to Mr Wm West, a local artist, at a nominal rent, the ruins of an old windmill, known as the snuff-mill, on Clifton Down, which had been destroyed by fire, October 30 1777. Mr West built a dwelling house on the spot, and reconstructed the tower, which he fitted up in 1829 with telescopes and a camera-obscura, and styled an observatory. Some years later, at considerable expense, he

excavated a passage from the building to the well-known 'Giant's Cave'. This was opened in July 1837. Photography appears to have been introduced to the people of Bristol at Mr West's abode. In an advertisement in a Bristol newspaper of April 27 1839, it was announced that 'various kinds of photogenic drawing' might be seen, and that 'superior photogenic paper' was sold at the observatory.[2]

A painting by William West, showing a view of the Avon Gorge from the top of the observatory can be seen in Bristol Museum & Art Gallery. He continued to live at the observatory until his death in 1861, after which it remained in the hands of his family until 1943. It has changed remarkably little since West's day, and the camera obscura and tunnel to the Giant's Cave can still be visited. In 2013, following a major restoration, it was put up for sale for £2 million.

On the far side of the bridge is Burwalls, a red-brick house built for the proprietor of the *Bristol Times* in 1872. After his death, it was bought by George Alfred Wills. During the Second World War it was requisitioned for military purposes, and was later taken over by the university. It was sold to developers in 2013.

A little further on, turn right up North Road. Alpenfels, the Tyrolean-inspired building on the right, was built around 1872 for Francis Fox, the chief engineer of the Bristol & Exeter Railway. Further on is a

An early twentieth-century view across the gorge to Alpenfels, here described as Swiss Cottage

house topped by an enormous belvedere that looks as though it could have been transplanted from Simla. Built around 1879, it is called, appropriately enough, Belvedere. Further along, on the corner of Vicarage Road, is Woodleigh, built in 1886 for Walter Melville Wills, with magnificently decorated gable ends. In 1959 the university botanic gardens were established in the grounds. The gardens have since been re-established in Stoke Bishop and the house has been converted to apartments, with further housing built in the grounds. The thatched cottage across the road was built around 1908 by Walter Wills as a playhouse for his children. It later became an estate office before being converted to a house.

A little further along, turn right through a kissing gate (KG) into Leigh Woods Nature Reserve, walk straight ahead uphill and carry on past a minor path branching off to the left. When you reach a clearing with a house over to the left, bear right along a broad path. The path soon narrows to wind through the ramparts of Stokeleigh Camp. As you carry on across the camp, look to the right across Nightingale Valley for a view of Belvedere ensconced amid woodland. As you approach the eastern edge of the camp – where no ramparts were necessary because of the precipitous terrain – what should be one of the most dramatic views of the gorge and suspension bridge is largely obscured by trees.

Stokeleigh Camp

Follow the path as it swings left to follow the edge of the escarpment. A little way along, when it forks, bear right and keep to the main path as it heads down through the ramparts. At a

LEIGH WOODS

Leigh Woods is one of the finest areas of ancient woodland in Somerset, and its unique character has been appreciated by Bristolians and visitors to the city for centuries. In 1819, Pierce Egan visited and penned a paean to its charms:

> *This wood, which contains the kingly oak, the lofty elm, ash, sycamore, box, and grave yew-trees, blending their various colours, with the addition of numerous others, render it so exuberant and attracting, that numerous parties, in summertime, frequently cross the river (what may be termed 'gypsying' it), taking their provisions, tea-kettle, etc, with them, and often concluding these excursions, on the verdant spot, to the sound of a fiddle, upon the 'light fantastic toe'.*

It was a favourite haunt of the Bristol School of Artists, which flourished in the 1820s. One member of the school, the Rev John Eagles, wrote of 'those woods opposite Clifton, separated from it by the muddy Avon', which divides 'the cares and trails of the everyday world from the region of Elysium'. Paintings of Leigh Woods by the school's most famous member, Francis Danby, can be seen in the Museum & Art Gallery, amply demonstrating that Danby shared Eagles' feelings.

Given its proximity to the city, however, it is not surprising that the survival of Leigh Woods has sometimes seemed in doubt.

In the 1830s, the wood's owners, the Smyths of Ashton Court, leased 170 acres to William Watkins as a rabbit warren. He cleared large swathes of it, fenced other areas off and charged visitors a penny for admission to those parts still open to them.[3]

Worse was to come, however. In the early 1860s it was announced that the Clifton Suspension Bridge, work on which had been abandoned in 1843, was to be completed. This meant that the undeveloped land on the west side of the gorge – hitherto accessible only by ferry from Hotwells or via a circuitous route through Bedminster – would be within walking distance of Clifton.

At around the same time, work started on a railway to Portishead, running along the west bank of the Avon and raising the prospect of a station at Leigh Woods. Sir Greville Smyth of Ashton Court, realising that Leigh Woods was now the most desirable piece of real estate in the area, announced that he was going to build on it.

The plans, unveiled in June 1863, were for 'a little town, comprising in all 435 houses', with an iron bridge spanning Nightingale Valley, a church and 'a hotel upon a scale of great magnitude and grandeur' near the suspension bridge.[4] Following numerous objections and 'bitter letters' in the newspapers, Smyth offered the council a short-term lease of the woods, but at such a high price that they turned it down.

In September 1864, the *Bristol Times* revealed that Smyth had sold Leigh Woods to a developer who planned to build 'some 800 tenements, many of them of a poor character, several of them small shops ... on the romantic site, thereby of course making it an eyesore to Clifton'. Faced with this threat, a number of wealthy citizens got together to buy the developer out. His terms were so exorbitant, however, that they decided to play for time – very wisely, for, after failing to come up with the first instalment of his payment to Smyth, he disappeared.[5]

The wealthy citizens could now deal with Smyth directly. They formed the Leigh Woods Land Company to undertake controlled development while preserving the view of the woods from Clifton and maintaining recreational access. Even this was too much for HA Palmer, a local philanthropist, who argued that 'no building scheme – however limited, however judiciously planned – can give to these woods ... the sublime and beautiful aspect they now present'. His attempt to raise enough money for a rival bid failed, however, and Smyth sold Leigh Woods to the Land Company for £40,000.[6]

Although development was limited to large villas in an area west of the suspension bridge, it impacted on other parts of the site. In 1869, it was revealed that the stone used to build North Road was being taken from Stokeleigh Camp, the iron age fort overlooking the gorge, significant parts of which had been destroyed.[7]

There were also large quarries further down the gorge, which were only too visible from Clifton. In 1886, the *English Illustrated Magazine* launched an attack on the destruction of the 'waving forest that had been the nursery of art to WJ Muller, Danby, Pyne and Turner, and the scenery that has given character to Clifton', transforming it into 'a record of an utilitarian age, whose sordid spirit could convert so choice a piece of landscape into crumbling stones for the sake of their value in money'.[8] In 1902, a group of leading citizens petitioned the council 'to urge that some steps should be adopted for the preservation of Leigh Woods from what appears to be impending destruction'. Bemoaning 'the gradual erosion of the quarrymen on the river's bank' and prophesying that, if no action was taken, 'the whole picturesque scene – one of superb grandeur and beauty – will be involved in destruction', they called on the council to buy the woods or, failing that, for a public appeal to save them.[9]

In the event, it was George Alfred Wills, who lived in Burwalls, one of the grandest houses built by the Land Company, who came to the rescue, presenting 80 acres of the woods to the National Trust in 1909. Unfortunately, the quarries did not form part of the gift. Not until 1936, when Walter Alfred Wills, George's brother, gave the National Trust a further 60 acres – including the last working quarry – did quarrying finally cease.[10]

In addition to the land owned by the National Trust, a further 300 acres of 'devastated woodland', most of whose trees had been felled during the Second World War, was acquired and replanted by the Forestry Commission in 1949.

Today, no metal bridge spans Nightingale Valley, no rows of terraces disfigure Leigh Woods, and nature has largely reclaimed the quarries so abhorred by Victorian lovers of the picturesque. Against overwhelming odds, Leigh Woods has been saved for future generations, and rapacious greed has given way to the careful management of this priceless green space at the city's edge.

T junction, turn right and – almost immediately – when the path forks, bear left. From here on, following a series of purple waymarks should make a convoluted trail relatively straightforward. Directions, should you need them, are as follows: go through a gate and bear right. When the path forks, bear left. At a crosspath turn right. When the path forks, bear left and carry on alongside a fence with a sheer drop into a quarry on the other side. When the fence ends, turn left, bearing right when the path forks. At a T junction turn right, and at the next T junction turn left into a car park, where the waymarks end.

Turn left and walk along a drive for 500m, before turning right along a footpath (ST551735). Go through a KG and follow a track straight on. When you reach the hedge on the far side of the field, turn left alongside it. Follow the hedge as it bears right and go through a KG. Cross a tarmac

drive, go through another KG and carry straight on alongside a hedge. When the hedge bears right, carry straight on to a KG. Go through it and follow a path towards Abbots Leigh church. After crossing a stile, walk up to the road and turn left.

The fifteenth-century church across the road was largely rebuilt after a fire in 1848. The first house on your left, despite its classical profile, is relatively modern. Beyond it are older buildings, including a former school and the eighteenth-century Abbots Leigh House, both looking out over open fields to Avonmouth and the Welsh hills beyond. Carry on along Church Road and at the end cross (using the pedestrian lights) to the George Inn, first recorded as a church house in

Abbots Leigh from across the fields

The Priory

1719 and handily-placed for a refreshment break.

Head up Manor Road, beside the George, passing the Tudor-style conservatory, dating from the 1830s, attached to the Priory. After 500m, bear right along a path beside the wall of a house called the Beeches. When the path forks, carry straight on, crossing a road, and, when you come to a rough lane, carry on along it. At the end, go through a KG and follow a bridleway – with some slippery steps – downhill beside a wall. After crossing a bridge at the bottom, turn left and left again across a small dam (ST535733). Bear right up steps to Abbot's Pool, where you will see a grotto-cum-boathouse designed for WM Wills in the early twentieth century. Turn right across a dam, and on the far side bear left and carry on until you come to a car park. Continue along a lane and, when you come to a road, cross and carry on along a bridleway for 250m.

ABBOT'S POOL

In the middle ages. Abbot's Leigh belonged to St Augustine's Abbey – now Bristol Cathedral. A stream west of the village was dammed to create a pool to supply the abbey with fish. After the Reformation, the pool passed into the hands of the lords of the manor, but in the early twentieth century it was acquired by William Melville Wills. He raised the level of the dam, built a boathouse designed to look like a cave, and installed rocky cascades – made from artificial stone – below the pool. After a recent restoration programme, supported by the Heritage Lottery Fund, Wills's work of enhancing this superbly atmospheric spot can be fully appreciated once again.

Carry on past a step stile in the fence on the right, but, a little way further on, turn right through a squeeze stile by a yellow post into Fifty Acre Wood, whose paths are popular with off-road cyclists (ST538727). Follow the path, bearing left by another marker when it forks, and carry on as it winds through the wood. After passing a red marker,

the path swings left. Carry on, following the red markers, as the path, after heading south, swings round towards the north. On entering a small clearing, bear left past a row of large boulders and turn left along a lane (ST535720).

At the main road, cross and head straight on along Longwood Lane. After 600m, opposite the entrance to Durnford Quarry, turn left through a gateway into Ashton Park and bear sharp right downhill along a broad path. Follow it as it curves left and carry on past paths branching left and right. After 850m, when you come to a T junction with a white marker ahead, turn right downhill. Follow the path as it zigzags left and right, before turning left at the bottom along Clerken Combe (ST543712).

A little way along, fork right by a white marker and carry on into a meadow and past a pond. When the path forks again, bear left through the meadow and, when you come to a stony path, turn right along it.

The path soon leads into parkland, with a deer park on your left and a view across the city to the clump of trees on Kelston Round Hill. Carry on as a path swings in from the

Top: Fifty Acre Wood

Above: In the deer park

Below: The view of the green hills of Somerset

ASHTON COURT ESTATE

The deer park at Ashton was established in 1392. It was acquired, along with much surrounding land, by the Smyth family in 1545. A medieval manor house came with the estate, and the Smyths embarked on a programme of enlarging and embellishing it that was to continue for over three centuries. The result is the building we see today, at once the grandest and the most muddled of the mansions around Bristol. At one time it was reckoned that the Smyths owned around two-thirds of Bristol, and, despite selling off parts of their estate (such as Leigh Woods), when the last of the line died in 1946 it still amounted to around 6,000 acres. The 850-acre park surrounding the house, which Humphry Repton helped to landscape in the early nineteenth century, had been designated as part of the 'green belt' in 1937, and it was anticipated

that the council would purchase it. A deal was finally agreed in 1949, but this did not include the court, which by now was in a parlous state. During the First World War it had been used as a military hospital, and during the Second World War it was a transit camp. In the run up to D Day, about 700 tanks and army vehicles were moved from Ashton Court to the south coast before being loaded onto ships heading for Normandy. As a result of these upheavals, large parts of the court had been more or less abandoned for over half a century. By the time the council eventually acquired the building in 1959, the process of dilapidation was well advanced.

Today, the estate is one of the most popular open spaces in the Bristol area, with over 1.6M visitors a year, and there has recently been a £4.4M Heritage Lottery Funded initiative to improve facilities and access. As for the house, although parts of it are used as a conference venue, much of it remains derelict. In 2011, a consultation was launched to determine how the long-term future of the building could be secured. The scale of what needs to be done, however, is daunting in the extreme, while the threats to its future grow ever more pressing. In August 2013, for example, a fire broke out in the northern wing, although prompt action by firefighters managed to confine it to two rooms.

right, and at a T junction turn right along a tarmac drive, which, as it curves, reveals Ashton Court ahead.

Bear left at another T junction, carry on as the drive curves round to the left of the house, and head for the visitor centre and café in the stables at the back. From here, carry on in the same direction, walk through the car park and go through a gateway at the end. Go through a tall KG behind the topograph on the right and head up through the red-deer park with a fence on your right. After going through a KG into woodland, bear left uphill when the path forks. Go through a KG at the top and bear right, following a well-worn track marked by short white posts. Back on high ground once more, there are superb views southwards to the green hills of Somerset.

Clifton Lodge

When you come to a T junction, turn right past a sculptured head with a toposcope and go through a KG. Carry straight on, and, when you come to Clifton Lodge, go through the gate, bear right to the pedestrian lights (ST558727), cross and carry straight on along Bridge Road to the suspension bridge.

Having crossed the bridge, carry straight on along the road for 300m. When you come to a zebra crossing, bear left along a path across the grass, heading for the spire of Christ Church. The memorials you can see on the right – one to the 79th Regiment and one to Pitt the Elder – were erected in the 1760s by General Draper in his garden at Manilla Hall, which stood to the right of the church. They were moved here in the late nineteenth century, and the site of the hall is now covered by terraced houses.

Carry on across three roads to the church, which was built between 1841 and 1885, head to the left of it and continue along Clifton Park. After 200m you will see Vyvyan Terrace set back behind gardens on the right.

Looking across the Clifton Suspension Bridge, and the views to north and south

Carry straight on along Clifton Park, and, when you come to Pembroke Road, cross and turn left. Take the first right along Oakfield Road, carrying straight on at the crossroads. Just past a former Congregational church (now Colkin House) is Oakfield House – designed in 1831 by Charles Dyer, who once again engraved his name on the porch.

Take the next left along Leigh Road (alternatively, if you are in need of refreshment at this stage, a right turn along Southleigh Road will take you to the Victoria pub). At the end, cross and turn right for a few metres before turning left along St John's Road. The Clifton Bethesda on the left was established in 1871 by the Christian Brethren, one of whose most prominent members was George Müller, the founder of the Ashley Down orphanages. At the crossroads carry on along St John's Road, and after another 125m turn right down to Clifton Down station and the end of the walk.

A mid-Victorian view of the path across to Christ Church, with Manilla Hall just visible through the trees in the distance

Further information online:
Avon Gorge & Downs Wildlife Project: *www.avongorge.org.uk*
Leigh Woods (National Trust): *www.nationaltrust.org.uk/leigh-woods*
Leigh Woods (Forestry Commission): *www.forestry.gov.uk/forestry/EnglandBathandNorthEastSomersetNoForestBristolWoodlandsLeighWoods*

12

COOMBE DINGLE, HENBURY, BLAISE CASTLE & KINGSWESTON

Starts at: *Sea Mills station*

Ends at: *Sea Mills station*

Distance: *9 miles*

Terrain: *Mostly on rough paths through woods and parkland*

Cafés:

> *Blaise Castle Estate Café, 250m west of Blaise Castle House by main car park; open 9-5 Apr-Oct; 9-3 (Mon-Fri) and 9-4 (Sat & Sun) Nov-Mar*
>
> *Café Retreat, Kingsweston House; open daily from 9.30; www.caferetreat.co.uk*

Access: *Blaise Castle Museum is open 10.30-4 , Wed-Sun, Apr-Oct (also Tues in Jul & Aug); weekends only Nov-Mar. For details see www.bristolmuseums. org.uk/blaise-castle-house-museum/*

Blaise Castle is open on certain Sundays and Bank Holiday Mondays throughout the summer. For details see www.friendsofblaise.co.uk/castle.html

Map: *OS Explorer 155*

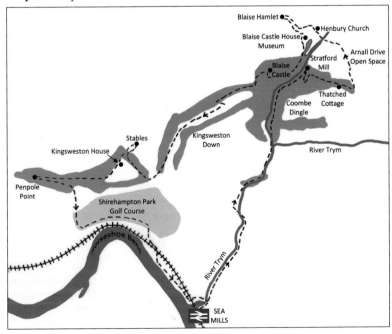

Opposite: View over Coombe Dingle from below Blaise Castle

*M*ost of this walk is through the parkland of two great estates – Blaise Castle and Kingsweston. En route it takes in scenery of almost Alpine splendour, a mill rescued from a flooded valley, whimsically picturesque thatched cottages, the eighteenth-century grave of a black servant, a famous viewpoint with its view now obscured by trees, a house designed by the architect of Blenheim Palace, a house converted to a fascinating museum, a panoramic view of the greatest hazard faced by ships sailing along the Avon, and much more.

On leaving Sea Mills station, turn right along the road. After going under the Portway, you will see one of the oldest buildings in the area, dating from around 1760, on the right, adjoining a block of modern flats.

Bear left across the grass and follow the River Trym upstream. Carry on across a road and follow a path into woodland before emerging on a busy road. Bear right along the pavement, cross the road (using the zebra crossing further along if traffic is heavy) and go down a footpath to the right of the Mill House Inn. After going through a squeeze stile, bear left when the path forks. A rough and uneven path leads along a causeway, across a sluice and into a meadow bordered by tall trees.

CLACK MILL, COMBE DINGLE.

Clack Mill, demolished in 1937

Coombe Mill, also demolished in the 1930s

Coombe Dingle, near Bristol.

After 200m you cross a tarmac path. A mill – known as Clack Mill – once stood alongside the river to your right (ST554769). In 1880, when the lease was advertised, it was described as a grist mill 'with two pair of stones driven by water power, together with two cottages, garden, and small paddock of pasture land'.[1] Shortly afterwards, it was converted to a smithy and repair shop, and the mill wheel was used to work punching and shearing machines.[2] It was demolished in 1937.

Carry on through the meadow, under a road bridge and along a causeway beside the river. When you come to a crosspath, bear left up to a lane and turn right. After a few metres, bear left into a car park and carry on through a kissing gate (KG) along a carriage drive. After 150m, the path passes through the site of another mill – Coombe Mill – demolished in the 1930s (ST558775).

After another 150m the River Trym curves off to the right, but, instead of following it, carry on to follow its tributary – the Hazel Brook – along Coombe Dingle, the sides of which soon begin to steepen. After the drive crosses a bridge to the right bank, it starts to climb before descending again. An ornamental bridge on the left heralds the approach to the most spectacular part of the walk along the valley. The pool on your left, built, like the drive, in the late eighteenth century, is known as the Giant's Soap Dish and provides a picturesque foil to the cliffs towering above. Even though Bristol has more than its share of scenic surprises, it still seems incredible that something so improbably alpine can be found less than four miles from the city centre.

Stratford Mill, moved from West Harptree in 1949

After another 300m, you come to a bridge with a boarded-up mill beyond it (ST561783). Known as Stratford Mill and dating from the late eighteenth century, it originally stood on the River Chew near West Harptree. The story of how it came to be here is on page 175.

Turn right to follow a drive as it zigzags uphill past an ochre-coloured cottage built in 1798. After another 250m, you come to a thatched cottage orné covered in strips of bark. Unfortunately, largely as a result of vandalism, it is in a parlous state: the bark is peeling, sheets of metal have replaced the thatch, and the doors are covered with security grilles.

The thatched cottage in Blaise Castle Woods around 1910; and as it appears today

171

BLAISE CASTLE ESTATE

In terms both of scenery and architectural heritage, the Blaise Castle estate is the jewel in the crown of Bristol's open spaces. Despite ongoing conservation issues, it remains the best preserved of the great landed estates now administered by the city council, and the one in which the intentions of its original owners can most readily be appreciated. The castle at its heart, a glorious folly set amid an iron age fort, dates from 1766, but the rest of what we see today is largely due to John Harford, a wealthy merchant and banker who acquired the estate in 1789. He commissioned a new mansion from William Paty, and hired Humphry Repton to landscape the park and design a series of picturesque lodges. Harford also engaged John Nash, the architect of London's Regent Street, to build an orangery, a thatched dairy and the cottages of Blaise Hamlet.

The 650-acre estate remained in the hands of the Harford family until 1925, when they put it up for sale for £20,000, giving Bristol Corporation first refusal. The *Western Daily Press* declared that 'Bristol cannot have too many open spaces, which have been aptly described as the city's lungs; and provided the terms of purchase are favourable – and they are so regarded – citizens generally will be keen on a acquiring this famous beauty spot.'[6]

Inevitably, there were those who opposed the purchase. 'The idea of purchasing the Blaise Castle estate as a free and open park appears to have captivated certain members of the sanitary committee,' wrote one correspondent, 'but I trust, in view of the crushing burden of local and national taxation, the proposal will not be pressed.'[7] Another was even more forthright:

To spend £20,000 on acquiring this property would be preposterous, in face of the fact that thousands of ratepayers are out of work or on short time. If this sum is available, why not spend it on building workmen's cottages? This property would cost an enormous sum to get it into anything like a semblance of a pleasure ground. Some 50 years ago I assisted to re-roof the model cottages, which were houses for aged servants of the Harford family. I then understood it took several woodmen to keep the paths clear of tangled brushwood and undergrowth. What would it mean now?[8]

But the council were not swayed by these arguments, and on 28 July 1925 voted to purchase the estate.

At the end of the drive, go through the gates of a castellated lodge, cross a busy road and turn left along the pavement (ST567781). On the left is Chesterfield House, built around 1770. A little further along, bear right through a chicane into Arnall Drive Open Space and follow a path parallel to the road. At the end, bear left as the path forks to return to the road. After crossing the end of Trymwood Close, cross the main road and follow a footpath sign through a KG and alongside a high wall. When the wall ends, fork right, go down steps and cross the Hazel Brook. Carry on through two tunnels under the garden of the old vicarage and up a flight of steps into Henbury churchyard. Follow the path to the left of the church – parts of which date from the thirteenth century – and head for

Tunnels under the vicarage garden

Gravestone in Henbury churchyard

the north porch, near which are the headstone and footstone of Scipio Africanus, 'negro servant to ye Right Honourable Charles William, Earl of Suffolk and Bradon, who died ye 21st December 1720, aged 18 years'. Little more is known about this chilling reminder – almost three centuries old – of Bristol's slaving legacy, but recent research suggests that the stones were moved to their present site in the mid-nineteenth century and were first painted in the mid-twentieth century. Their current garish appearance is due to an over-zealous makeover in 2006.[3]

Most of the buildings you pass as you head through the churchyard gates are nineteenth century, but Close House, on the left, dates from 1624. Bear left beside it and, when you reach the main road, look right to see the Blaise Inn, originally the Henbury Porter Stores. After being closed for some time, it reopened following a full refurbishment in the summer of 2014.

Bear left along the main road before crossing and turning right down Halland Road. After 100m, go through a gate on the left into Blaise Hamlet. This group of nine cottages set around a green was designed by John Nash in 1811 as almshouses for retired workers on the Blaise Castle estate, and is now owned by the National Trust. Its bucolic rusticity and design features such as those disproportionate chimneys bespeak a peculiarly English kind of whimsical wistfulness.

After making a circuit of the hamlet, leave by the gate through which you entered and head back

Blaise Hamlet in the mid-nineteenth century

up Halland Road. Cross at the top, turn left and, when you come to Church Road, go through a gateway on the right. This leads between high walls and past a stable yard to Blaise Castle House, home to perhaps the city's most approachable museum and the one where the charms – and tribulations – of a bygone age can be sensed most strongly. Although established in a house built for one of Bristol's wealthiest families, it is very much a museum of the people – and of childhood. On the ground floor you will find old doll's houses, dolls, train sets and toy soldiers alongside a fully-equipped early twentieth-century schoolroom; upstairs the focus is on the clothes our ancestors wore and the gritty reality of domestic life, including a memorable display of vintage toilets. There are also paintings of Bristol in the eighteenth and nineteenth centuries and an exhibition on the history of the estate.

Carry on past its entrance or – if visiting the museum – turn left when you leave. When the path forks, bear left. After a diversion to the left to see Nash's orangery and thatched dairy, return to the path, carry on along it until it starts to head downhill, and bear right up a gravel path. After 125m, as the path enters woodland, turn left. A few metres further on, turn right at a T junction. Carry straight on uphill, with a steep drop on your left, past the Butcher's Cave, one of three grotto-type caves on the estate. Just beyond it, a viewing platform commands a view over Coombe Dingle, with the tower of Sea Mills church straight ahead. Carry on along the path to an even more spectacular viewpoint on the edge of Lover's Leap, to look down at the dingle you walked along earlier.

Turning round, another surprise awaits – Blaise Castle, hidden until now by a bank of trees, stands before you in lordly isolation. Climb up to the open space surrounding it – originally an iron age hillfort – head

for a path 25m along on the left and head down it to emerge in a meadow (ST557783). Bear left, follow a path up into the woods and bear right along a broad path. After 400m, turn left up a crosspath – easy to miss as it is not especially wide, but look out for a white arrow painted on a tree on the left (ST552780). When the path emerges into the open, bear right to follow a well-worn track across Kingsweston Down, a long strip of meadow bordered by woods. After 750m (just after passing a mast on the left), the path joins a gravel track. As you continue through a KG, you

A MUSEUM IN BLAISE CASTLE HOUSE

The idea of creating a museum in Blaise Castle House was raised almost as soon as the council acquired the estate. In November 1925, when Henbury Council met to consider – and oppose – proposals to include part of Henbury within the city, the vicar suggested that 'Blaise Castle House would make ... an excellent museum.'[9] The idea was not taken up, but neither were alternative suggestions to turn it into a hospital or a youth hostel.

By the mid-1930s the idea of creating a museum at Blaise Castle was gathering momentum, along with a notion of the form it should take. At a meeting of the Bristol Development Board in 1936, a speaker

> laid before the meeting the question of a folk museum for Bristol, and the gathering together of houses such as their forefathers lived in was discussed. They had in Gloucestershire and Somerset many good examples of barns, thatched cottages, etc, and he suggested that Blaise Castle could be the site of such a museum.[10]

War intervened before anything had been decided, but when peace returned there was renewed enthusiasm for the idea. 'There are proposals afoot for the establishment of a folk museum in Bristol with headquarters at Blaise Castle House,' reported the *Western Daily Press* on 15 November 1945. 'Discussions are to take place between the corporation, city architect and Bristol museum authorities. Old tithe barns and cottages may be built.' When the council approved the proposals the following year, it was announced that

> the folk museum will contain exhibits of the working conditions of men engaged in handicraft work of years ago, with examples of transport used at the time arranged in the yard. The park will contain specimens of farmhouses, weaving sheds and mills.[11]

Less than three years later, on 6 May 1949, when the museum opened, the chief attraction was 'the reconstruction of a domestic hearth and a kitchen'.[12] There was no sign of the barns and cottages, nor were they to follow later. One building that did move here, however, was Stratford Mill from the Chew Valley. This fell into disuse after the First World War and in 1939 was acquired by the Bristol Waterworks Company, who were planning to flood the area to create a reservoir. In 1941, it was brought back into use as a wartime emergency measure, but in 1949 the waterworks company offered it to Bristol Corporation for re-erection at Blaise Castle.[13] The cost of moving it was estimated at around £2,500, but, as it was the only mill 'standing in the West of England in working condition and actually grinding corn now in the old-fashioned way', it was approved by the council and the mill was rebuilt beside the bridge below Blaise Castle House.[14]

It was to have been the first of many such rebuildings, but sadly it was to be the only one and the project was quietly forgotten about. To get some idea of the opportunity lost, you only have to visit the National History Museum at St Fagans near Cardiff. This was founded as a folk museum a year earlier than Blaise Castle, and in 2011 *Which?* Magazine named it the UK's biggest visitor attraction. Although Blaise Castle remains one of the country's finest small museums, it could have been so much more.

will see the old Kingsweston Inn on your right (ST544772). In 1793, it was described as 'much resorted to by those who visit [Kingsweston House], as being a convenient place to leave their carriages and servants at'.[4] It closed around 150 years ago, but reopened as a tea room before becoming a private house.

Carry on across a footbridge over Kings Weston Road, and go up steps through a gap in the wall on the right. Carry on past a loggia known as the Echo and designed, like Kingsweston House, which you can see ahead, by Sir John Vanbrugh around 1710.

Head towards the house, but, just before you reach it, turn right along a path past an old brewhouse. At the road, cross and head up the road opposite for 75m to see the old stable block on the left and two lodges flanking a lily pond on the right. They were all built about 50 years later than the house. The medieval stone cross on the far side of the pond is known as Bewy's Cross and has only stood here since the 1950s. It was previously in the formal gardens of Kingsweston House, but originally stood near the River Severn in what is now Avonmouth.

Lodge and lily pond opposite Kingsweston stables

Head back to the house and bear right along the north side of it, where there is not only a panoramic view over Avonmouth but also an

KINGSWESTON HOUSE

Around 1710, after Sir Edward Southwell had inherited the Tudor mansion of Kingsweston, he ordered it to be demolished and hired Sir John Vanbrugh – already at work on Blenheim Palace and Castle Howard – to build him a new one. Kingsweston House remained in the Southwell family until 1833, when it was bought by Philip John Miles. His son, Philip William Skynner Miles, was the driving force behind the development of Avonmouth Docks and of the railway from Hotwells to Avonmouth. After his death in 1881, it passed to his son, Philip Napier Miles, who was more interested in music than commerce. He achieved some fame as a composer and counted Ralph Vaughan Williams among his friends. It was at Miles' instigation that Vaughan Williams' most popular work, *The Lark Ascending*, received its first performance

Kingsweston House as a hospital in the First World War

in Shirehampton Public Hall. In 1904, he leased 93 acres to Shirehampton Golf Club, and during the First World War the house became a war hospital. After the war he bequeathed a large part of the estate – including the golf course – to the National Trust, prompting a correspondent in the *Times* on 21 November 1918 to declare that 'those who know the neighbourhood ... will not need to be told that the park is one of exceptional beauty, rich in grassy glade and noble trees, and rising, in its upper portions, to a considerable height above the river, over and across which it commands magnificent views towards the Leigh Woods ... The nearness of the park to Bristol adds greatly, of course, both to its value as a place of public enjoyment and to the generosity of the donor. It is at present partly used as a golf course, and this use will, of course, continue, at any rate during the remainder of the lease held by the club.'

After Miles died in 1935, the rest of the estate was broken up and the house was bought by Bristol Municipal Charities for use as a school. In the 1950s, the chimneys which formed such a striking part of the building's design were taken down after they became dangerous, but they were restored in 1968. Between 1970 and 1995, the house was used as a police college, after which it lay empty for five years before being leased to a local businessman and partially restored as a conference centre and wedding venue. A new leaseholder, who took over the house in December 2012, has ambitious plans for its further restoration, and will live in it while continuing to hire it out for weddings. Some 220 acres of the estate survive in the ownership of Bristol City Council and the National Trust, with open access, except across the golf course, where access is restricted to public footpaths. In 2011, the Kingsweston Action Group was founded to conserve and enhance the historic landscape around the house.

Sundial, Penpole Point, Shirehampton.

PEMPOLE POINT, SHIREHAMPTON. 1896.

Top: Penpole Lodge and sundial around 1916

Above: The view once enjoyed from Penpole Point

Left: The view today, with the sundial dwarfed by tall trees

excellent tea room. Carry straight on along a stony track for 250m, before bearing right along a broad path with large stones across it. Carry on across crosspaths, and, when the path forks, bear right along the broader path and carry on through the woods. Eventually, you will emerge into an open space (ST532772). The two low ruined walls flanking the path here are all that survives of Penpole Lodge, which led from the Kingsweston estate onto Penpole Common. It was demolished in 1950 after falling into disrepair.

A little way ahead you will see a large sundial, now without a gnomon to tell the hours. It stands on Penpole Point and once commanded one of the finest prospects in the area. According to John Latimer, when the Shirehampton turnpike road opened, 'it opened out that district to the fashionable throng at the Hot Well, and excursions to Kingsweston Inn and Penpole Hill became popular. For the accommodation of visitors to the latter, a building called the Breakfasting Room was erected, the patrons of which were permitted to ramble in the shrubberies of Kingsweston House.'[5] When the railway to Avonmouth opened, many more people were able to take the trip, and on Bank Holidays thousands of Bristolians flocked to this promontory. In February 1877, when the Bristol Port & Channel Dock opened at Avonmouth, a huge bonfire was lit here to round off the celebrations, and crowds gathered to enjoy a spectacular firework display. It is difficult, standing in this neglected spot today, surrounded by a dense screen of trees, to imagine how well-known and well-frequented it once was.

THE VIEW FROM PENPOLE POINT IN 1793

'From Shirehampton, a back road leads to Pen-pole, an abrupt knoll at one of the terminations of Lord de Clifford's park. On the extreme northern point of this knoll is a dial pedestal, which attracted us to the best view we had yet found here ... It extends to the Old or Aust Passage House, where a gentle, but formal swell of hills closes the view. The new Passage House in Gloucestershire, and the opposite one in Monmouthshire, are very discernible, as opaque white spots, which are relieved by woods and fields. The valley is decked with a richness rarely to be met; coppices and hedgerows are grouped in graceful confusion, till the whole resolves itself into a continued wood. Immediately above the vale, and on a gentle acclivity, stands the mansion of Lord de Clifford, surrounded by woods, and sheltered by King's-Weston down.'

JC Ibbetson, *A Picturesque Guide to Bath, Bristol, Hotwells, &c*, 1793

Turn round and head back, but, when you come to the ruined lodge, head straight on to the right of it. When you come to a road with a football club on one side and an academy on the other, carry on along it for 100m before turning right down a footpath along the side of a playing

Left: The lodge on Park Hill around 1905

Below: Two views of the Avon from Shirehampton Park before the building of the Portway

field. This leads to a busy road – Park Hill – with one of the lodges to the Kingsweston estate across the road. Cross and go to the left of it into the golf-club car park. Follow the hedge on the right as it leads round to a narrow path heading down into woodland. (Unfortunately there are no signposts or waymarks to assist you here.) At the bottom, when you come to a KG (ST536767), don't go through it but turn left along a path and follow it as it winds along the southern edge of the golf course. After 200m, the undergrowth clears and you get a superb view of Horseshoe Bend, the greatest shipping hazard between Bristol and the mouth of the Avon.

After passing the 12th tee, a track leads steeply down to a road (ST544767). This is the Portway, which – as there are lights controlling traffic along to the left – you should be able to cross with care and patience. If you would rather not chance it, stay on the golf course, carrying on past the exit and follow a footpath sign along a rough track. When the track curves left, carry on, following a path diagonally uphill to emerge on Sylvan Way. Turn right downhill, and at the bottom use the pedestrian lights to cross Sylvan Way and the Portway. Bear right along the pavement for a few metres before going through a KG on the left. Follow the path until you come to a T junction, where you turn left.

If you decide to cross the Portway, go past a gate on the other side into a field with a National Trust sign. Cross the field, bearing slightly left towards a waymark on the far side. Go down steps by the railway and up more steps, where the footpath from Sylvan Way comes in on the left.

Carry on, forking right along a footpath past a playing field and go under the railway (ST545765). Go past a gate on the other side and turn left, following waymarks for the Severn Way. This path tends to become overgrown. It can also flood when there are exceptionally high tides, and if this is the case you have no option but to head back to the Portway and walk along the pavement to return to Sea Mills.

At the end – assuming you can follow the Severn Way – go under the railway bridge and the road bridge, turn right across a footbridge and right again to return to Sea Mills station.

Further information online:
Blaise Hamlet: *www.nationaltrust.org.uk/blaise-hamlet*
Friends of Blaise: *www.friendsofblaise.co.uk*
Blaise Castle House Museum: *www.bristol.gov.uk/page/leisure-and-culture/*
blaise-castle-house-museum
Kingsweston Action Group: *www.kwag.org.uk*

13

LOST GARDENS, SPAS & RAILWAYS OF THE AVON GORGE

Starts at: *Sea Mills station*

Ends at: *Temple Meads station*

Distance: *7 miles*

Terrain: *A mixture of rough paths and pavements, with some steps*

Pubs & other amenities:

Adam & Eve, Hope Chapel Hill, BS8 4ND; open from 5.30 Tue-Fri, from 12 Sat & Sun, closed Mon; dogs welcome; 0117 3292025

Bag of Nails, St George's Road, BS1 5UW; open from 5 Mon-Thu, from 12 Fri-Sun; 07941 521777

Three Tuns, St George's Road, BS1 5UR; open 12-2.30 & 4-11 Mon-Thu, from 12 Fri-Sat, 4-10.30 Sun; dogs welcome; 0117 9070689; arborales.co.uk

Small Bar, King Street, BS1 4DZ; open from 12 daily; dogs welcome; 07709 449708; www.smallbarbristol.com

Cornubia, Temple Street, BS1 6EN; open from 12 daily (closed Bank Holidays); dogs welcome; 0117 9254415; thecornubia.co.uk

Map: *Geographers' A-Z & OS Explorer 155*

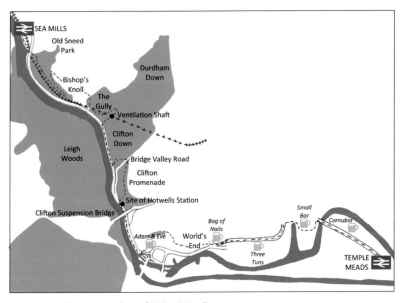

Opposite: The Lost Gardens of Bishop's Knoll

*S*tarting at Sea Mills, this walk heads south alongside the Avon. Along with several crossings of the Portway and hikes up and down the gorge, there is some surprisingly untamed country en route, including lost gardens, lost spas and a gully grazed by wild goats. After passing the site of the old station at Hotwells and crumbling wharves where generations of Bristolians boarded paddle steamers, it threads its way through a maze of hidden footpaths to the World's End. From there a precipitous flight of steps leads – past a bus stop where no bus has ever stopped – down to the harbourside, and a chance to visit some of the city's finest hostelries on the way to Temple Meads.

Good footwear is essential, as a couple of footpaths are steep and potentially slippery. The crossings of the Portway all make use of central reservations or lights, except one, where there is a hatched area in the middle of the road.

O n leaving the train at Sea Mills, you will see a ruined wall stretching partway across the river. Although the Romans had a port here, this structure dates from 1712, and was part of a floating harbour in use for around 50 years before being abandoned. It was the first attempt to develop a dock near the mouth of the Avon and avoid the navigational hazards and inconveniences entailed by sailing into Bristol. It failed because the prospect of carting goods overland along rough

and hilly roads, at the mercy of highwaymen and other ne'er-do-wells, was even less desirable than that of carrying on upriver. But the idea did not go away, and, as ships got bigger, the need for a dock downstream grew ever more pressing. Three hundred years on, the ports of Avonmouth and Portbury are the direct descendants of the failed enterprise at Sea Mills.

Take the footpath under the railway and turn left along the river bank by the old signal station. The new signal station, built to replace it in the 1950s, is a little further on. After 350m, bear left up a flight of steps and cross the Portway. To the left of the railway bridge, you will see two flights of steps – take the one on the right. After 30m, when the path forks, bear right. Carry on downhill (ignoring a path branching up to the left), and follow the path as it curves down to the right. At the bottom, with the railway line ahead, turn left. Go through a kissing gate (KG) into Old Sneed Park Nature Reserve, head straight on across the meadow and go through another KG. This leads into the grounds of Bishop's Knoll, a house built in 1874 for Peter Prankerd,

Bishop Knoll Red Cross Hospital, Bristol.

During the First World War, Bishop's Knoll became a hospital for Australian soldiers

who, after emigrating from Langport to Australia, where he made his fortune, retired to Bristol. Much of the seven-acre site was planted with specimen trees to form an arboretum, but ornamental terraces were constructed at the southern end. The house was demolished in 1970, to be replaced by flats, and the grounds were acquired by the Woodland Trust. A major restoration programme has seen paths and steps cleared, and the stonework on some of the terraces restored, but the magic of these long-abandoned gardens, with their hidden paths and secret gates, remains.

Head up the path, which leads through a gate onto a lane. A short diversion down the lane to the right brings you to a railway bridge where the overgrown trackbed of the line to Hotwells can be seen beside the line to Clifton. The junction of the two lines was 175m to the west – roughly midway towards the bridge under the Portway.

On the far side of the bridge, a twelve-acre former sports ground has been acquired by the Avon Wildlife Trust to create a new nature reserve. The trust hopes to open the Bennett's Patch & White Paddock Reserve in 2015, but this depends on enlisting the help of hundreds of volunteers and raising sufficient money through an appeal.[*]

To continue with the walk, head back up the lane, and, a few metres past the gate you came through earlier, turn right through a KG. Take the stepped path forking right downhill, and at the bottom turn left alongside the railway. Follow the path uphill, with the railway below you on the right and the arboretum up to your left. After 250m, you will see a flight of steps heading steeply uphill to the left. You will be climbing it shortly, but for now carry on past it to enter the terraced gardens of Bishop's Knoll, one of the most atmospheric places in the city. A metal arbour, still largely intact, leads down to a sudden drop to a sunken area where beehives were once kept, while beyond it steps lead down to a metal gate and a tunnel under the railway. Further up, steps lead to a high terrace with a ruined gazebo at the far end and more terraces, ruinous and hidden in the undergrowth, above.

_____

[*] Information on the project can be found at www.avonwildlifetrust.org.uk.

After savouring this extraordinary lost world, head back to the flight of steps you passed earlier, climb it and turn left at the top. After 30m, bear right up a couple of steps and carry straight on uphill. Go through a gateway at the end and turn right up Bramble Lane.

Carry straight on along Knoll Hill, and follow it as it curves left. An optional diversion along Cook's Folly Road, on the right, will allow you to admire the ersatz medievalism of Cook's Folly. As it is a dead end, however, you will have to return to Knoll Hill. After passing the junction with Goodeve Road, carry on along Seawalls Road. After 150m, when the main road swings right, carry straight on along Seawalls Road and go

Tower Hirst

Ventilation shaft in the Gully

through the gate at the end. Bear right alongside a wall and you will come to an extraordinary house with an octagonal half-timbered turret. Known as Tower Hirst, it was designed by a local architect called JH Hirst in 1861.[1]

Carry on past the public toilets, and look down to your right to see the Severn Beach line emerging from Clifton Down Tunnel. Follow the pavement round the edge of the escarpment, and, when it forks, bear right. When the path ends, head through a KG and bear left to follow a rough and narrow path alongside the perimeter fence.[*] Keep close to the fence, carrying on past two KGs as the path curves south. After entering woodland, bear right when it forks, and, when you come to a broad, steep and slippery path, head down it. As you carry on down Walcombe Slade, otherwise known as the Gully, keep a lookout for goats, introduced in 2011 to control scrubby undergrowth and give the wildflower grassland, home to several rare species, a chance to re-establish itself.

Partway down, you pass a ventilation shaft for Clifton Down Tunnel. After going through a KG at the bottom, you will see, to your left, the pumping station for the Northern Stormwater Interceptor, whose southern end featured in the fourth walk.

Turn right alongside the Portway for a few metres (staying within the barrier) to see the Black Rocks, site of one of the numerous quarries that once lined the gorge, towering above you, before crossing at the central reservation and turning left along the pavement. Opposite the pumping station, look over the wall to see the outfall of the interceptor.

---

[*] For an easier option, don't go through the KG but carry on with the fence on your right for 400m, passing two more KGs, but going through the third and taking the steep path down Walcombe Slade.

THE LOST PLEASURE GROUNDS OF COOK'S FOLLY

The original Cook's Folly was a lookout tower built in the 1690s by John Cook, the owner of Sneed Park House. Morgan's *New Guide to Bristol, Clifton, etc*, published in 1851, declared that from the tower – entrance to which cost threepence – 'is obtained an uninterrupted and expansive view of Kingroad, which is much enhanced by vessels at times in full sail; also of the Welsh mountains.' Nearby was a small tavern called Folly Cottage. In 1853, the 'cottage and walks, which have so long been the favourite resort of the inhabitants of Clifton and Bristol' were advertised to let.[2] They were taken by Mrs Haste, who hoped, 'by keeping a superior stock of all kinds of refreshments, to merit a large share of patronage'. The stock included 'fine ales and porter, both in bottle and draught.'[3]

In July 1855, the estate was acquired by a Captain Goodeve who drew up plans for a medieval-style mansion beside the tower, with further houses in the grounds. A few weeks later, on 18 August, the tavern made national headlines after a girl living in a cottage by the river was sent there by her father to fetch some beer, but was murdered on the way home. The perpetrator of this dreadful crime was never apprehended.

A week after the murder, the *Bristol Mercury* carried news of a farewell bash at Folly Cottage:

The romantic grounds of Cook's Folly, so long a favourite resort of the public and the admiration of tourists, are, as most readers are aware, doomed to be invaded before long by buildings, when lovers of the picturesque will be debarred from access. There are few who will not feel regret at this popular region being converted into sacred private property, and to give effect to this sentiment the present tenant, Mr Kelly, has resolved on holding a grand fete, to take place on Monday next, which shall enable the public to take something like a formal farewell ... A programme of the entertainments ... includes the performances of Mr Ward, a world-renowned gymnastic professor, of Mr C Gomez, an exhibitor of amazing Herculean feats, and of other artistes in different lines, in addition to which there are to be a display of fireworks by Burns, and a variety of amusements, the whole promising a merry day.[4]

In the event, the fete was postponed for a week 'owing to the threatening aspect of the weather'.[5] The exequies, however, seem to have been a little premature, for the following spring Mr Kelly announced that Cook's Folly was 'open for the season in all its beauty', with 'refreshments of every description' available 'at moderate charges'.[6] The tavern's end, when it came, was sudden, for on the night of 14 June 1857 it was almost totally destroyed by fire.[7]

The loss of the tavern signalled the end of public access to Cook's Folly. Roads were soon built across what had been open country and the memory of one of Bristol's most popular pleasure grounds slowly faded. The seventeenth-century tower adjoining the mansion survived until 1933, when it was demolished to make way for an extension to the house.[8]

THE NEW HOTWELL

The disused drinking fountain alongside the Portway, 150m south of Walcombe Slade, was supplied with water from St Vincent's Spring, whose history John Latimer outlined in *The Annals of Bristol in the Eighteenth Century*:

> *The existence on the shore of the Avon, near the mouth of the great ravine on Durdham Down, of a copious spring of water, as much entitled to be called 'hot' as the ancient well at St. Vincent's Rocks, must have been always well known. The first record of its having been turned to profitable account does not occur, however, until 1743, when its owners, the Merchants' Society, ordered that the lessees (unnamed) should be sued for arrears of rent ... As there was no carriage road by the river side, and pedestrians had some difficulty in traversing the rocky pathway, the place offered little temptation to the speculative; but in October 1760 the proprietors succeeded in leasing the well to – Newcomb and John Dolman, for a term of 21 years, at a rental of £24 per annum. One or two cottages were then erected for the accommodation of visitors, and it appears from John Wesley's diary that he took up his abode at this secluded spot in 1764 for the purpose of drinking the waters 'free from noise and hurry'. The visit of so prominent a personage was naturally made the most of by the lessees ... The extreme solitude of the spring, however, proved fatal to its popularity ... In September 1778, the premises, then in bad repair, were offered to be let by auction; but no bidder appeared ... In 1792 a passing visitor noted that the pump room was falling in ruins, and that the adjoining cottages had been converted into dwellings for quarrymen.[9]*

The following year, another visitor wrote that

> *a solemn stillness is here interrupted by nothing, but the innumerable kites and daws which hover over the lofty rocks ... The New Hot-well house was erected here to rival the other ... but the access to it being extremely dangerous, it has gone to decay, and is now converted to a hovel for the miners.[10]*

Exactly a century later, in 1893, the *Bristol Mercury* reported that a 'new drinking fountain' was to be built 'over the warm spring which rises near the Gully [to] preserve the hot spring water which rises at the spot, and which about a century ago was in much repute, being known as the New Hot Well ... It is intended to call it 'the St Vincent's Spring'.[11] It is the crumbling remains of this last attempt to revive the fortunes

of this little-known spot that stand rusting and forlorn beside the roaring tide of traffic along the Portway today.

After 150m, look across the Portway to a disused drinking fountain on the site of New Hotwell. Another 150m futher on, you will see a parking area, popular with climbers, on the other side of the road. This was the site of another quarry, known as Great Quarry, which was in operation until 1877. Carry on for another 300m, and, just after passing a small brick pumping station on the other side of the Portway, you will see a viewing platform above the road, with a path leading up to it. Look

Great Quarry, with Black Rocks Quarry in the distance, around 1860

A view from roughly the same spot around 40 years later, with railways on both sides of the river. The Portishead line, on the left, is still in use, but the Portway now runs on the course of the line to Hotwells

Looking south towards Hotwells station and the suspension bridge around 1910, with Bridge Valley Road on the left

A view, taken around the same time, of Hotwells station from the suspension bridge

out for the bottom of the path and cross over to it. Unfortunately – and somewhat bizarrely, as the path is well maintained – there is no central reservation here. There are, however, hatched markings in the middle of the road, indicating that it should, if you are patient, be safe to cross. Be aware, however, that, although city-bound traffic may be travelling slowly, vehicles in the bus lane beyond it may be travelling much faster.

Walk up the path and, when you come to a crosspath at the top, bear right across Bridge Valley Road – another tricky crossing – and head on up another path.* When you emerge from woodland, head straight across the grass to Clifton Promenade and bear right. After 250m, turn right along a broad track. Follow it downhill in the same direction for about 200m, before carrying on along a narrow path between railings, leading to steps high above the Portway.

---

* There are plans to build a footbridge to replace the crossing.

Clifton Rocks Railway, with Hotwells station in the distance

The steps date from the early 1920s when the path was rerouted and Bridge Valley Road set back around ten metres to make way for the Portway. Ahead is the blocked-up portal of a tunnel that led to Hotwells station. If you look over the wall near the bottom you will see the blocked-up entrance to another tunnel. During the Second World War, this served as an air-raid shelter, while the tunnel nearer the old station was used to store archives. In the early 1960s the northern tunnel also hosted a couple of prototype raves, with jazz bands playing around braziers.

After crossing Bridge Valley Road, cross the Portway at the lights and turn left. On the other side of the road is the site of Hotwells station, with the Giant's Cave high above. There was once another quarry here, as Pierce Egan discovered when he came this way in 1819:

The men employed in blowing-up the rocks, which is rather a service of danger, have tables set out by the side of the river with selections of various pieces of the rock, termed bacon, blue, and black spar, with some variegated Bristol stone for sale, left to the generosity of the purchaser. Some parts of this stone are polished, and made into chimney-pieces, but it is principally burnt for lime. The echo is thunder indeed when the blowing-up is performed; and the men on the rocks, engaged in sending some of the fragments down, appear like little boys. Near to the top of one of the above high rocks is to be seen the 'Giant's Hole'. From the great curiosity which frequently induced numerous persons to ascend, to explore the two cavities which it contained, an outer and an inner chamber, where, according to tradition, a giant formerly dwelt, all approach to it now has very properly been blown up, in order to prevent any farther danger or accidents. Persons walking by the side of these rocks appear truly diminutive; and the majestic appearance of the above venerable cliffs must be pronounced one of the grandest scenes in nature.[12]

Carry on under the suspension bridge and past the Avon Gorge Gallery, built to protect vehicles from rock falls. As you carry on, there are views across to the entrance to the Clifton Rocks Railway, the Colonnade and Rock House, and plenty of time to contemplate the ramshackle ruins of the old paddle-steamer wharves on your right. Beyond St Vincent's Parade, there were once many more buildings, including at least two pubs, but they were swept away for road widening in the early 1960s.

Follow the road as it swings round to the lock at the entrance to the floating harbour, and head north to cross a footbridge over several

RAILWAY TO PORTWAY

When the railway from Hotwells to Avonmouth opened in 1865, there was nothing at the northern terminus save the hopes of the promoters. So successful was the plan to develop a port at Avonmouth, however, that, less than 50 years later, as road transport started to increase, there were calls for a new road to the port, bypassing the hilly route across Durdham Down.

The problem, given Bristol's topography, was where to build it. The only practical solution was to take it along the Avon Gorge, but part of this route was used by the railway, which ran at the foot of the cliffs for the first mile north of Hotwells. Although the service between Hotwells and Avonmouth was still well used by dock workers in the morning and evening rush hours, most trains now ran through to Bristol, and it was decided to close the line to Hotwells in order to build what was initially known as the 'Low Level Road between Bristol and Avonmouth'.[13] A temporary platform had been built a little way north of Hotwells station, on the far side of the two tunnels, during the First World War, and, when Hotwells station closed on 19 September 1921, trains terminated there.[14] This was only a temporary reprieve, however, and the branch closed completely on 1 July the following year.[15]

At the time, the Portway was one of the most ambitious and most expensive roads ever built. It cost around £800,000 and its opening had to be delayed for over a year after 180m of newly-built embankment collapsed into the river. When it opened on 2 July 1926, the speeches at the official ceremony concentrated so much on 'the aesthetic and scenic character of Portway ... that the dock chairman thought it desirable to emphasise the part it was destined to play in facilitating the commercial business of the future'.[16] Those speakers who praised 'the excellent qualities of the road and the new viewpoints it offered of the Avon and its rocky gorge' could not have foreseen the phenomenal growth in road use over the ensuing century. Looking at the scenery while driving along the Portway today is not recommended, and appreciating it on foot is seriously compromised by the incessant flow of vehicles. Imagining the gorge as it was when wealthy visitors drank the waters at Hotwell Spa, or when the silence was only disturbed by the whistle of an occasional train is well nigh impossible, and one of the most scenic riverside walks in the country has effectively been lost to us.

Not that the history of the Portway has been trouble free. After a major rock fall at Black Rocks in November 1972, the road closed in 1974 for the cliffs to be made safe, and did not fully reopen for two years. Further rock falls near the suspension bridge led to the construction of a shelter – known as the Avon

Portway by night.

28

Portway, the goodly heritage of the citizens of Bristol, while superb by day is no less beautiful at night. The picture shows some four miles of the road electrically lighted in all its beauty of curve, line and reflections, as it follows the windings of the river through the Avon Gorge.

Gorge Gallery – below the bridge, which opened in 1981. In July 2001, a burst water main blew a large crater in the road and sent part of the embankment crashing into the river, and in 2010 Bridge Valley Road was closed for 18 months for work to be carried out to stop it slipping down the hillside. But, whatever challenges the cliffs of Avon throw in their way, it seems unlikely, given the Portway's strategic importance, that the highway engineers will fail to meet them, whatever the cost.

For years now there has been talk of closing

This page: Three postcard views of the Portway published shortly after it opened. The bottom one also includes a view of Sea Mills station.

Opposite: The Portway today

PORTWAY. BRISTOL. 374

PORTWAY HORSESHOE BEND

the Portway on summer Sundays. It does close occasionally for rock inspection, maintenance work, marathons and other sporting events, but the idea would be for people just to come along to enjoy the gorge without the traffic. There is much opposition to the idea, but we can only hope that it does eventually come to pass.

lanes of traffic. As you cross, you have a splendid view of a truncated row of four early eighteenth-century lodging houses on the far side that managed to escape the devastation visited on this area. The footbridge leads down to Granby Hill, where there is a well-preserved nineteenth-century shopfront at No 3. A little way up Granby Hill, turn right along Cumberland Place, then left up Albemarle Row, with a date of 1763 in its central pediment.

At the top, cross and carry straight on along Polygon Lane (although, if you are tempted to take a break at this stage, the Adam & Eve is 50m down to the right). After 50m, when the path divides, bear left uphill. Carry on past turnings to Glendale and Polygon Lane South, following the path as it winds uphill between high walls. You emerge on Cornwallis Crescent, which is in two parts, with a gap left to preserve access to this footpath. The gap was originally wider – the three houses to your right are later additions. Turn right and walk to the end of the crescent, where you will see a row of converted coach houses on the left. When the road forks, bear left uphill and take the next right down Goldney Road. At the end, turn right down Goldney Lane. At the bottom turn left up Ambra Vale East, and at the T junction carry on in the same direction. At the crossroads, with the Lion pub on the corner, turn left. At the end of the row of brightly-painted houses on the right, turn right along a footpath. At the end, carry on to a T junction, and turn right down a cul-de-sac. As it swings left, there is a spectacular view of the cathedral backed by tower blocks.

When you come to World's End House, turn left up a footpath. A right turn at a T junction leads downhill – where you need to watch out for intermittent steps – past secret gardens and a bus stop where no bus has ever stopped. The steps are known as White Hart Steps because an inn called the White Hart stood on the left at the bottom. It was demolished in 1877 and replaced by a church. There was another church on the right at the bottom of the steps. This dated from 1833, but, as the population of Hotwells grew, was found to be too small – hence the construction of a new church next door. The old church was bought

Above: The bus stop on White Hart Steps

Left: The White Hart, demolished 1877

Looking west along Hotwells Road around 1905, with the library housed in a former church

by the corporation and converted to a library, but both old and new churches were demolished in 1938. The site is now occupied by a block of flats, through which an archway leads to the road, with the SS Great Britain straight ahead on the far side of the harbour. Cross the bottom of Jacob's Well Road to the Bag of Nails, one of Bristol's most splendidly idiosyncratic pubs. It opened around 1862 as the American Eagle, after a packet ship which sailed between London and New York.

Bear right and head round the corner into St George's Road, where a few doors along is an example of that increasingly endangered species – a good second-hand bookshop.* Carrying on along St George's Road – originally known as Limekiln Lane – you come, after 150 metres, to the Three Tuns, brewery tap for Arbor Ales. Carry on past the library and the cathedral, which was founded as an abbey around 1140. Although much of the eastern end of the building is medieval, the nave and west front are Victorian. After passing the Marriott hotel – whose modern extension

The Floating Harbour in the late nineteenth century

* Dreadnought Books, opened in November 2013, specialises in history – including local and industrial history – but also carries a wide range of titles in other areas. Opening hours are 10-6 Tue, Wed, Fri, Sat; 1- 8 Thu; closed Sun & Mon (dreadnoughtbooks.blogspot.co.uk).

stands on the site of St Augustine's church, demolished in 1962 – carry on across the road at the lights, follow the pavement as it curves down to the Centre, bear right at the lights and – with the Watershed on your right – carry on across the top of the cascade. The arm of the floating harbour into which it flows is part of the River Frome. Although its former course through the city centre lies under ground, until 1938 the area to your left, where fountains now play, was still part of the floating harbour, and, in the aftermath of the First World War, captured German U Boats were moored in front of the Hippodrome.

Carry on across another road to the Radisson Blu and bear right. Follow the pavement as it curves left, cross at the lights across the bottom of Marsh Street and carry on past the late seventeenth-century Merchant Venturer's Almshouses, which displays a somewhat unrestrained version of the Merchant Venturer's crest. The Chinese restaurant next to it was Bristol's first public library, built around 1740.

King Street, which lies ahead, not only contains some of Bristol's oldest and most attractive buildings, including the Theatre Royal, but is also home to three of the city's finest pubs, with an awesome array of keg, cask and bottled beers. Astonishingly, they all opened, in their current incarnations at least, in 2013. On the right is the Famous Royal Navy Volunteer and the Beer Emporium, while on the left is the Small Bar, which, despite its name, is only small by comparison with the other two. It also has more beers on offer than you will find in most medium-sized towns, along with a minimalist makeover that makes the most of the building's eighteenth-century pedigree, and a bar menu that is a perfect match for the drinks on offer. It has even got a small brewery at the back, with plans for local microbrewers to collaborate on one-off beers for the pub.

At the far end of the street, two more iconic pubs beckon. The Llandoger Trow is one of the few surviving examples of the timber-framed jettied houses built by wealthy Bristol merchants in the seventeenth century. The pub originally occupied one building – No 5 – in a row of five. Nos 1 and 2 were destroyed in the 1940 Blitz, and in 1962 the Berni Brothers extended the Llandoger into the two adjoining buildings to create a restaurant. Its name goes back to when it was owned by the captain of a trow which ferried goods across from Llandogo on the River Wye. Opposite is the Old Duke, originally known as the Duke's Head. It is unclear which duke it was named after, but, as Bristol's oldest and best-known jazz pub, it is appropriate that it is now Duke Ellington that looks down from its signboard.

The Llandoger Trow around 1900

At the end, turn left along Welsh Back before bearing right across Bristol Bridge. From here, you could carry straight on along Victoria Street to Temple Meads, but, for a quieter route (with another excellent pub en route), cross and take the second left along Counterslip. After turning first right along Temple Street, you will see a remnant of the maze of streets that once characterised this area in the shape of the Cornubia on the right. This is yet another pub named after a ship, in this case a paddle steamer which ran between Bristol and Hayle from 1858 to 1861. She was later used by the Confederates in the American Civil War before being captured and used by Union forces.

Just past the Cornubia, turn left along Water Lane, where, through a archway on the right you will see the bombed-out shell of Temple church, founded by the Knights Templar in the twelfth century. Turn right at the end, and, at the dual carriageway, bear right for a few metres before crossing at the lights. Carry straight on past a shard, representing a templar stone, and a statue of Brunel in little tramp mode. River Gate, a little further along, follows the line of the medieval port wall, and viewing holes enable you to look down at the foundations uncovered when the site was redeveloped. Before the railway arrived, the port wall marked the end of the built-up area, beyond which lay Temple meads – or meadows. From here, carry on, heading diagonally across The Square and continuing across a zebra crossing to Temple Meads station.

Further information online:
The Friends of Old Sneed Park Nature Reserve: *www.spnaturereserve.com*
Bishops Knoll: *www.woodlandtrust.org.uk*
Avon Gorge & Downs Wildlife Project: *www.avongorge.org.uk*

14

PILL, PARADISE BOTTOM & THE AVON WALKWAY

Starts at: *Shirehampton station*

Ends at: *Temple Meads station*

Distance: *11 miles*

Terrain: *Mostly on rough paths (many shared with cyclists), but including the Avonmouth Bridge and a final section largely on pavements*

Pubs & other amenities:

Orchard Inn, Hanover Place, BS1 6XT; open all day from 12 (11 Sat & Sun); snacks served all day; dogs welcome; 0117 9262678; www.theorchardinn.co.uk

Seven Stars, Thomas Lane, BS1 6JG; open all day from 12; dogs welcome; 0117 9272845; www.7stars.co.uk

Map: *Geographers' A-Z & OS Explorer 154*

Good footwear is essential, as parts of the route may be muddy. The riverside path is a busy cycle route, and you may need to watch out for cyclists on blind corners and keep dogs under control.

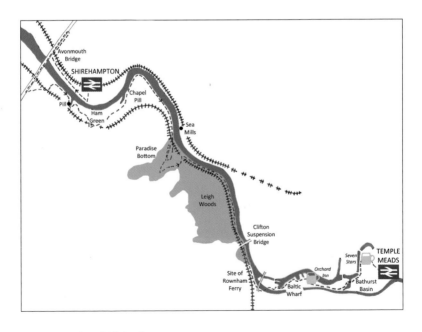

Opposite: Chapel Pill Creek

Starting at Shirehampton, this walk heads north alongside the Avon before crossing the M5 bridge and heading south past the village of Pill – once home to the pilots who navigated ships along the river – to the city's docks. The scenery is magnificent, with creeks and mudflats echoing to the cries of curlews and oystercatchers, but the legacy of the slave trade hangs in the background like an insistent ostinato. Not only does the walk follow the route of slave ships as they hied the last few miles for home between the wooded banks of the Avon; it also explores pleasure grounds laid out by one of Bristol's biggest slave owners, visits a folly from where he could survey the river, and ends at a dockside pub which played a key role in the abolition campaign. On a lighter note, the walk also passes the sites of several lost ferries, as well as some historic shipyards.

Head out of Shirehampton station and turn left along the road. After going under the railway, look on the right for a milestone in the wall indicating that Bristol is five miles away. After passing a group of Georgian buildings, you come to the Lamplighters Inn. First recorded in 1768 as

The Lamplighters in the 1940s

Lamplighters Hall, its name suggests that the original landlord was responsible for lighting lamps along the river to guide shipping.* In 2014, after it had stood empty for four years, the owners of Kingsweston House started refurbishing it, and by the time you read this it should have reopened.

For centuries a ferry ran to Pill from the Lamplighters. Celebrated in song by Adge Cutler in 'Pill, Pill, I Love Thee Still', it last ran in November 1974. Passengers also disembarked from Bristol-bound boats here. Among them was King William III, who landed here on 6 September 1690 after his victory at the Battle of the Boyne, and stayed with Sir Robert Southwell at Kingsweston House before continuing on into Bristol the following day.

Just over a century later, the Lamplighters was the scene of a bitter forced departure. On 8 December 1792,

a local journal reported that a wealthy citizen had just sold a 'black servant girl, who had been many years in his service', into perpetual

---

* There is, however, a tradition that its first landlord built it with the money he made after winning the contract for lighting oil lamps in the streets of Bristol.

bondage, and that the price of the unhappy woman, who was shipped to Jamaica, was £80, colonial currency. When she 'put her feet into the fatal boat at Lamplighters' Hall, her tears ran down her face like a shower of rain.'[1]

Turn right along the road opposite the Lamplighters, following a signpost for Avonmouth. After 200m, follow a path into Lamplighters Marsh. Avonmouth Bridge, which you can see ahead, opened in May 1974, sounding the death knell for the Pill Ferry. Follow the path out of the nature reserve, carry on under the bridge, cross a road and turn right over a level crossing. At the main road, turn left for 100m, cross at the

Looking across to Pill from the Lamplighters today

Looking across to the Lamplighters from Pill when the ferry still ran

lights and head straight on across rough ground. Cross a minor road and turn left along a footpath running parallel to the bridge. After 250m, carry straight on up steps and turn left across the bridge.

Looking over to your left, you will see the wooded promontory of Penpole Point (visited in Walk 12) to the left of two blocks of flats. The views from the bridge, which had to be built over 30m above high-water mark so as not to impede shipping, are spectacular. It also crosses two railway lines – the Severn Beach line and a spur off the old Portishead line serving Royal Portbury Dock.

On the far side of the bridge, follow the path as it curves down to the left and carry straight on past a pair of sculptures commemorating the strengthening of the bridge in 2001 (ST516762). Running parallel to the path on the right is the trackbed of the old line to Portishead, closed to passengers in 1964 but due to reopen as part of the Bristol Metro project. After 350m, just after going under the line to Royal Portbury Dock, cross a stile on the left (ST520762). Follow a path curving round the houses on the right and carry on along a levee. Go through a kissing gate (KG) and follow the path as it bears left alongside an access road before curving right between trees alongside the river. Go down steps and carry on along Marine Promenade, where modern buildings predominate, with only a handful – such as Mariner's Cottage – surviving from earlier times.

When you come to the mouth of Pill Creek, you will see the Lamplighters less than 200m away across the river. On the other side of the creek is a customs station, known as the Watch House. A customs station was first established here in 1693, but the present building dates from 1850.

Pill was described by JC Ibbetson in 1793 as

a place famous for pilots and boat-men, who conduct the vessels to and from Bristol. It is principally inhabited by this description of persons, and by fishermen, and is an irregular, ill-built, dirty place. There is a never-ceasing enmity between this village and Bristol; the people of Pill vent their rage on those of Bristol, by every species of imposition and rapacity; while contempt and opprobrium are liberally returned to them.[2]

Above: Marine Promenade and Pill Creek
Opposite: One of the narrow lanes that characterised Pill in the early twentieth century

Pierce Egan, who visited in 1819, was similarly unimpressed. He declared that 'near the river it has something like the appearance of Wapping', although he admitted that, 'at its extremity, towards the country, it possesses the neatness of a village'. Egan also remarked on the large number of public houses, 'among which the Waterloo Inn, Red Lion, and Duke of Wellington, are the most conspicuous'.[3] Time seems to have lent some enchantment to the view, however, for in 1944 CFW Dening declared that, 'from the artist's point of view, the quaint village with its old-world houses presents the appearance of a foreign port, and one must travel far before anything of a similar nature is encountered.'[4] Sadly, most of the old village has been swept away in the name of progress and flood prevention. To see a few of its surviving houses turn right alongside the creek and carry on to the right of the Duke of Cornwall pub and Prospect House up Back Lane. At the top of the steps, turn left past Cumberland House, and, as Chapel Row swings right, bear left down a footpath and steps between modern buildings.

As you turn right at the bottom, you will see a railway viaduct ahead. Bear left round the head of the creek and continue round to the left along the other side. Before you reach the Watch House, turn right along a footpath past the garage of No 9. After following the path past seventeenth-century Mulberry House, carry on up a field, keeping close to the hedge on your left. At the top of the rise, turn to take in the view over the river before carrying on alongside the hedge. After passing a community orchard, follow its fence around to the right. At the end, head across the grass to a drive and bear left. The small tump you can see over your right (ST528756) stands roughly on the site of Ham Green Farm.

At a T junction, turn left, right, then almost immediately left again along Cycle Route 41. At a road, carry straight on for a few metres before turning left along Chapel Pill Lane. The buildings on your left stand on a site once occupied by the ancillary buildings of Ham Green Hospital for Infectious Diseases, established in the 1890s and closed in 1992. A little way along Chapel Pill Lane, you come to the entrance to Ham Green House, once the main hospital building but now home to Penny Brohn Cancer Care. Carry straight on down a private road, looking

Top: The view over Pill
Above: Ham Green House
Below: The lake at Ham Green

out for the top of a gazebo, built around 1760 and restored after years of dereliction in 1999, to the right of the house. If you look back, you can see that the eighteenth-century house had a large extension added – dwarfing the original building – in the early nineteenth century.

As you carry on down past the old stables, a view opens up across a lake. At the bottom, follow the path past a metal gate and, when you come to Chapel Pill Farm, carry on along the River Avon Trail. After 250m, you will see the mouth of Chapel Pill Creek on your left.

The white building across the river dates from around 1755 and was a magazine where ships bound for Bristol offloaded gunpowder, which could not be taken into the docks. As you carry on, look to the right to see the tower of Sea Mills church rising above the crest of the hill. Ahead lies the most treacherous stretch of the river, the notorious Horseshoe Bend, where many vessels came to grief.

As you carry on round, look out for the tower of Sea Mills emerging from behind the trees on your left – a vivid demonstration of just how sinuous Horseshoe Bend is. A little further on, look for the remains of Sea Mills' eighteenth-century harbour through the railway bridge across the river. After this, the track winds into woodland, with the cliffs of the gorge visible in the distance. Eventually, you come to a railway viaduct on the right (ST548752). Below the third arch are the remains of a dry dock where Bath stone was offloaded for building Leigh Court in the early nineteenth century. A path leading through the second arch, after winding through a muddy patch, follows the course of a late nineteenth-century tramway through a valley landscaped with the help of Humphry Repton and graced with the oxymoronic name of Paradise Bottom.

The Powder Magazine

After 175m, fork right as the path follows the course of the tramway uphill through woods carpeted with wild garlic in spring. After another 250m, when you come to a clearing (ST545748), look to the right to see a sign to the Grotto. Follow it for 500m – the last part of which can get very overgrown in summer – and, after passing two small caves, you will come to a viewing platform and grotto overlooking the river. Trees now hide what must once have been a spectacular view, but in winter, when

The view from the grotto is best in winter

the leaves have fallen, if you look up river you can just make out the spire of Christ Church in Clifton. The spire you can see across the river is that of St Mary Magdalene in Sneyd Park.

Paradise Bottom

The Portishead line disappearing into a tunnel

The path once continued on past the grotto, but is now impassable. Head back to the clearing and carry on along the path you were on before (don't take the one heading up to the right). After 250m – with the private entrance to Leigh Court on the right – turn left along a drive. After 125m, turn left past bollards along a path heading downhill (ST543745), through the most spectacular part of Paradise Bottom. After passing a giant redwood, the path rises briefly before continuing downhill with a spring scouring an ever deeper cleft below you on the left. After dropping down to a pool, follow the path as it crosses a small dam before bearing right alongside the pool and turning left uphill beside a spring. Go through a KG and bear left along a broad drive. Carry on uphill as it curves to the right and, when you come to a T junction, turn left along Cycle Route 41 (ST548748). After 250m, look to your left to see the Portishead line disappearing into a tunnel below you. When you reach the riverside path, bear right along it.

SUGAR AND STONE AT PARADISE BOTTOM

Leigh Court, in which the future Charles II had lain concealed for several days after his defeat at the Battle of Worcester, was acquired in 1811 or 1812 by Philip Miles, scion of one of Bristol's richest families. His wealth came from shipping, sugar and banking – in other words from slavery – and he wasted no time in commissioning a grand new Palladian mansion near the old court, which was then demolished.* To take delivery of the large quantities of Bath stone needed for the new house, a dock was constructed on the Avon, from where a cart track – or possibly a rudimentary tramway – was built to carry the stone up to the construction site. Miles also engaged Humphry Repton to draw up plans for landscaping the estate and laying out woodland walks, waterfalls, ornamental pools and a grotto.

There were also quarries on the estate, one of which is believed to have provided stone for the abutments of the Clifton Suspension Bridge, and this may have been shipped out from the dock on the Avon. In the 1880s, however, large quantities of a highly-prized mineral called celestine (strontium sulphate) were discovered on the estate and Sir Henry Miles, then squire of Leigh Court, granted the extraction rights to a Mr Withers of Pill. The dock was refurbished and a two-foot gauge tramway was laid on the track up which the stone to build the court had come. Ironically, given the source of the family's wealth, celestine was mainly used at the time for refining sugar beet – a product which had undermined the West Indian sugar trade. In the early twentieth century, however, demand for celestine increased as radiography and cathode ray tubes – both of which used strontium – were developed. The operation at Leigh Court, however, came to an end in 1912, and shortly afterwards Leigh Court was sold to become a hospital. It has now been converted to a business and conference centre.

---

* An idea of the extent of Miles's wealth can be gained from the amount of compensation he received from the government when it abolished slavery throughout its dominions in 1833: a total of £47,403 9s 6d for the 2,043 slaves he owned in Jamaica and Trinidad. The slaves, however, received nothing.

If you look across the river, you will see the walls, high above the Portway and the railway, of the lost gardens of Bishop's Knoll (visited in Walk 13), with Cook's Folly a little further along. As you carry on, look across to see three large restraining arches protecting the Clifton Extension Railway from rock falls just before it enters the mile-long tunnel under Clifton Down.

On your right is the Portishead line on a high embankment through which, every so often, archways run to long-abandoned quarries. The next section of the walk is, if you time it right, magical. To see the late afternoon sun throwing the cliffs on the other side of the river into sharp relief is one of Bristol's finest visual treats, while climbers scaling the vertiginous crags provide a human dimension.

Above: Looking south towards the suspension bridge around 1910

Left: The Paragon and Windsor Terrace

Below: Rownham Ferry, with the New Inn on the left

As you approach the Clifton Suspension Bridge, an archway with a KG leads into Nightingale Valley (ST563732). If you look through it, you will see the gateway to Nightingale Valley Halt, opened in 1928 and closed in 1932. As you carry on under the suspension bridge, there is much to see from a new perspective – Clifton Rocks Railway station, the terraced gardens above the Colonnade, the crumbling paddle-steamer wharves, and – perhaps most striking – the Paragon and Windsor Terrace high above the river.

A little further on, you will see the lock gate leading into the floating harbour. Rownham Ferry, dating at least as far back as the twelfth century, once ran across the river here. Originally operated by the monks of St Augustine's Abbey, it later passed to the dean and chapter of the cathedral. A public house, known as the New Inn, stood alongside the river to cater for those making the crossing; there was another inn – the Rownham Tavern – on the other side. In 1865, as the corporation drew up plans to build a new entrance into the floating harbour, they acquired the ferry for £10,000. Two years later, when the railway to Portishead was being built, there was talk of tunnelling under the river here to take the line into Hotwells, but this came to nothing.[5] The following year, however, work started on building the new entrance to the floating harbour, and the ferry was moved 150m upstream, beyond the old entrance to the floating harbour, where it continued to operate until 1932.[6]

THE PORTISHEAD LINE

The nine-and-a-half mile line from Parson Street Junction to Portishead opened in 1867. It was built by the Bristol & Portishead Pier & Railway Company, but was operated from the outset by the Great Western Railway. As with the line to Avonmouth, it was built to serve new docks near the mouth of the Avon. Although work on a dock at Portbury began in the 1840s, several years before work started on one at Avonmouth, it did not achieve anything like the same success. The Portishead line closed to passengers in 1964 and to all traffic in 1981. The construction of a high capacity freight terminal at Royal Portbury Dock, however, led to the line to the dock being reinstated in 2002. Since then there have been repeated calls for the line to be reopened to passengers; for information on the campaign, visit www.portisheadrailwaygroup.org.

Carry on alongside the New Cut and, after going under a road bridge, turn left across Ashton Swing Bridge. Turn right for 250m before turning left across the railway. Carry straight on – with care – across two roads, turn right and, after 100m, turn left through the harbourmaster's yard and right along Baltic Wharf, through which timber from the Baltic, Canada and Russia was imported in the nineteenth century. The Cottage Inn was originally an office for the timber company.

Launching of the "New York City" at Hotwells, Bristol. 16-vi-17. II.

After 400m, follow the path as it bears right and then left alongside the water's edge to the gates of Albion Dockyard. This historic shipyard, owned by Charles Hill & Sons, was once much larger, extending eastward over the area now occupied by a marina. When it closed in 1977, it was the oldest shipbuilding concern in the country, with a history dating back to 1772. Another shipbuilding and repair company has since taken over part of the site.

Turn right, following old railway tracks past a building with a brick clocktower. Just beyond it you will see the Orchard pub, a traditional local with one of the finest selections of cider in the country, plus a range of beers from the barrel and pasties and rolls served all day.

Bear left, following the railway tracks before heading along an alleyway. The building on your left is a malthouse, built in the late nineteenth century and currently derelict. At the end of the alleyway, a left turn would take you to the SS Great Britain. We, however, will be turning right – past Aardman Animations – to follow a less-frequented route before returning to the waterfront.

Look to your right when you reach Cumberland Road to see a building with pilasters and acanthus capitals, once the offices of Charles Hill & Sons. Turn left past the Phidias Stone Yard and, after 200m, you will come to a fascinating group of buildings from around 1840. First comes Gothic Cottage, a picturesque villa flanked by modern extensions.

Then, after a short terrace, an extraordinary pair of semi-detached Greek Revival-inspired villas with an elongated niche in the middle. Finally, an asymmetrical row of three with a pediment over the two on the left – not the product of architectural waywardness or bankruptcy but demolition. This row – known as Cumberland Terrace – originally consisted of ten houses: the other seven went to make way for the railway which still runs under the road.

After carrying on past late nineteenth-century semis and Perrott's Court, comes another surprise – a little chunk of St Raphael's Church, built in 1859 with six almshouses for aged seamen attached. The Mud Dock Deli, a little further on, occupies an old workshop built for the nearby gaol. Opposite, the bridge over the New Cut was opened in 1935, replacing a ferry known as the Coronation or Gaol Ferry. A little further on – now part of the Wapping Wharf redevelopment scheme – is the gatehouse of the old gaol. It was built in 1833 to replace a gatehouse burnt down two years earlier during the Bristol Riots. The gaol closed in 1887.

At the end, cross to the Louisiana, built in 1816 and originally known as the Bathurst Hotel. Head to the right of it alongside Bathurst Basin, built between 1804 and 1809, on the site of an old millpond, to link the floating harbour to the New Cut. The connection has now been sealed off, but the rotting lock gates which controlled access can still be seen on the right. Steam Packet House, just past the Louisiana, was for many years the Steam Packet Tavern. Further down, in the wall of the house at the end of the row, is a stone which until 1835 marked the boundary between Bristol and Somerset.

A little further on is one of Bristol's most splendid façades – a warehouse from 1874, with two-tone brick teased into exotic exuberance, and now converted to flats. The old General Hospital, facing it across Bathurst Basin, is also being converted to residential accommodation.

Cross the footbridge over Bathhurst Basin and turn left past the Ostrich Inn. Before the millpond was converted to Bathurst Basin, there was a mill, known as Trin Mill, where it met the river. There was also a ferry across the floating harbour, which stopped running in 1931, although its slipway still survives.

Carry on round to the right along Phoenix Wharf. Originally known as Alfred Wharf, this was renamed Midland Wharf in the early twentieth century after the Midland Railway established a warehouse

The Steam Packet Tavern

Right: A map of around 1900 showing the Guinea Street and Redcliff ferries

Below: The Benjamin Perry Boathouse on Phoenix Wharf in the 1930s, and today

Opposite: Redcliff Wharf transformed into an urban beach in July 2007

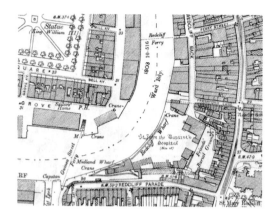

here. It acquired its present name after renovation work was funded by the Phoenix Assurance Company. The Benjamin Perry Boathouse, now used as a scout hut, is typical of the timber warehouses built on the dockside in the nineteenth century.

Beyond it lies Redcliff Wharf, the last undeveloped part of the harbourside, where, despite its dereliction, something of the feeling of a working wharf still lingers. Plans for its transformation have been drawn up, however, and soon this last remaining link with a centuries-old tradition will be gone.

Head through the gateway at the far end, cross the road and, just before the bascule bridge, bear right down a slope alongside the river. This is Redcliff Back, so called because of the merchant's houses that once backed onto it. After 50m, as you head along a cantilevered walkway, look up to see three cantilevered goods hoists above you. This building, built between 1909 and 1912 for the Western Counties Agricultural Society, was converted to social housing in 1997.

Beyond it, the way ahead is blocked. Until it closed in 1930, this was the embarkation point for a ferry to Welsh Back. Turn right between high walls and bear left when you emerge onto a road. On the left, old warehouses await renovation. Beyond them is a warehouse-style development called Mill House. Turn left into Buchanan's Wharf, passing a double Archimedes screw (presumably used in a nearby silo), and carry on through a covered area to continue along the harbourside. After going down a short flight of steps, turn right up more steps to a sculpture celebrating 'Bristol's seafaring heritage'. Head past it towards St Thomas's church, to the right of which, on Thomas Lane, is the Seven Stars, one of Bristol's finest traditional pubs, which – as described overleaf – played a crucial role in the campaign to abolish the slave trade.

Beyond the Seven Stars is a former wool warehouse, built in 1828-30 and now converted to a music venue called the Fleece with offices upstairs. Turn left at the end of Thomas Lane and, at Victoria Street, turn left for the city centre or right for Temple Meads.

Further information online:

Paradise Bottom: *www.forestry.gov.uk/forestry/ englandbathandnortheastsomersetnoforestbristolwoodlandsparadisebottom*

Friends of the Avon New Cut: *www.franc.org.uk*

THE PUB THAT CHANGED THE WORLD

In 1787, a national association for the abolition of the slave trade was formed. One of its principal members was Thomas Clarkson, a 27-year Cambridge-educated clergyman determined to devote his life to the abolition of slavery. As he wanted to gather as much evidence as possible to use against the slave traders, it was natural that one of the first places he should visit was Bristol.

On seeing the city for the first time, he wrote that, 'it filled me, almost directly, with a melancholy for which I could not account. I began now to tremble, for the first time, at the arduous task I had undertaken, of attempting to subvert one of the branches of the commerce of the great place which was now before me.' Not surprisingly, he found most doors closed against him. 'The owners of vessels employed in the Trade there,' he wrote, 'forbad all intercourse with me. The old captains, who had made their fortunes in it, would not see me. The young, who were making them, could not be supposed to espouse my cause to the detriment of their own interest.'

Clarkson had been told, however, that sailors had 'an aversion to enter and were inveigled, if not forced, into this hateful employment'. Disgruntled sailors would, he figured, be the best source of information about the slave trade. The problem was finding them. He was a middle-class clergyman; the men he wanted to interview would be found in the roughest parts of one of the roughest cities in the land. Not only that: he was, as far as the slave traders were concerned, a marked man. He was almost killed in Liverpool, England's other main slave-trading port, by a bunch of hired thugs, and he was obviously keen to avoid a similar confrontation in Bristol.

Fortunately, not all of those who wanted the slave trade abolished were middle class. Clarkson was introduced to a man called Thompson (we don't know his first name), the landlord of the Seven Stars. Clarkson described him as a very intelligent man who received sailors discharged at the end of their voyages and helped them find places on other ships. He refused to have any dealings with the slave trade, aware that his reputation – and the reputation of his inn – would be ruined if he sent those who entrusted themselves to his care onto slave ships.

With Thompson as his guide, Clarkson made 19 visits to various public houses in Marsh Street used by masters of slavers to pick up crew members. They generally set out around midnight and returned two or three hours later. From his own observations and from information given him by Thompson, Clarkson gathered ample evidence to confirm his suspicions that sailors were inveigled onto slave ships by lies and fraud. Getting them blind drunk or cracking them over the head in a dark alley were also regarded as legitimate means of recruitment.

Clarkson was also able to prove, using information from muster rolls, that, far from being a 'nursery for British seamen', as anti-abolitionists claimed, far more sailors died on slave ships than on all the other vessels sailing out of Bristol put together.

The evidence Clarkson collected provided the abolitionists with an unanswerable case for reform. Hard facts, rather than opinion and hearsay, could be used to counter the anti-abolitionists' claims that the slave trade was well-run and well-regulated. It took 20 years from the time Clarkson stepped over the threshold of the Seven Stars for the slave trade to be abolished, but his work in Bristol created a momentum that was unstoppable.

Clarkson's work in Bristol would have had far less impact had not been for the courage of the landlord of the Seven Stars. It was Thompson who provided him with an entrée to places he would not have dared go and to people who would not otherwise have trusted him.

Given the importance of the Seven Stars not only to Bristol's heritage, but also to national and international history, it is astonishing it is so little known. Admittedly, the Civic Society put a blue plaque above the door a few years ago, but that was about it until local historian Mark Steeds decided that something more was needed.

He came up with the idea of a large plaque commemorating Clarkson and Thompson. Bristol Radical History Group took up the idea and the plaque was unveiled by Richard Hart, a civil rights lawyer and former Attorney General of Grenada, on 1 May 2009, the 202nd anniversary of the abolition of the slave trade. Other speakers at the ceremony included Paul Stephenson OBE, the local civil rights campaigner who influenced the framing of the government's first anti-discrimination laws in 1965, Roger Bell from the Bristol Radical History Group and Madge Dresser from the University of the West of England,

The plaque on the Seven Stars is a first step towards raising the profile of Clarkson in a city that has so far paid him scant recognition. That it will also raise the profile of one of Bristol's finest traditional pubs is another bonus.

15

PILNING, PATCHWAY & BRADLEY STOKE

Starts at: *Severn Beach station*

Ends at: *Bristol Parkway station*

Distance: *11 miles*

Terrain: *Mostly on rough paths, with some stiles*

Map: *OS Explorer 167 & 155; although the Geographers' A-Z is useful for the latter part of the walk, the section from Severn Beach to Cattybrook brickworks is not included in it*

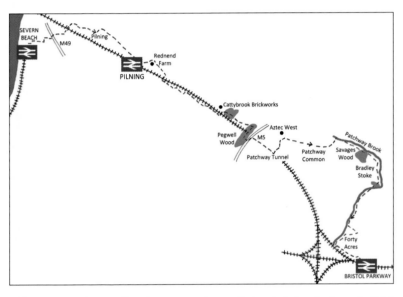

Starting at Severn Beach station, this walk heads inland, through fields and woods, and alongside the main railway line to South Wales, before negotiating the business park at Aztec West. From there – although housing estates are never far away – it follows a ribbon of greenery across old commons and alongside brooks, through Patchway and Bradley Stoke, before ending at Parkway station. This is an area that has only recently been developed. Had you walked through it as recently as the late 1970s, it would almost all have been open country. We can, however, like the residents of these new suburbs, enjoy and celebrate what has been saved from the developers.

Opposite: Rhine at Rednend Farm

217

Arriving at Severn Beach, turn right out of the station. At the mini roundabout, turn left into Gorse Cover Road, then right into Church Road. After 300m, follow the road round to the left. After another 100m, follow Church Road as it swings right. Cross the footbridge over the motorway. Carry on and, when you reach the main road, turn left along the pavement, which, after 175m, takes you across the main railway line to South Wales. Although you cannot see it, as it runs through a short tunnel and there are high banks on either side of the road, you will be seeing a good deal of it later. A little further on, when the pavement ends, cross over, turn left and bear right along a lane past Pilning Forge.

Above: Pilning High Level in 1960, with a car train in the siding and Pilning Low Level signalbox station visible on the far side of the yard

Below: The same view today

At the end of the lane, turn right along Redwick Road. Carry on for 600m before crossing the road and turning up a footpath to the left of St Peter's Church (ST557850). The allotments near the end stand on the trackbed of the section of the Bristol & South Wales Union Railway that ran to New Passage Pier. It closed when the Severn Tunnel opened in 1886, but in 1900 part of it reopened as part of a new line from Pilning to Avonmouth. Although a section of this line – from Severn Beach to Avonmouth – is still open, this section closed – for the second and final time – in 1964.

Go through a kissing gate (KG) and turn right along a lane. As you walk along, you will see traces of the old railway on your right. After 1100m, turn right at a T junction. After 125m, you will see a footpath on the left leading to Rednend Farm. Before heading along it, if you cross the road you can visit Pilning station, one of a handful of 'ghost' stations served by only one train a week in each direction. Before the Severn Road Bridge opened in 1966, however, motorists could load their

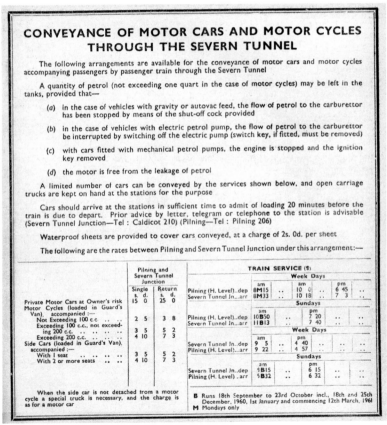

Arrangements for conveying cars and motorcycles to South Wales in 1960-61

cars onto special trains here to carry them through the Severn Tunnel, thus avoiding a lengthy journey via Gloucester. Although the station is known simply as Pilning today, it was once called Pilning High Level to distinguish it from Pilning Low Level, which was served by trains to Severn Beach and Avonmouth.

From here, head back and walk along the drive to Rednend Farm. After 175m, cross a stiled footbridge on the left and turn right alongside a rhine (or ditch) through a field with horses. After 225m, cross a stiled bridge back over the rhine. Carry on across another stile and turn right along a farm track. After 125m, follow the track as it swings left (ST572843). Carry on for 300m and turn right along a lane. Go under the railway and turn left along a bridleway (ST573839). The tranquillity of this tree-lined green lane, with views across open country, is only disturbed by occasional trains rushing past on the main line.

Follow the bridleway as it curves through the fields. Don't take the footpath under the railway but carry on with the line on your left. When you reach a lane, turn left. After 50m, just before some cottages, go through a white gate on the right (ST583833) and bear left beside the hedgerow alongside the railway. At the end of the field, cross a metal stile and carry straight on past two houses.

When the track bears right, turn left to cross a footbridge over the railway (ST587831), which has a superb view of Patchway's twin tunnels. The two lines are at different levels because they were built at different times. The down line (on the right looking towards the tunnels) came first in 1863; when the up line was added in 1887, it was built at a lower

Green lane alongside the main line

level to make the gradient easier for eastbound trains – an important consideration when many of those trains carried coal from South Wales to London.

Cattybrook brickworks, on the far side of the footbridge, was established in 1865 by Charles Richardson, who was in charge of building the railway and had been impressed by the quality of the clay excavated from Patchway tunnel. From here came many of the bricks for lining the Severn Tunnel, as well as the red and buff-coloured bricks in some of Bristol's most iconic late nineteenth-century buildings.

Head straight on to the right of the brickworks and turn right, following a footpath sign up a road past extensive clay pits. After 250m, when the road swings right, bear left up a footpath (ST591830) and carry on past three rows of houses. At the road (which may be busy), turn left for 50m, cross and go through a KG.

Head up the field, with the hedge on your right. On top of the wooded hill to your left are the ramparts of an ancient hillfort. In 1570, Thomas Chester, Mayor of Bristol, built a mansion, incorporating a fifteenth-century lookout tower, within the ramparts. Known as Knole Park, it was demolished in 1970, but part of the lookout tower was spared and now forms part of a modern house.

Follow the hedge as it bears left and then right up to a KG (ST596828). Bear right through Pegwell Wood along a well-worn track. After 400m, when you meet a path heading up through the woods, turn left along it and cross a footbridge over the motorway.

Cross a stile on the far side of the bridge and turn left alongside the motorway. After 175m follow the path as it bears right through an area known as the Tumps. The twin bores of Patchway tunnel are directly below; the tumps are the spoil heaps created when the tunnels were built. After 650m, when you come to a service road, turn left along it towards Aztec West. This business park, established in the early 1980s to attract technology-based businesses to the area, is now home to over 100 companies employing

Pegwell Wood

around 7,000 people. Little more than 30 years ago, though, this was all farmland, and was part of the Hempton Court estate. Hempton Court itself, which stood to the right of the path you are walking along, has given its name to the office blocks that stand there today.

After passing a lake with two fountains, bear left along a road, and at a T junction turn right along a broad boulevard. After 200m turn right along a footpath to Patchway Common and Bradley Stoke (ST604826), and carry on along Hempton Lane, once a tree-lined track between fields. Just before you come to a dual carriageway, follow a footpath sign to the right and go through a subway. Climb the steps on the far side and turn right (passing over the subway) past North Patchway Hall. As you turn right along the Common (ST608824), look over to your left to see the Traveller's Rest. Originally known as the New Inn, it is one of Patchway's oldest buildings, but has been greatly extended.

As you carry on along the Common, you will see the occasional old cottage or farmstead amid modern buildings. One of the oldest is Pond Farm, set well back from the road, 200m along on the right. When you reach a main road, cross and carry on along The Common East. After 200m, you will see a pond on the right. Until around 30 years ago, Manor Farm stood on the left, with orchards behind it. Follow the lane as it bears left past Manor Farm Cottages and carry on across a footbridge over a road (ST615825).

Ahead, where once lay fields, is Bradley Stoke, whose earliest houses date from 1986. Today, with a population of over 27,000, it claims to be Europe's largest new town. The land on either side of the brooks running through it, however, was preserved, to form a network of green arteries. When you get to the far side of the bridge, you will see Patchway Brook below you on the right. Head down to it and follow the path along its left bank. When you come to a metal footbridge, cross it and carry on along the right bank through Savage's Wood.

Carry on through a gate and, when you reach a wooden bridge, turn right, keeping to the path. When you reach a large pond with two stone

Savage's Wood

Stoke Brook

bridges, bear right alongside Stoke Brook (ST626814). Go under a road bridge and, 100m further on, turn left across a wooden footbridge and then right into the woods.

Follow the path straight on out of the woods, keeping close to the brook. When you come to a road, cross and carry on along a footpath. At Stean Bridge Road, cross and carry on along the footpath beside the road. At Winterbourne Road, cross the dual carriageway at the lights, turn left for 100m and then right across a footbridge over a ditch.

Carry on along a path through woodland, and, when it branches to left and right, carry straight on up a slight rise. Head towards a play area, but, before your reach it, turn right along a tarmaced path.

Cross the road at the lights and go through a KG into Forty Acres. There is a choice of two paths here – take the one straight ahead, and follow it as curves to the left alongside a brook. When you come to a crosspath, with a bridge on the right, carry straight on and follow the path as it curves right. After crossing a stone bridge, you come to another crosspath. Carry straight on and follow the footpath as it curves left, with the backs of houses on your left and a railway embankment high above the stream on your right.

After crossing another footbridge, near which the stream disappears into a culvert under the railway, follow the path as it bears right past the backs of more houses. After 200m, just after a short avenue of trees, the path curves left through a gap in a fence.

Straight ahead you will see a modern half-timbered house. Head towards it, but before you reach it, turn right. Take the next left and turn right at a T junction. Carry straight on at the end along a path between houses. When you reach the main road, cross at the lights and turn right along the pavement. After crossing the end of North Road, bear left to Parkway station and the end of the walk.

Further information online:
Three Brooks Nature Conservation Group: *www.three-brooks.info*
Friends of Forty Acres: *sites.google.com/site/40acresfriends/home*

16

SEVERN SHORE & SEVERN BRIDGE

Starts at: *Severn Beach station*

Ends at: *Severn Tunnel Junction or Chepstow*

Distance: *13 miles (to Severn Tunnel Junction); 9 miles (to Chepstow)*

Terrain: *Mostly on rough paths, but including the Severn Bridge*

Pubs & other amenities:

Boar's Head, Aust, BS35 4AX; open 11.30-3.30 & 5.30-11 Mon-Sat, 12-10.30 Sun; food served 12-3 & 6-9 Mon-Sat, 12-4 Sun; dogs welcome; 01454 632278; www.boarsheadpub.co.uk

Millers Arms, Mathern, MP16 6JD; open all day from 12; food served 12-2.30 & 6-9 Tue-Sat, 12-3.30 Sun (advance booking recommended); dogs welcome; 01291 622133; www.millersarms.co.uk

Map: *OS Explorer 154 & 167*

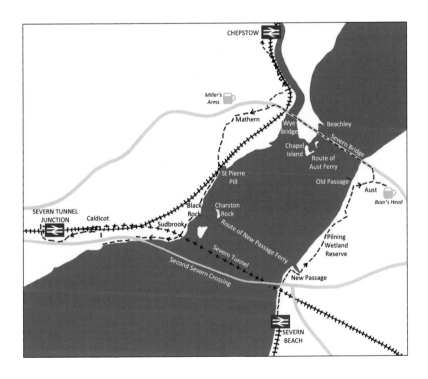

Opposite: The walkway across the Severn Bridge

This walk not only finishes in a different country from the one it starts in, but also offers a choice of endings. Setting off from Severn Beach, it heads north-east alongside the Severn, past a ventilation shaft for the Severn Tunnel, under the Second Severn Crossing, and past the embarkation points for two long-closed ferries, before crossing the Severn Bridge into Wales. There, you have the choice of heading into Chepstofw to catch a train back, or, for a longer walk, heading along the Wales Coast Path past a lost harbour, another ferry embarkation point, the Severn Tunnel pumping station, a ruined church and an iron age fort, before catching a train back from Severn Tunnel Junction. Either way, it is a superb walk in good weather – don't even think about attempting it in rain or high wind – with plenty of reminders of the dangers of crossing the Severn in days gone by, and a wealth of estuarial birdlife.

Leaving Severn Beach station, turn left, carry on to the sea wall and turn right. As you pass a slipway, look to the right to see Tubbies Burger Bar – a forlorn vestige of Severn Beach's heyday as a holiday resort. South of it, the land between the sea wall and the road, now covered by houses, was the site of the Blue Lagoon sea-water swimming pool.

Above: The Blue Lagoon, seen here in the 1930s, has long gone, but the row of shops in the background survives

Left: Tubbies Burger Bar

Depending on the tide, you can drop down at this point to carry on along the concrete walkway below the railings. When the walkway rises to rejoin the upper path, look to the right to see Salthouse Farm, around four centuries old and now surrounded by park homes. After another 70m, bear right along a narrow path and, after passing a gate, turn left to see, through a high-security gate, a ventilation shaft for the Severn Tunnel. The Sea Wall Pumping Station once stood here, and until recently the structure behind the shaft had a gantry over it, which has now been removed.

Heading north towards Sea Wall Pumping Station in the 1920s

The pumping station and cottages built for men working on the Severn Tunnel

A little further on, turn right to carry on along the Severn Way. The cottages on the right were built for men working on the tunnel. From here, take the lower path again if you wish and continue under the Second Severn Crossing (SSC). Built between 1992 and 1996, it is, at 3¼ miles, the longest bridge in the country. The old Severn Bridge, which you can see in the distance, opened in 1966; the cantilever bridge to the left of it carries the motorway over the River Wye.

After rounding a bend, the remains of New Passage Pier, from where a ferry ran to Portskewett, comes into view ahead (ST543864). Just before it is Severn Lodge, raised up above the flood plain, with an interesting collection of derelict outbuildings at the back.

When the railway to New Passage opened in 1863, lines were laid on the pier but the passenger station was built inland, where a lawn and a modern building stand today. It lasted a mere 23 years, closing when the Severn Tunnel opened in 1886. The ferry operators and the landlord of

THE BEACH NEW PASSAGE. 15.

Above: New Passage in the 1920s, with Severn Lodge on the right and the New Passage Hotel in the distance

Left: Chestle or Chiswell Pill

the New Passage Hotel, which lay just to the north, may have bemoaned the loss of trade, but it is unlikely that many others mourned the demise of the service. Crossing the Severn here was notoriously dangerous; hundreds, if not thousands, lost their lives over the centuries when their boats were overtaken by the tide. This spot, for many, would have marked their last sight of land – for ever.

The hotel managed to stay in business, catering for daytrippers from Bristol, but was demolished in 1973, and houses now occupy the site. Carry on past them and follow the path as it bears right alongside Chestle or Chiswell Pill. After curving left over flood gates, the path goes through a kissing gate (KG) to head north along a levee through Pilning Wetland Reserve, created in 2011 when a military firing range and sheep fields were landscaped to create areas of freshwater flooding. Even with the distant roar of traffic, this is an atmospheric stretch of coastline, with skylarks trilling above and the distant cries of oystercatchers and other waders.

After crossing Cake Pill, turn left along a road for 700m, bearing left just past 30mph signs. After passing Wharf Barn, look to the left to see the disused entrance to the Aust car ferry, which closed on 8 September 1966, the day before the Severn Bridge opened. The dilapidated turnstile was the entrance to the gents.

Wharf Barn at Aust around 1910

The entrance to the the Aust car ferry

Bear right uphill past Wharf Barn. The building you can see ahead is Old Passage House, dating from the sixteenth century. Turn left and continue uphill, from where you can look down on the crumbling remains of the old pier.

After passing the old vicarage and a heavy-duty pylon, you come to a junction on the left, signposted to Severn Bridge and Chepstow (ST570891). Although this is the path you will be taking, there is the option of visiting Aust Village – and the Boar's Head Inn – first.

For Aust, carry straight on, cross the dual carriageway, and, a little way along to the right, turn left into the village. Despite its proximity to the Severn Bridge and several busy roads, Aust has a semi-rural air, along with several buildings – including the Boar's Head, 350m along on the left – dating from the seventeenth century. From here, head back across the dual carriageway and take the turning to Severn Bridge and Chepstow.

Following signs for Chepstow, stay on the left-hand side of the motorway, and after going under a height barrier, you will find yourself on the bridge, high above the Severn. Even if, so far, you have felt nothing more than a gentle breeze, the chances are that the wind will hit you as you walk out of the lee of Aust Cliff. Undertaking this crossing in driving rain or when the wind is high does not bear contemplating. Neither – speaking personally – does the thought of clambering upwards, although, as robust defences and copious signs indicate, this aversion is not universal.

The scope and scale of the bridge is, seen up close like this at walking pace, monumental, and the views are magnificent. On the island ahead, known as Chapel Rock, are the ruins of a chapel believed to date from the fourth century. It was originally dedicated to St Tecla, the daughter of a nobleman from Gwynedd, who retired to the island to live as a Christian anchorite, but was murdered by raiders from the sea. It was later rebuilt

The Second Severn Crossing from the Severn Bridge

and rededicated to the sixth-century St Twrog, but fell into disuse some time before the eighteenth century. It is a fitting introduction to the land of saints and legends you are fast approaching.

First, though, there is the last of England to cross, for the Beachley peninsula, bounded by the Severn and the Wye, is part of Gloucestershire (although it was part of the Kingdom of Gwent until the ninth century). Looking down as you approach it, with tall trees below you, is curiously reminiscent of coming into land at an airport, albeit at a somewhat slower pace. The slipway from where car ferries once crossed to Aust is unfortunately out of sight on the other side of the bridge, but you do have the slightly surreal experience of walking high above the barracks of 1st Battalion The Rifles – complete with rifle range.

Leaving the Beachley peninsula, the cantilever bridge over the Wye takes you into Wales, where the footpath drops down to a crosspath and the choice of following the Wales Coast Path (WCP) east to Chepstow or west to Severn Tunnel Junction.

For Chepstow, turn right under the motorway and carry straight on, passing Samuel Rogers Crescent on the right. At a T junction, turn right for 100m, before turning right along Tenby Lane. At the end, bear left along a track with a view over the Wye Bridge. After passing a stile on the right (leading to a riverside footpath closed due to subsidence), carry on through woodland. After climbing to a viewpoint high above the river, follow the path downhill. Carry on up a tarmac path and, when you come to a road, bear right uphill and turn left at the T junction at the top. After 50m, turn right along a path beside a bungalow.

Looking up the Wye towards Chepstow

Carry straight on and, after passing an industrial estate and the entrance to Bulwarks Fort, you will see a large disused quarry on your right. Continue along a path which once wound through the landscaped gardens of a large house called Hardwick Court. The house was demolished in the 1960s to make way for a housing estate, but the path – along with an open space known as Piggy's Hill – survived. Carry on into Wye Crescent and turn left uphill at the end. At the crossroads at the top, follow WCP waymarks to the right.

As the road starts to curve left alongside the medieval Port Wall, you again have a choice. If you want to head to the station, carry straight on through a gap in the wall, bear left downhill at a T junction, turn right at the bottom and bear right at the crossroads.

If you want to head into the town, follow the road as it curves alongside the wall, cross the main road and carry straight on along a footpath to emerge at the top of the High Street. The castle and museum – both well worth a visit – are on Bridge Street at the bottom end of town.

Returning from Chepstow to Bristol, you have to change at either Newport or Severn Tunnel Junction – you will need to check the timetable or ask the conductor on the train to see which applies.

For Severn Tunnel Junction, follow the WCP waymark straight on and follow the path as it sweeps through a landscaped area with warehouses down to the left. When the path forks, follow a WCP waymark right alongside a fence (ST534913). At the road, cross and carry straight on along the path. Go through a KG and carry on. After going through the next KG – where the going may be muddy – bear diagonally to the right towards a stile in the far corner of the field. Cross the stile, bear left alongside a fence and cross another stile (ST524910).

If you feel in need of refreshment, you can turn right along the lane after crossing the stile, carry on under the motorway and after 600m you will see the Millers Arms on your right. Otherwise, carry straight on along a lane across crossing the stile, and, when it forks, bear right to pass to the north of Mathern church. This is dedicated to St Tewdrig, sixth-century king of the Celtic kingdom of Morgannwg. He abdicated in favour of his son and retired to live a life of Christian contemplation, before being recalled to lead his people against invading Saxons. He won the battle, but was mortally wounded and laid to rest on the spot where Mathern church now stands. The building south of the church is Mathern Palace, once home to the Bishops of Llandaff. The ruined arch in the churchyard is thought to be a fragment of a medieval priest's house.

At the end of the lane, go through a gate and turn left. The turret up to your right belongs to Moynes Court, dating from the middle ages and described in 1803 as a 'deserted ecclesiastical mansion ... occupied as a farmhouse'.[1] At the end of the field, go through a gate and carry on for a few metres before following a WCP waymark diagonally to the left across a field. Go through a KG, cross a footbridge and follow a WCP waymark to another waymarked footbridge. After going through a KG, bear right across another bridge and carry straight on. Pill Cottage (ST520901), which you pass on the right, was a custom house for the lost port of St Pierre. The manor house of St Pierre, 400m to the west, was for centuries home to the Lewis family, the biggest landowners in the area, who also owned the New Passage Ferry. It is now a golf and country club.

A MONMOUTHSHIRE LYONESSE

Parishes along the shore have quaint and sometimes beautiful names: Mathern, Portskewett, Caldicot, Rogiet, Undy, Magor, Redwick, culminating in Goldcliff before one finds the Usk. All have lost territory to the sea, and off Portskewett the names of vanished farms are still remembered in the Dumplings, Lady Bench, and Crab Hole. If any doubt this, there is the evidence of a man on oath at Monmouth Assizes less than 200 years ago; he stated that in his youth ... he had mown hay in a meadow on the Charnston [Charston] Rock, then joined to the shore by a strip of land.

Brian Waters, *The Bristol Channel*, 1955

Carry on and go through a wooden gate, across a footbridge, and through another gate at the far end (don't go through the metal gate on the right). Carry on alongside a fence, continue through a gateway and head straight on through several more KGs, one of which leads onto the main railway line from Gloucester to Newport.

After crossing – with care – you will see a levee ahead. The coast path bears right along it – there is a ramp a little way along – but it is worth diverting to the left to see St Pierre Pill. This small tidal creek was once a large harbour, first recorded in the ninth century, which has gradually silted up. As you walk along the levee, you should, unless it is very hazy, be able to discern the buildings across the water at both Old and New Passage.

The lighthouse you can see ahead, on Charston Rock, was built in 1868 and is maintained by the Gloucester Harbour Trustees.

St Pierre Pill

After going through a KG, you pass Passage Wharf Pill on the left. When the path forks, bear left to continue along the shoreline (ST513883). After passing under a red cliff, go through a KG, and, a little further on, look to your right, where, beyond a lawn, you will see a bridge. The railway line that ran beneath it continued onto Portskewett Pier to meet the ferry from New Passage. The station – unlike the one at New Passage – stood at the end

Charston Rock Lighthouse, with New Passage in the distance

The bridge that once spanned the railway to Portskewett Pier

of the pier. The Black Rock Hotel, which catered for passengers, stood on dry land, however, its site now occupied by a large car park. The small building on the far side of the car park houses the nets and tackle of the last lave net fishery on the Severn.* From here, local fishermen set out at low water during spring tides to catch salmon in hand-held nets using techniques dating back centuries.

Carry on along the coast path and, as you approach Sudbrook, you will see, opposite the electricity substation, a large yard on the left. This is where many of the bricks for lining the Severn Tunnel were made. Once the tunnel was built, the brickworks was converted to a shipyard, which built over a hundred ships before closing in 1922. Continue past a terrace, built by the GWR for men working on the tunnel, towards Sudbrook Pumping Station. This massive structure was built to pump water from the Great Spring, an underground watercourse which flooded

---

* Information on the Blackrock Lave Net Fishery can be found at www.blackrocklavenets.co.uk.

234

The disused railway line leading
to Sudbrook Pumping Station

Mural of the Severn Tunnel in
Sudbrook History Centre

into the tunnel workings in 1879 and held construction up for over a year. Estimates on how much spring water is pumped out of the tunnel vary wildly. Network Rail puts the average figure at around 12 million gallons a day, although the daily figure can peak at over 20 million gallons. Most of it is discharged into the Severn, but around two million gallons a day is pumped to the InBev brewery seven miles away at Magor. The pumping station also controls large fans to keep the air in the tunnel fresh.

Follow the road as it bears right past the pumping station and turn left over a disused level crossing. The line here, which once carried coal to the pumping station, is directly over the tunnel.

Turn left, and on your left you will see a history centre, which, if open, is well worth visiting to discover more about this fascinating area. There was, to all intents and purposes, nothing here before work started on the tunnel. The first building to go up was the short terrace on the right, consisting of six cottages and an office, and known, appropriately enough, as Old Row. A little further on, though, as the road dwindles to a rough path, is something much older – the ruins of a church, founded in Norman times but abandoned in the seventeenth century. The village that stood around it seems to have been a casualty, like other settlements along the Bristol Channel coast, of the great flood of 30 January 1607, believed to have been caused by a tsunami. It is estimated to have killed

SUDBROOK'S RUINED CHAPEL

'Sudbrook Chapel has not been used for church service now for two centuries and more. The last certain notice of its use dates back to 1755, and to the burial of a sea-captain, by name Blethyn Smith. The old place appealed to him, as did Mathern to more than one bishop. He asked in his will to be buried 'in the eastern end of the chancel of the decayed church of Sudbrook, as near the wall as may be, attended by six seafaring men as bearers – my coffin covered with the ensigns of colours of a ship instead of a pall'. A brass plate was put on the wall over his grave,

but it has long since disappeared. At Sudbrook you can still picture the ship-master's funeral – especially if there should be a Bristol barque going down channel to help you to recall the old days before steam came in. Then the ship's boat and the six sailors give way to a Viking's war-vessel, such as that they dug out of the mud in making Newport Docks, and the chapel vanishes and you see the Danish pirates run into the neighbouring pill and prepare to use the camp as a base for their next raid inland. Much history lies embedded in the mud bank at Sudbrook.'

Ernest Rhys, *The South Wales Coast from Chepstow to Aberystwyth*, 1911

around 2000 people and rendered many more destitute. It is not known if anyone chose to hang on after the village had been devastated, but by 1858 there was not a single dwelling within half a mile of the church.

As you carry on, you find yourself within the mighty ramparts of Sudbrook Camp, an iron age fort now used as a playing field, much of which has crumbled into the estuary. As you head through the ramparts on the far side, you will notice, atop them, the concrete base of a World War Two observation post. It is something of a scramble to climb up to it, but in such flat terrain it is worth it not only for the view but also to see how robustly defended the fort was. The disused paper mill to the west opened in 1958 and was supplied with water from the Great Spring. It closed in 2006 and there are plans to build over 300 homes on the site.

Carry on along the WCP, and, after 1250m, follow it as it bears left under the motorway (ST492873). After emerging on the other side – with a view across to the wind turbines at Avonmouth – you cross Caldicot Pill. Carry on through two KGs, and, after another 500m, when the path drops down, follow a WCP waymark through a KG on the right

The Second Severn Crossing from the ramparts of Sudbrook Camp

(ST481871). Another KG takes you onto a bridge across the motorway. Go through a KG on the far side, carry on past pylons and go through another KG.

Ahead is a bridge over the Gloucester-Newport railway line, with the western portal of the Severn Tunnel just beyond it. Instead of crossing the bridge, however, bear left, following a WCP waymark. After 600m (with Caldicot station on the right), bear left along what soon turns into a tree-lined country lane, with a reen – or drainage ditch – running alongside (ST474875).* The ever-present sound of traffic inevitably compromises its character, however, and, as it curves alongside the motorway and power cables cluster overhead, any hope of bucolic reverie seeps ineluctably away.

When you come to a T junction (ST461873), don't follow the WCP waymark left, but turn right to Severn Tunnel Junction. You need to continue on for some distance after crossing the railway before turning right along the access road towards the station, from where there are regular direct services to Bristol.

Further information online:
Severn Estuary: *www.severnestuary.net*
Severnside Birds: *www.severnsidebirds.co.uk/index.html*
Wales Coast Path: *www.walescoastpath.gov.uk*
Sudbrook: *www.sudbrook.info*

---

* Reens also occur in Gloucestershire – they featured in the walk from Severn Beach to Parkway – but there the word is spelt 'rhines', while in Somerset it is spelt 'rhynes'. In all three counties, however, it is pronounced 'reens'.

OLD PASSAGE v NEW PASSAGE

In 1803, JT Barber wrote that

> *New Passage [is] the principal entrance into Monmouthshire from the south-western counties. The breadth of water from this place to the Bristol coast is three miles and a half, while the ferry of Aust, or the Old Passage, four or five miles higher up the Severn, is only two miles across; but this advantage is considered to be overbalanced by the more commodious landing at the former. Both these concerns, being monopolies, are, like all other monopolies, hostile to the interest of the publick; for there being no competition for preference between the boatmen, they are extremely rude in their manners, indifferent to the accommodation of the publick, and by no means unpractised in various arts of extortion.[2]*

The incivility of the boatmen was legendary. A letter in the *Bath Chronicle* on 2 October 1777 suggests that drunkenness was also commonplace:

> *If anybody would communicate to the public, and to Mr Lewis of St Pierre any abuse they see practised with respect to the boats, or any ill-treatment they receive from the landlord (who, one would think, had served on board a pirate, rather than an English privateer) we might hope Mr Lewis would at length be stimulated into working a reformation amongst such his tenants [sic] ... I should be glad to be informed, if it is Mr Lewis's interest to permit a skittle-alley immediately under his nose; to the great injury of every young farmer who comes there, with his pockets full of money, to be taken in at best, for as much beer as the boatmen can swallow, to the imminent danger of all who trust themselves afterwards to these drunken savages.[3]*

By 1793, however, when JC Ibbetson visited the New Passage Inn – 'long ... resorted to by companies for dinner and tea' – he reported that

> *the accommodations and entertainments have been much and justly complained of, but new inhabitants have retrieved its character. A coach sets out every morning, at seven o'clock, from Bristol for the New Passage House ... The mail coach for Milford, with the Waterford mail, leaves Bristol about eleven in the forenoon, and is a sure conveyance across the Severn in the packet boat, which is kept in the pay of government for this express purpose.[4]*

Despite Ibbetson's assurances, passengers crossing the Severn often took their lives into their hands. Plaques at New Passage recall John and Charles Wesley's trips on the ferry; they do not mention Charles's experience in October 1743, when 'the boat in which [he] was crossing the Severn, at the New Passage, was carried away by the wind and in the utmost danger of splitting upon the rocks', before he was delivered by 'God, when all human hope was past'.[5] Nor do they mention a trip made by John Wesley the previous year:

> *We then hastened to the passage; but the boat was gone half an hour before the usual time: so I was obliged to wait till five in the afternoon. We then set out with a fair breeze; but when we were nearly half over the river, the wind entirely failed. The boat could not bear up against the ebbing tide, but was driven down among the rocks, on one of which we made shift to scrabble up; whence, about seven, we got to land.[6]*

Steam packets replaced sailing boats on the New Passage ferry around 1826, but the crossing remained hazardous. This report of an incident on the New Passage ferry in August 1844 is, unfortunately, typical of many:

Four boatmen had taken two gentlemen safely over from the Monmouth shore to the opposite side, in about 15 minutes, and were on their return with a passenger ... The wind ... was blowing in frightful gusts; and shortly after the ill-fated men left the shore, their perilous situation was observed by the boatmen, passengers, and several other persons at the Old Passage, and when about half a mile from the Black Rock, a succession of waves was observed to break over the boat which sank, drawing the five men into the vortex. To the great credit of the master and men of the Old Passage, their boat was immediately put out in the hope of rendering assistance to the unfortunate fellows; but they were too late, and a hat, the boat's rudder, and a few small articles, were all that could be picked up.[7]

In 1863, the centuries-old rivalry between the Old and New Passage ferries seemed to have been finally resolved in favour of the latter, when the Bristol & South Wales Union Railway opened branches to the ferry termini at New Passage and Portskewett. A year later, the *Western Daily Press* described the transformation effected at New Passage:

Those who knew the Passage Hotel as it formerly existed ... could scarcely have contemplated that such a magnificent hotel and grounds as those which now adorn the New Passage would have been brought into existence. But the promoters had other objects than those of the comfort of the passengers crossing the river ... It was found that a remunerative excursion traffic might be started and maintained between Bristol and New Passage, provided something were done to obviate the monotony of an afternoon's sauntering by the water. That something has been done, and those who undertook to do it are now being rewarded by public approval. The old hotel has been so renovated, altered, and enlarged that its very builders could not now identify it as the offspring of their labour and capital. New bedrooms

New Passage Hotel.

have been added, old windows pulled out, and splendid bay windows, bordered by ornamental balconies, inserted; and a suite of sitting-rooms has been erected. A new dining hall, for the accommodation of excursionists, has been entirely built ... The roof of the building has been so adapted that the bands which may accompany large numbers of excursionists will be enabled to perform upon it, and yet be observable from the terraces in front ... A splendid bowling green has been laid out in front of the building ... Around this green a spacious terrace has been erected, one side of which forms a sort of breakwater, and at the outer base of which the tide flows. Then there are flower and fruit gardens of considerable extent, well laid out and stocked, and other objects of attraction to those who desire to spend a few hours on the banks of the Severn.[8]

It was a similar story at the Black Rock Hotel, adjacent to the pier at Portskewett. An advertisement in May 1866 urged 'tourists and excursionists [to] visit this delightful place on the banks of the Severn', for 'on and after Whit Monday a Quadrille Band will play on the lawn every afternoon.'[9]

Portskewett Pier

A map showing New Passage Ferry and the Severn Tunnel

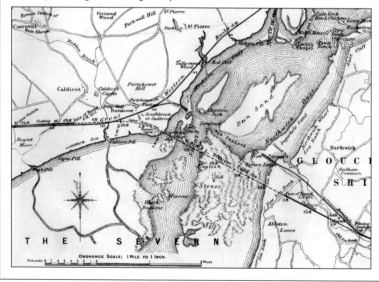

The glory days were short-lived, however. In 1886, the Severn Tunnel opened, and a year later the *Bristol Mercury* reported that 'not a relic of the Portskewett pier now remains ... and the waves of the Severn estuary now roll on the Black Rock shore without let or hindrance'. It went on to report that

the pulling down of the New Passage pier on this side of the river will be commenced this week ... The hulks that formerly floated at the heads of both piers are now being broken up on the New Passage side of the river; and the huge cables that held these landing stages in position are now being drawn ashore opposite the New Passage Hotel, which we may say is still open.[10]

The New Passage Hotel survived until 1973, relying almost entirely on excursionists; not so the Black Rock Hotel, which, when it closed in September 1893, prompted the following meditation upon mutability:

From Portskewett station a junction line ran down to the low cliffs overlooking the water at Black Rock, and here, in receipt of much custom, stood the Passage House, the Black Rocks Hotel, overlooking the turbid channel, and in view of the level lands of the English shore. In mid-channel stands the reef that gives the place its name and on it rises a little lighthouse. Now the place, saving indeed the lighthouse, is deserted. No ferry boats ply upon the water; traffic rumbles below the river bed in over three miles of burrow, and the junction line that received the voyagers is grubbed up and its cuttings are overgrown with weeds and wild flowers. A deserted railway is a rare sight in England. And now the hotel licence is withdrawn, and the building retires, after over a hundred years' public service, to the status of a private residence. The hotel, with its outbuildings and its singular situation, isolated from Portskewett village, upon the verge of the water, wear a mild and lovely air, significant of some unacted drama, whose fulfilment they seem passively to await.[11]

Despite closing, it opened its doors on at least one occasion, to accommodate Ernest Rhys – the founder of Everyman's Library – who came this way to summon up memories of the time when ferries still plied across the Severn:

My recollection of Portskewett dates back to the time when there was no Severn Tunnel, and travelling from Bristol to Carmarthen, we alighted on the Somerset side, to cross by broad-decked paddle-boats: a sort of miniature Holyhead-to-Kingstown experience. Out of all these crossings one made at Easter comes back clearly to mind. It was blowing and raining hard. The Severn was rough and dirty enough for any open sea, tumbling and rolling with choppy muddy yellow billows before a west wind. It was more daunting than Holyhead itself in the teeth of a gale – the flooded Severn, about an hour after high water, looked so malevolent. The wind, too, in the station at Portskewett – crying, buffeting, howling, and whistling – was such as only Dickens with his uncanny faculty of describing the elements at odds with roof and walls, could describe. I have often thought of that crossing when being sucked through the Severn Tunnel in an air-tight, sulphurous cylinder of a railway compartment in about a tenth part of the time: a great saving, no doubt, but a traveller's experience not at all to be compared with the other.

More than a generation later, a September evening took me again to Portskewett. The old waterside hotel was an hotel no longer; but it let me have pleasant quarters for the night; and after supper I walked under the stars to the waterside, and heard the lazy flap of the tide against the causeway, while in the distance sounded what seemed to be a noise of forge-hammers, or heavy clamping, possibly from the works at Sudbrook.[12]

The former hotel, after being damaged by fire in 1948, was demolished in the 1970s.

Despite the opening of the Severn Tunnel, ferry traffic across the Severn was set for one last revival. On 6 July 1926, as road traffic grew inexorably, the Lord Mayor of Bristol presided at a ceremony to reopen the Old Passage ferry, which had last run in 1861. The *Western Daily Press* explained that

the principal desire of the revival of this method of communication was to create a short cut for heavy road traffic, but at the moment the scheme has had to be whittled down to pedestrian or light traffic, such as motor-cycles, motor-combinations, and ordinary bicycles.[13]

The service only lasted two years before a storm destroyed the pier at Aust, but in 1931, after it had been repaired, a ferry capable of carrying eight vehicles started running. A second vessel was introduced in 1935.

The Beachley-Aust car ferry, August 1937

As early as the 1920s, there were calls for a road bridge across the Severn, but these were 'rejected by successive governments on the ground that inquiries were being made regarding the Severn barrage'.[14] Reports on the feasibility of a barrage were published in 1933 and 1945, but eventually it was decided to go for a bridge, which opened in 1966.[15] Since then, it has been joined by another – but the barrage idea has not gone away. Who can say what the crossings over the estuary will look like in a century's time?

For the present, we must count it a rare privilege to drive high above an estuary which so many crossed in fear and trepidation. It is an even rarer privilege to walk high above the whorling waters, gazing down at the shining spools of mud, reconfigured by the tides as the light shifts and breaks.

Vessels still ply up and down the estuary, but the ferries that once crossed it are a distant memory, the piers dismantled or crumbling into the mud, and the landing stages peopled only by ghosts. The most potent evocation of a tradition stretching back centuries is a photograph taken at Aust on 11 May 1966, when the ferry from Old Passage to Beachley had less than four months to run. Bob Dylan had played at the Colston Hall in Bristol the previous night and was en route to a gig in Cardiff. Six days later, at the Free Trade Hall, Manchester, would come the famous incident when a member of the audience yelled 'Judas' in protest at Dylan's decision to 'go electric', but already his non-acoustic numbers had been greeted with heckling, and the boos from a section of the Colston Hall audience would still have been ringing in his ears as he stepped out of an Austin Princess onto the slipway at Aust that damp and chilly morning. Above him loomed the still-to-be-opened Severn Bridge, but for the moment there was no choice but to watch the river flow and wait for the superannuated ferry to cross to the other side. No wonder he looked hacked off as Barry Feinstein raised his camera to take the most iconic photograph of one of the most iconic musicians of all time.

It is also possible that he was musing on the significance of his assumed name. Dylan is Welsh for 'wave', and in the *Mabinogion,* it was given to a boy who, as soon as he was baptised, made for the sea, 'where he took the sea's nature, and swam as well as the best fish in the sea.' Dylan Thomas was named after him, and it is often claimed that Robert Zimmerman changed his name to Bob Dylan in homage to Dylan Thomas. It seems, however, that, although he adopted the name while at high school, he initially spelt it Dillon, possibly after Matt Dillon, the US Marshal in the TV series *Gunsmoke*, only changing the spelling after moving to the literary and cultural milieu of Greenwich Village. Or so it is said. As with so much about Bob Dylan, disentagling fact from myth is beset with as many snares as investigating the origin of medieval Welsh folk tales.

The end of the pier at Aust

THE SEVERN BEACH LINE: A BRIEF HISTORY

A lthough this is a book of walks, it is useful to know something of the history of the line from whose stations the walks start, and which features so prominently in several of them. There are few, if any, lines of comparable length, however, whose history is so convoluted, and the potted history that follows can only provide the barest of outlines.

The first piece in the jigsaw was the Bristol & South Wales Union Railway (B&SWUR), opened in 1863, which Severn Beach trains follow for the first two miles out of Temple Meads. Built by Brunel, and absorbed into the Great Western in 1868, this ran to a pier at New Passage on the Severn, from where passengers took a ferry to Portskewett, before continuing their journeys to Newport, Cardiff and points west by train. In 1886 trains were rerouted through the newly-opened Severn Tunnel and the pier at New Passage closed.

Originally mounted above the eastern portal of Patchway Tunnel, this plaque was moved to platform 3 at Temple Meads in 1986.

The next line to open was one of the most speculative and unusual ever built. Not only was it isolated from the rest of the railway system, its northern terminus stood on a virtually uninhabited stretch of coastline. It owed its construction to an increasing dissatisfaction with Bristol's docks and the hazards of the tidal and tortuous River Avon, which lay between the docks and the sea. By the mid-nineteenth century, Bristol's docks, the bedrock of the city's prosperity for centuries, were in decline, and, as the size of ships increased, it was clear that, whatever steps were taken to improve the docks, this decline was bound to accelerate. The only practicable solution was to build new docks near the mouth of the river. This had been tried, once before, at Sea Mills, in the early eighteenth century, but had proved unsuccessful, largely due to the difficulty of carrying goods overland between Sea Mills and Bristol.

The promoters of the new dock at Avonmouth, to ensure they did not run up against similar problems, decided that a railway needed to be

Opposite: A map published in 1903 showing the railways north of Bristol. Both the original southern terminus of the BPR&P line at Hotwells and the northern terminus at Avonmouth are shown, although the northern terminus closed the year the map was published. Also shown – as a mineral railway – is the line from Pilning to Avonmouth, opened in 1900, with Severn Beach conspicuous by its absence.

in place before the dock opened. The name of their company – the Bristol Port Railway & Pier Company (BPR&P) – summed up their aspirations and business plan succinctly. The railway, 5¾ miles long, opened on 6 March 1865, and ran from a station called Clifton – directly below Brunel's newly-opened suspension bridge – to Avonmouth.

The directors of the BPR&P realised that, for the project to have any hope of success, their line had to link up with the rest of the railway network, and they started negotiations with the two major companies serving Bristol – the Midland and the Great Western – as well as with Bristol Corporation. There was much talk at this time of building a grand central station in or near Queen Square. Had it been built, the BPR&P line could have been extended to it either through Hotwells and along the harbourside, or through a tunnel under Clifton Wood and Brandon Hill.

In the event, the grand central station never materialised and a new joint station was built at Temple Meads instead. This left the BPR&P directors with several options – to built a line east from Avonmouth to join the B&SWUR at New Passage; to build a line from Sea Mills up the Trym valley to Westbury-on-Trym and from there carry on to join the B&SWUR near Horfield; or the one that was eventually adopted – to tunnel under the Downs, emerging in Clifton and heading eastwards through Montpelier to join the B&SWUR north of Baptist Mills.

The Clifton Extension Railway, as the new line was known, left the BPR&P line at Sneyd Park Junction, a quarter of a mile south of Sea Mills, and climbed steeply before entering a tunnel, just under a mile long, at the far end of which it emerged near Whiteladies Gate, where a large station – called Clifton Down to avoid confusion with the original Clifton station below the suspension bridge – was built. From here, the line headed downhill through Redland – which had to wait until 1897 before it got a station – to Montpelier. East of Montpelier the line divided at Ashley Hill Junction, one line curving south to join the B&SWUR at the evocatively named Narroways Junction, the other heading straight on to link up with the Midland Railway at Kingswood Junction.

Work on the new line had barely started when, in 1869, the company ran into financial difficulties and responsibility for building it passed jointly to the Midland and Great Western Railways. The tunnel under the Downs took five years to complete, with the first goods train running through it on 24 February 1877, the same day that the dock at Avonmouth opened. Passenger and goods trains had already been running to Clifton Down station from Bristol since 1874, but due to operational concerns and disagreements the first passenger train did not run through the tunnel until 1885. When it did, the original line from Sea Mills to the terminus under the suspension bridge was downgraded to secondary status. The old Clifton station – renamed

Hotwells in 1890 – remained busy, however, as it was also the terminus of a tram service from Brislington. Services along this section of the line were finally withdrawn in 1922 so that the Portway could be built.

The new line not only gave the Midland and Great Western Railways access to what, they clearly hoped, was going to be one of the biggest docks in the country, but also to the populous and well-heeled suburbs of Clifton and Montpelier. In attempting to kill two birds with one stone, however, a serious miscalculation had been made, a miscalculation that became ever more apparent as goods traffic from Avonmouth increased. While lightly-loaded passenger trains could handle the gradients on either side of Clifton Down station without too much difficulty, it was a different story with goods trains. Not only were extra engines needed to haul them uphill – burning more coal and using more manpower – but brakes had to be applied before they travelled downhill to stop them running away. This took a great deal of time and effort, as well as increasing costs, and

Above: A goods train heads west through Clifton Down station in 1957

Left: An eastbound goods train leaves Clifton Down Tunnel in 1947

the ensuing congestion threatened not only the viability of the line but future growth prospects for Avonmouth docks.

To get round the problem, in 1900 the Great Western opened a new line, with no appreciable gradients, from Pilning on the B&SWUR along the coast to Avonmouth. Part of this line used the trackbed of the old line to New Passage which had been abandoned 14 years earlier. Initially it was only used by goods trains, but in the 1920s a station was opened at Severn Beach and a passenger service was introduced.

In 1903, the original terminus at Avonmouth, along with a hotel and pleasure gardens, which the promoters had hoped would attract excursionists to the line, closed to make way for the massive Royal Edward Dock, which was opened by King Edward VII on 9 July 1908. With the original terminus gone, passenger services terminated at Avonmouth Dock station, half a mile to the south and still open – but now known simply as Avonmouth – today.

In 1910, the Great Western opened another line to Avonmouth. This left the B&SWUR at Filton and provided direct access to the newly-opened main line to London via Wootton Bassett. Although passenger services on this line were withdrawn in 1964, it is still open for freight and there are plans to reintroduce passenger services as part of the Bristol Metro scheme.

There is no longer any regular goods traffic on the Clifton Extension Railway, or on the surviving section of the BPR&P between Sea Mills and Avonmouth. The line from Narroways Junction to Avonmouth was

Avonmouth Dock station around 1914. The number of workers using the station rose dramatically during the First World War as the government established munitions factories and a remount depot nearby, and in 1918 an extra platform was built on the right.

singled in 1970, with a passing loop provided at Clifton Down. Beyond Avonmouth, passenger trains still run to Severn Beach, but the line beyond was closed to passengers in 1964 and to all traffic four years later. The spur from Ashley Hill Junction to Kingswood Junction closed in 1965 and parts of it have been converted to footpaths which feature in Walks 3 and 6.

Passenger services on the Severn Beach line were recommended for withdrawal in the Beeching Report in 1963. Plans to close the line in the spring of 1964 were turned down, but on 10 February 1967 another closure proposal was announced. A few months later, staff were removed from the stations along the line and a conductor-guard scheme was introduced. The threat of closure hung over the line until June 1969 when the Labour Transport Minister, Richard Marsh, announced its reprieve, on the grounds that it would cause hardship to the workers who were its main users. Whether or not his decision was influenced by the impending General Election is unknown, but when it was held a year later the Conservatives won a surprise victory. Two of the seats they won from Labour were Bristol North East and Bristol North West.

Today, the Severn Beach line is busier than ever and both reliability and frequency of services – which just a few years ago hit an all-time low – have improved enormously, largely thanks to vigorous and persistent campaigning from Friends of Suburban Bristol Railways (FOSBR). This in turn has led to a seemingly unstoppable rise in the number of passengers using the line. In 2013, 1,063,000 journeys were taken on the line, an increase of 13.7% from the previous year, and an astonishing turnaround – a decade earlier annual passenger figures were less than 350,000.

Nevertheless, there is much more that could be done to realise the line's potential. Cancellations and delays due to train breakdowns and the problems inherent in having two long sections of single track continue to frustrate and deter passengers. Unstaffed stations mean that fares are often not collected, so that revenue does not fully reflect usage. Restoring double track to at least part of the line would mean more trains at peak times and improved reliability, while a new station adjacent to the Portway Park & Ride would boost passenger numbers. Given an appropriate level of investment, the future of this jewel in the crown of Bristol's public transport network is indeed bright.

A TRIP ALONG THE LINE

The Severn Beach line is not just the gateway to some superb walks; it is perhaps the strangest and most diverse branch line in Britain, and was once rated by Thomas Cook as one of Britain's top scenic rail routes.

A journey along the line starts amid the splendour and bustle of Temple Meads, the 34th busiest station in the country, with over nine million passengers boarding or leaving trains every year.

As the train pulls out of Temple Meads, flats and offices can be seen on the left, where once sidings, warehouses and factories stood. Alongside the line are the sheds and sidings of Barton Hill Depot, used by the LNWR (London & North Western Railway) train maintenance company, where you may glimpse a steam locomotive being prepared for an excursion.

The forecourt of Temple Meads around 1920

A Severn Beach Line train runs into Temple Meads on 2 September 2013

Just past it, at Dr Day's Junction, a spur from the Bristol to Bath line curves in from the south. The junction was named after a well-known doctor – William Edward Day – who lived at nearby Barton Hill House.

As the train rattles through a brick-lined

cutting, you can see that, where there are now two tracks, there were once four. The other two tracks were taken out of use in 1984 but, as the frequency of train services has increased, so has congestion, and there are now plans to reinstate them.

Opposite: A Severn Beach Line train at Narroways Junction on 24 July 2007

Lawrence Hill, the first stop, is a shadow of its former self – only two platforms in use, all its buildings demolished and the site of its goods yard – on the left – occupied by a supermarket and builder's yard.

Leaving Lawrence Hill, the train passes under a bridge that once carried the Midland Railway line to Gloucester and Birmingham, but now carries a railway path. Just past it, on the left, rusty rails, leading to a disused waste transfer depot, trail off into the undergrowth.

After emerging from a cutting, the train scuttles along an embankment with streets of terraced houses on either side. Until the late nineteenth century, the low-lying land on the left was home to several brickworks, located here because of the abundance of clay soil. Beyond them, a couple of hundred metres west of the line, was Easton Colliery, closed in 1911.

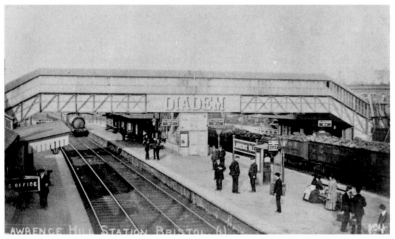

Lawrence Hill station around 1905

The same view on 17 May 2013

Stapleton Road station around 1910 – milk churns on the platform, porters in abundance and a refreshment room on the centre platform. This photograph was taken from the southern end of the platform on the east side of the station, the track serving which was lifted in 1984.

A train for Severn Beach pulls into Stapleton Road on 22 June 2014, with the tower of St Mark's visible in the distance

As the train slows for Stapleton Road, look out on the right for St Mark's church, with muppet-like carvings adorning the roof of its tower. Built in 1848, it was converted to housing in 1989. St Mark's Road, beside the church, is home to the famous Bristol Sweet Mart, while Stapleton Road station is home to a mural depicting life in Easton past and present, and the Eastside Roots Community Garden has been established between the abandoned platforms on the right.

Left: The turret at the north end of Stapleton Road station, once a gazebo in the garden of Stapleton Manor

Below: On 27 July 1978, a southbound engine – No 33113 – clatters over the bridge into Stapleton Road station. In the distance can be seen a large gasholder – recently demolished – and, on the horizon, the former Muller orphanages at Ashley Down. The two tracks seen here were lifted in 1984 and their course through the station is now the site of a community garden, with all trains using the tracks on the left.

At one time, some trains between South Wales and the South Coast ran via the spur at Dr Day's Junction and called at Stapleton Road rather than Temple Meads, thus avoiding the need to reverse – an important consideration in the days of locomotive-hauled trains.

As the train pulls out of the station, look out on the left for a turret on the corner of Stapleton Road, originally a gazebo in the garden of nearby Stapleton Manor. After crossing Stapleton Road, the bridge continues over a path following the old course of the River Frome which still flowed here when the railway was built.

Once over the motorway, the train runs past St Werbugh's, its streets built on the site of yet more brickworks. As the train continues to climb, the view extends westward as far as the heights of Clifton, dominated by the tower of the university physics building in the grounds of the Royal Fort. Nearer to hand is the chimney of Brook's Dye Works, which closed in 2007, and whose future is uncertain. The land on the right was until recently the site of a large railway-served gasworks, which has now been cleared with a view to redevelopment. Further east is the BT tower on Purdown.

The train now slows for Narroways Junction, where it leaves the main line, curving uphill along a single track past the tower of St Werburgh's

A train entering Montpelier tunnel around 1968. The malthouse in the background was built in 1876, two years after the line opened, and has now been converted to housing.

Montpelier station around 50 years ago, with both platforms still in use and lines on the left – beyond the signal – leading into the goods yard, which closed in 1965 and is now home to industrial units

church, which gave its name to the suburb and was moved here from Corn Street in central Bristol in 1879. After crossing a road, the train passes the site of Ashley Hill Junction, where a line trailed in from the east (a photograph of the junction appears on page 86). The line closed in 1965 and in 2000 the cutting through which it once ran, along with the surrounding land, was designated a Millennium Green.

Left: Montpelier station on 24 July 2007

Below left: Redland station on 1 June 2013

Below: An invitation to wake up and smell the coffee at Redland station

Bottom: Redland station in the 1960s

After passing under a couple of bridges, the train runs through a 263m tunnel before pulling into Montpelier station. The former station building, covered with a vibrant mural, is now home to a period fireplace company. The main building, which stood between it and the footbridge, was destroyed by bombing on 16 March 1941. There was also a large building on the up platform, which survived until the 1970s.

Heading out of Montpelier, the train runs high above Cheltenham Road on an impressive bridge before pulling into the next station, Redland. A recent and very welcome innovation here is the presence of a coffee trike from which refreshments are served to passengers on weekday mornings. An ornate cast-iron bridge across the line links the two sections of Lovers' Walk, visited in Walk 8 and 9.

A little further on, look out for the wicker nose of Redland on the wall of a building on the right. Just past it comes a double-track section where trains can pass each other. After a short tunnel – created when shops were built above the line alongside Whiteladies Road – the train pulls into Clifton Down station. The grandiose station building on the up side survives as a bar. The other buildings have gone, as have the glass

canopies above the platforms – the last of them were removed in 1971 but the marks where they were fixed can still be seen on the down side. A large coal yard on the south side of the line is now covered by flats and a shopping centre.

Just past the station comes a 1601-metre tunnel under the downs, most of which

Top left: The wicker nose of Redland

Top right: A train bound for Avonmouth approaches Clifton Down station on 1 June 2013

Centre: A train for Temple Meads pulls into Clifton Down station on 12 June 2014

Bottom: Clifton Down station a century ago

Left: Retaining arches above the western entrance to Clifton Down tunnel

Below: A northbound train passes the site of Sneyd Park Junction around 1968

Bottom: A bus heads south along the Portway in 1926, with Sea Mills station in the background

Portway Sea Mills.

Left: A train crossing the bridge over the River Trym as it pulls out of Sea Mills station on 25 September 2009

Below: A train heads south alongside Horseshoe Bend in the 1930s, with the Portway high above

is downhill. The train gradually gathers speed, clattering through the darkness before bursting into the light high above the shining mud (or water) of the Avon, with Leigh Woods on the far bank. If you look back along the gorge you can glimpse the cliffs of Black Rocks Quarry, while to your right are high retaining arches. A little further along on the right, the lost gardens of Bishop's Knoll – visited in Walk 13 – pass in a blur.

The Portway, directly below you for the first 200 metres or so, following the course of the old Hotwells line, curves away as the cliffs recede, and after a while you will see the grass-grown trackbed of the old line – disused for over 90 years – before it merges at the site of Sneyd Park Junction.

After going under the Portway, the line runs through a cutting before pulling up at the up platform of Sea Mills station, exactly six miles from Temple Meads, as a post on the platform indicates. After crossing the River Trym, where the remains of an eighteenth-century dock can be seen on the right, the line runs past sports grounds, with views across the Avon to Somerset. Ahead lies Horseshoe Bend, with a white building where ships once offloaded gunpowder before continuing upstream.

Shirehampton station around 1916

A train from Temple Meads pulls into Shirehampton on 25 April 1980. Although the goods yard closed in 1965, it had by this time been brought back into use as an oil depot. The main station building also survived in private use, but was demolished after a fire in the 1990s.

Unfortunately, trees prevent you seeing much of Horseshoe Bend as the train rattles past it, before entering a cutting and coming to a halt at Shirehampton's up platform. The site of the goods yard is now home to a vehicle-hire company. As the train pulls out of the station, you can see Pill, once linked to Shirehampton by ferry, across the river.

North of Shirehampton, the land on the right-hand side of the line, extending almost to Avonmouth, was, during the First World War, the site of a remount depot, where horses and mules were kept before being

On 24 September 2009, a southbound train heads past the Avonmouth Park & Ride, occupying a small part of the site of the First World War remount depot

The 1635 from Temple Meads after arrival at Avonmouth on 12 June 2014

shipped out to the Western Front and other theatres of war. Around 250 men worked at the depot, which could handle up to 7,000 animals at any one time.

After passing the car park for the Park & Ride – unfortunately without the station that would boost the line's revenues – the train goes under the M5. The land on the left, site of brickworks in the late nineteenth century and ironworks in the early twentieth, is now occupied by large sheds. A little further on, long lines of sidings on the left of the line have given way to trees and undergrowth.

Avonmouth station still has two tracks and two long platforms built for the trains that carried dockers to and from work

when dock work was more labour intensive than it is today. This was not Avonmouth's original station – which lay further to the north – and only opened in 1877, twelve years after the opening of the line. Originally known as Avonmouth Dock, it has been rebuilt and expanded several times, and in 1966, having long been the town's only station, its name was shortened to Avonmouth.

Most trains terminate at Avonmouth before running back to Temple Meads. Those continuing to Severn Beach head over a level crossing along a grass-grown track which, after 250m, having reverted once again to a single line, takes a sudden lurch to the right. The original line carried straight on for around 750m to the original terminus, the site of which now lies under the Royal Edward Dock.

A little further on comes another level crossing, guarded by a signalbox – St Andrew's Junction – dating from 1910. On the other side of the line, the disused CWS Flour Mills, built of reinforced concrete in 1907-8, tower over a conveyor along which coal from Royal Portbury Dock travels under the Avon in an 800m tunnel before ascending to a high tower. From there, it crosses the Severn Beach Line to a loading hopper, down which it is fed to trains, bound for power stations at Aberthaw, Ratcliffe and Rugeley, passing slowly underneath.

St Andrew's Road, where some trains stop briefly, originally opened in 1917 to serve a large First World War munitions factory adjacent to the line where chemical weapons – notably mustard gas – were made.

Beyond St Andrew's Road, to the south of the line, are the sidings of the Bristol Bulk Handling Terminal, which opened in 1993. After the freight-only line to Filton curves off to the right at Hallen Marsh Junction, the

St Andrew's Junction signalbox controls the Bristol Bulk Handling Terminal and other lines in the Avonmouth area. It is scheduled to close in 2025, when the area comes under the control of the Thames Valley Regional Operations Centre at Didcot.

These three photographs show how dramatically St Andrew's Road has changed. Above, the 1312 Temple Meads to Severn Beach calls on 31 July 1978.

On the left, the 1423 Temple Meads to Severn Beach calls on 22 June 2014. Only one platform survives, the semaphore signals have gone, and the scene is dominated by the loading hopper down which coal is fed to trains passing underneath.

Below, the 1512 from Severn Beach arrives on 22 June 2014, with the sidings of the Bulk Handling Terminal in the background.

A train from Severn Beach passes Hallen Marsh Junction on 9 October 1976. Here too there have been many changes. The signalbox and semaphore signals have gone and Severn Beach line trains now use a new track to the left of those seen here to keep them clear of freight trains using the Bulk Handling Terminal. The skyline is also dominated by the Seabank gas-fired power station which opened in 2000.

Seabank power station seen from Severn Beach station as a train for Temple Meads pulls out on 10 April 2014.

Severn Beach train, gathering pace, bounces, rattles and rolls on its single track past Seabank gas-fired power station. The tunnel under the road, just beyond the power station, provided rail access to ICI Severnside, a chemical plant built in the early 1960s and now largely demolished. Although the track has been lifted, the course of the siding that served the plant can still be seen on the right. On the left, meanwhile, is a vast empty landscape of sky, marshes and mud, with the Second Severn Crossing ahead.

And then the brakes go on for the long unlovely platform at the end of the line. Nothing can prepare you for the otherness of Severn Beach. When the line opened there was nothing here, not even a station. Then, in the 1920s, an entrepreneur called Robert Stride persuaded the railway to open a station and proceeded to develop the Severn estuary's answer to Blackpool. Soon, there were amusement arcades, gardens, a holiday camp, hotel, and swimming pool. The only problem was the beach: despite the name bestowed on the fledgling resort, there wasn't one.

Today, the trappings of holiday fun have largely disappeared, to be replaced by modern houses, but it is not too difficult to imagine crowds of children, on a day trip from Bedminster or Brislington, bucket and spade in hand, catching sight of the mud-fringed estuary and crying out, 'is that it'?

There is not even a pub at Severn Beach any more, although the old Severn Beach Hotel – later renamed the Severn Salmon – was once a noted music venue. Its guests included Adge Cutler, whose 1968 song, 'Aloha Severn Beach' described the resort as 'a little bit of heaven, Down

Severn Beach station on 4 August 1976. The main station building – now demolished and replaced by houses – can be seen on the left. On the right the former through line to Pilning has been downgraded to a siding for storing vans conveying fertiliser from ICI Severnside

Top: The main station building at Severn Beach, which stood at right angles to the platform, in 1976

Above: The 1416 to Temple Meads (not Par as indicated on the destination blind) on 20 November 1978. A corner of the Severn Beach Hotel is visible on the right.

Left: The Severn Beach Hotel in the 1940s

there by the River Severn'. The hotel was demolished around 2002 and houses have since been built on the site.

Many of the West Country's holiday resorts have declined, but few have dropped so completely off the radar as Severn Beach. Yet, while towns along the channel coast such as Clevedon, Burnham, Minehead, Ilfracombe and Porthcawl lost their stations decades ago, the trains still run to this place that time forgot. And, within minutes of leaving the train, you can have left its streets behind and be striding alongside the estuary on a long-distance path called, appropriately enough, the Severn Way, which, if you were to follow it to its end, would lead you to the slopes of Plynlimon.

Left: A postcard sent from Severn Beach to Littlehampton on 11 September 1926. *'We are sat here watching the tide,'* reads the message. *'It is really very nice. Our first visit, but I think we shall like to come again.'*

Below: Severn Beach today

Further information online:
Friends of Suburban Bristol Railways: *www.fosbr.org.uk*
Severn Beach Line (Timetables & other information): *www.severnbeachline.org*

References

Abbreviations:
BM, Bristol Mercury;
WDP, Western Daily Press.

Introduction
1. Andrew Foyle, *Bristol: Pevsner Architectural Guide*, New Haven & London, 2004, p. 3.

Walk 1
1. William Worcestre, *The Topography of Medieval Bristol*, ed. Frances Neale, Bristol, 2000, pp. 57-59.
2. *BM*, 19 June 1890.
3. *BM*, 19 June 1890.
4. *BM*, 23 June 1890.
5. *BM*, 23 June 1890.
6. *BM*, 23 June 1890.
7. *BM*, 24 June 1890.
8. *BM*, 24 June 1890.
9. Letter to George Montagu, 22 October 1766.

Walk 2
1. John Latimer, *The Annals of Bristol in the Eighteenth Century*, Bristol, 1893, pp. 506-7.

Walk 3
1. *WDP*, 21 August 1878.
2. *WDP*, 25 November 1889; *WDP*, 21 March 1895.
3. *BM*, 8 May 1882.
4. *WDP*, 25 April 1888: *WDP*, 1 May 1888; *WDP*, 31 January 1894.
5. *WDP*, 11 October 1928.

Walk 4
1. *London Gazette*, 30 January 1857; *BM*, 24 October 1857.
2. *WDP*, 10 October 1859.
3. *WDP*, 31 August 1861.
4. *WDP*, 29 August 1888.
5. *BM*, 27 February 1891.
6. *BM*, 26 May 1887.
7. *BM*, 9 June 1887.
8. *WDP*, 6 June 1888.
9. *BM*, 29 August 1899.
10. *WDP*, 13 January 1926.
11. *WDP*, 28 September 1932.
12. *WDP*, 2 April 1937; 29 January 1938.

Walk 5
1. John Latimer, T*he Annals of Bristol in the Seventeenth Century*, Bristol, 1900, p. 202.
2. John Latimer, *The Annals of Bristol in the Nineteenth Century*, Bristol, 1887, pp. 250-51.
3. *BM*, 10 September 1844.
4. *BM*, 4 January 1845.

Walk 8
1. *WDP*, 9 November 1938; *Transactions of the Bristol & Gloucestershire Archaeological Society*, 36 (1913), p. 112.
2. Latimer, *Nineteenth Century*, p. 45.
3. Latimer, *Nineteenth Century*, pp. 317-18.
4. *WDP*, 24 February 1922.

Walk 9
1. Quoted in David Harrison, 'The Hangman Hanged and the Crate Frustrated' in James Belsey et al, *Bristol: The Growing City*, Bristol, 1986, p. 57.
2. Latimer, *Nineteenth Century*, pp. 241-42.
3. Latimer, *Seventeenth Century*, p. 130.
4. Julius Ibbetson, John Laporte & John Hassell, *A Picturesque Guide to Bath, Bristol, Hot-Wells, the River Avon, and the Adjacent Country*, London, 1793, pp. 166-70.
5. Latimer, *Nineteenth Century*, p. 71.

Walk 10
1. Egan, Pierce, *Walks through Bath ... also an Excursion to Clifton and Bristol Hot-Wells*, Bath, 1819, pp. 243-44.
2. Latimer, *Seventeenth Century*, p. 352.

Walk 11
1. Egan, p. 249.
2. Latimer, *Nineteenth Century*, pp. 124-25.
3. Latimer, *Nineteenth Century*, pp. 264-5; see also *WDP*, 27 April 1935.
4. *BM*, 20 June 1863.
5. Latimer, *Nineteenth Century*, pp. 407-8.
6. *BM*, 12 November 1864.
7. *WDP*, 29 March 1869.
8. Latimer, *Nineteenth Century*, p. 265.
9. *WDP*, 30 September 1902.
10. *WDP*, 3 January 1936.

Walk 12
1. *WDP*, 23 October 1880.
2. *WDP*, 24 April 1888.
3. Colin Godman, 'The Unquiet Grave: A Fresh Look at the Scipio Africanus Story', *The Regional Historian*, 18 (Summer, 2008), pp. 13-17 (p.17).
4. Ibbetson, p. 204.
5. Latimer, *Eighteenth Century*, p. 331.
6. *WDP*, 22 May 1925.
7. *WDP*, 25 May 1925.
8. *WDP*, 16 June 1925.
9. *WDP*, 1 December 1925.
10. *WDP*, 31 October 1936.
11. *WDP*, 10 January 1946.
12. *WDP*, 6 May 1949.
13. *WDP*, 9 August 1941.
14. *WDP*, 13 December 1949.

Walk 13

1. *WDP*, 25 May 1861.
2. *BM*, 12 November 1853.
3. *BM*, 20 May 1854.
4. *BM*, 25 August 1855.
5. *BM*, 1 September 1855.
6. *BM*, 15 March 1856.
7. *BM*, 20 June 1857.
8. *BM*, 9 June 1933.
9. Latimer, *Eighteenth Century*, pp. 264-66.
10. Ibbetson, p. 186.
11. *BM*, 21 September 1893.
12. Egan, p. 246.
13. *WDP*, 26 June 1922.
14. *WDP*, 20 September 1921.
15. *WDP*, 26 June 1922.
16. *WDP*, 3 July 1926

Walk 14

1. Latimer, *Nineteenth Century*, p. 29.
2. Ibbetson, p. 192.
3. Egan, pp. 254-55.
4. CFW Dening, *Old Inns of Bristol*, Bristol & London, 1944, p. 83.
5. *WDP*, 10 June 1867.
6. *WDP*, 21 December 1868; 24 December 1932.

Walk 16

1. JT Barber, *A Tour throughout South Wales and Monmouthshire*, London, 1803, p. 244.
2. Barber, pp. 238-40.
3. *Bath Chronicle*, 2 October 1777.
4. Ibbetson, pp. 223-30.
5. John Wesley, diary entry for 22 October 1743.
6. Wesley, diary entry for 28 March 1742.
7. *Hereford Journal*, 20 August 1844.
8. *WDP*, 20 July 1864.
9. *WDP*, 19 May 1866.
10. *BM*, 14 November 1887.
11. *Bath Chronicle*, 28 December 1893.
12. Ernest Rhys, *The South Wales Coast from Chepstow to Aberystwyth*, London, 1911, pp. 27-28.
13. *WDP*, 6 July 1926.
14. *Gloucester Citizen*, 1 August 1931.
15. Brian Waters, *The Bristol Channel*, London, 1955, p. 8.

Bibliography & Online Resources

Bristol City Centre Policy Report, 1966, Bristol, 1966

Barber, JT, *A Tour throughout South Wales and Monmouthshire*, London, 1803

Belsey, James et al, *Bristol: The Growing City*, Bristol, 1986

Bettey, JH, *Bristol Observed: Visitors' Impressions of the City from Domesday to the Blitz*, Bristol, 1986

Bowerman, Veronica, *The Henleaze Book*, 2nd Edition, Bristol, 2006

Charlton, J & DM Milton, *Redland, 791 to 1800*, Bristol, 1961

Coules, Victoria, *Lost Bristol*, Edinburgh, 2006

Dening, CFW, *Old Inns of Bristol*, Bristol & London, 1944

Egan, Pierce, *Walks through Bath, Describing Every Thing Worthy of Interest ... also an Excursion to Clifton and Bristol Hot-Wells*, Bath, 1819

Ernest Rhys, *The South Wales Coast from Chepstow to Aberystwyth*, London, 1911

Foyle, Andrew, *Bristol: Pevsner Architectural Guide*, New Haven & London, 2004

Foyle, Andrew & Nikolaus Pevsner, *Somerset: North and Bristol (The Buildings of England*, New Haven & London, 2011

Godman, Colin, 'The Unquiet Grave: A Fresh Look at the Scipio Africanus Story', in *The Regional Historian*, 18 (Summer, 2008), pp13-17

Ibbetson, Julius, John Laporte & John Hassell, *A Picturesque Guide to Bath, Bristol, Hot-Wells, the River Avon, and the Adjacent Country*, London, 1793

Jeremiah, Josephine, *The Bristol Avon: A Pictorial History*, Chichester, 2005

Jones, Donald, *A History of Clifton*, Chichester, 1992

Lambert, David, *Historic Bristol Parks*, Bristol, 2000

Langley, Martin & Edwina Small, *Estuary & River Ferries of South West England*, Albrighton, 1984

Latimer, John, *The Annals of Bristol in the Eighteenth Century*, Bristol, 1893

Latimer, John, *The Annals of Bristol in the Nineteenth Century*, Bristol, 1887

Latimer, John, *The Annals of Bristol in the Seventeenth Century*, Bristol, 1900

Maggs, Colin, *Bristol Railway Panorama*, Bath, 1990

Maggs, Colin, *The Bristol & Gloucester Railway*, Lingfield, 1969

Mellor, Penny & Mary Wright, *Kingsdown: Bristol's Vertical Suburb*, Chichester, 2009

Morris, GR, *The Mid Frome Valley*, Bristol 1974

Oakley, Mike, *Bristol Railway Stations, 1840-2005*, Bristol, 2006

Stone, George Frederick, *Bristol: As It Was and As It Is*, Bristol, 1909

Thomas, Ethel, *Down the 'Mouth: A History of Avonmouth*, Avonmouth, 1977

Vincent, Mike, *Lines to Avonmouth*, Oxford, 1979

Walker, Thomas A, *The Severn Tunnel: Its Construction and Difficulties, 1872-1887*, London, 1888

Ward, Owen, 'The Mills of the Bristol Frome', *BIAS Journal*, xi (1978), pp 27-33

Waters, Brian, *The Bristol Channel*, London, 1955

Worcestre, William, *The Topography of Medieval Bristol*, ed. Frances Neale, Bristol, 2000

Wright, Mary, *Montpelier: A Bristol Suburb*, Chichester, 2004

Avon Gardens Trust: *www.avongardenstrust.org.uk*

Avon Local History & Archaeology: *www.avonlocalhistandarch.co.uk*

Avon Wildlife Trust: *www.avonwildlifetrust.org.uk/reserves/royate_hill.htm*

Bristol Parks Forum: *www.bristolparksforum.org.uk*

Bristol Parks: *www.bristol.gov.uk/page/leisure-and-culture/parks-and-open-spaces*

Forest of Avon Trust: *forestofavontrust.org*

Know Your Place (Historic Maps of Bristol): *www.bristol.gov.uk/page/planning-and-building-regulations/know-your-place*

Acknowledgements & Picture Credits

Shorter versions of some of the walks first appeared in *The Bristol Magazine* and I am grateful for permission to reproduce them here. Thanks also for George Ferguson for writing the foreword.

Thanks to the R Blencowe Archive for the photographs on pages 5 (bottom), 28 (bottom) & 247 (top); to the R Blencowe Archive/ET Gill for the photograph on page 218 (top); Simon Castens for the photographs of Severn Beach on pages 265 & 266 (top); and Garry Stroud for the photographs of the Severn Beach line on pages 254 (bottom), 260 (bottom), 263 (top), 264 (top) & 266 (centre).

Other black & white railway photographs from the 1940s, 1950s and 1960s were acquired at railway fairs over the course of several years, with no indication as to the photographers, and, despite making enquiries, I have been unable to establish this.

All other photographs are from the Akeman Press Archive.

General Index

Pub Index

Note: All pubs listed below were trading at time of writing

Also from AKEMAN PRESS

On Foot in Bath
Fifteen Walks around a World Heritage City

Andrew Swift

Literary Walks in Bath
Eleven Excursions in the Company of Eminent Authors

Andrew Swift & Kirsten Elliott

The Ringing Grooves of Change
Brunel & the Coming of the Railway to Bath,
with a Brunel Trail from Keynsham to Box

Andrew Swift

Somerset Follies

Jonathan Holt

Queen of Waters
A Journey in Time along the Kennet & Avon Canal

Kirsten Elliott

**For a list of other titles and details of how to order
go to www.akemanpress.com**